ALSO BY JOE KANE

Running the Amazon

SAVAGES

Joe Kane

SAVAGES

ALFRED A. KNOPF

NEW YORK

1995

This Is a Borzoi Book
Published by Alfred A. Knopf, Inc.

Copyright © 1995 by Joe Kane
Photographs copyright © 1995 by Zbigniew Bzdak
Map copyright © 1995 by David Lindroth, Inc.

Portions of this book were originally published in *The New Yorker* in slightly different form as "Amazon Showdown: A Stone Age Tribe Fights American Oil" (9/27/93) and "An Amazon Indian in D.C.'s Jungle" (5/2/94).

Library of Congress Cataloging-in-Publication Data

Kane, Joe.
    Savages / Joe Kane.—1st ed.
        p. cm.   213
    Includes bibliographical references.
    ISBN 0-679-41191-7
        1. Huaorani Indians—Land tenure.   2. Human ecology—Ecuador.
    3. Human ecology—Amazon River Valley.   I. Title.
    F3722.1.H83K36   1995
    333.3'0981'1—dc20   95-4258
                                                              CIP

Manufactured in the United States of America
First Edition

For Clare

Contents

*An eight-page insert of color
   photographs follows page 178.*

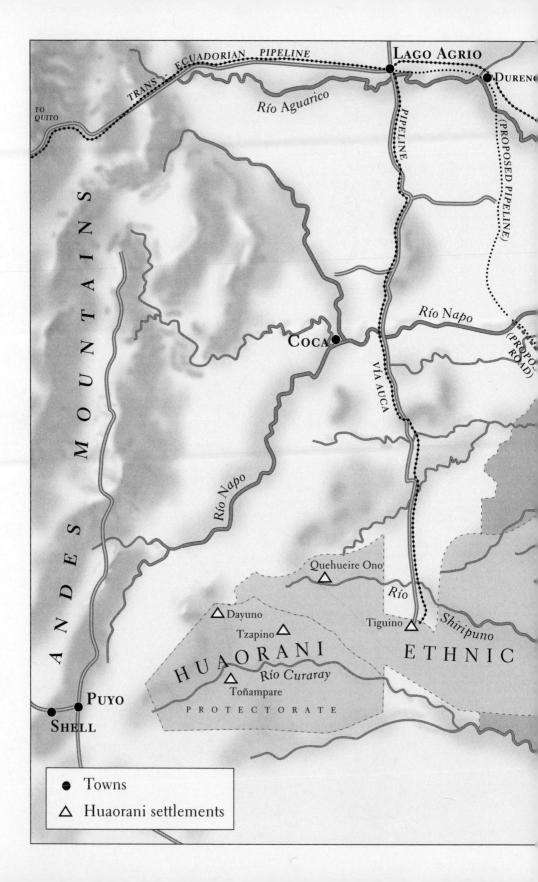

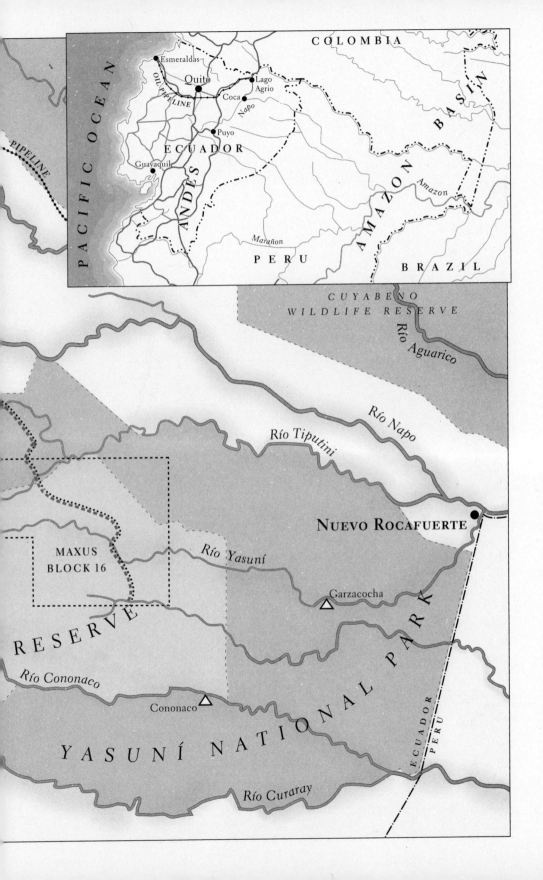

A Pronunciation Guide
to Some Huaorani Names

Amo: *ah*-moe
Dayuma: dye-*oo*-mah
Enqueri: en-*ker*-ee
Mengatohue: meng-gah-*toe*-way
Moi: *moy*
Nanto: *nahn*-toe
Quemperi: kem-*per*-ee
Quimonca: kee-*mone*-kah

Huao: *wow*
Huaorani: wow-*rahn*-ee
Quehueire Ono: kay-way-*i*-ray *oh*-no
Toñampare: toe-nyahm-*pahr*-ee
Yohue: *yoe*-way

SAVAGES

Prologue

T HOUGH MOI hit the streets of Washington, D.C., at the evening rush hour, he walked in the city as he does in the forest—in slow, even strides. He kept his eyes to the ground and his knees bent, and he planted his broad feet deliberately, heel and toe, yet lightly as raindrops. It was the walk of a man accustomed to slippery terrain. I found myself stutter-stepping all the way down Pennsylvania Avenue, but Moi slid through the pedestrian horde like a fish parting water. He stopped only once, to study a squirrel climbing a maple tree: meat.

Moi wore dark khaki pants, a starched white dress shirt, a blue-and-gray striped tie, and brown leather shoes. The shoes were borrowed but the clothes were new, and though he was not entirely comfortable in them, he cut a handsome figure. Only the unusually high set of his cheekbones, the distinctive cut of his thick black hair—straight across his eyes, halfway down his back—and the rack of shoulders that threatened to burst the seams of his shirt hinted at the distance Moi had come: His journey had begun deep in the Ecuadorian Amazon, in the homeland of his people, the Huaorani, a small but fearsome nation of hunter-gatherers who have lived in isolation for so long that they speak a language unrelated to any other on earth. It had taken Moi nearly two weeks to reach Washington. Traveling by foot, canoe, bus, rail, and air, he had crossed centuries.

Tucked into the small handwoven palm-string bag he'd brought from home were his passport, his toothbrush, his bird-feather crown, and a letter addressed to the President of the United States of North

America. The letter invited the president to visit the Huaorani. Moi wanted the president to explain to the People, as the Huaorani call themselves, exactly why it was that the United States of North America was trying to destroy them. "The whole world must come and see how the Huaorani live well," the letter said. "We live with the spirit of the jaguar. We do not want to be civilized by your missionaries or killed by your oil companies. Must the jaguar die so that you can have more contamination and television?"

At the White House gate Moi reached into his bag and carefully removed his crown. It was made from owl, eagle, toucan, parrot, and wild turkey feathers, and when he jammed it down on his jet black hair a thousand colors seemed to burst from the plumes. But the gate was closed, and for a long time Moi stood and stared silently through the iron fence.

Then he said, "That house looks pretty small. Are you sure the government lives here?"

"The president lives here, with his family."

"Where are the soldiers? Are they underground?"

"Probably. And in back, and inside."

He gripped the fence, as if testing its strength, and his eyes narrowed in calculation: He went into the Huaorani zone, as I'd come to think of it. When he returned he said, "I believe I can climb this fence and reach the front door before the soldiers get me."

"It will not work, Moi."

"It will not work if I do not try."

"The soldiers will be on you like a boa on a tree rat."

"I will climb the trees and hide. I will pretend I am hunting monkeys."

But I dissuaded him, at least for the moment, and we walked on. The sidewalks were full. Traffic roared.

"There are so many cars," he said. "How long have they been here? A million years?"

"Much less."

"A thousand years."

"No. Eighty, perhaps."

He was silent then, but after a while he asked, "What will you do in ten more years? In ten years your world will be pure metal. Did your god do this?"

Dusk turned to night, and as we approached our hotel Moi stopped beneath a streetlamp. He pointed to the street. "More people, more cars, more petroleum, more chaos," he said. Then he pointed straight up at the light. "But *there* are the Huaorani, all alone in the middle of the world."

MOI HAD BEEN brought to Washington by a team of lawyers from the Sierra Club Legal Defense Fund, which, on behalf of the Huaorani, had filed a petition with the Inter-American Commission on Human Rights, an arm of the Organization of American States. Since 1967 American oil development in the Oriente—as the Ecuadorian Amazon is known—had proceeded virtually without regulation. Every day the petroleum industry was dumping millions of gallons of untreated toxic pollutants into a watershed extending over fifty thousand square miles of rain forest, and it had opened the area up to such rapid and uncontrolled colonization that it was on a pace to be almost completely deforested early in the next century. No one was arguing whether oil exploitation had damaged the Oriente—with the possible exception of gold mining in Brazil, it was the worst case of toxic contamination in the entire Amazon. The debate was over the extent of the damage. The Ecuadorian government had estimated the cost of cleaning up the mess made by Texaco and Petroecuador, the state oil company, at $5 billion. Texaco—whose pipeline had dumped into the Oriente more than one and a half times as much oil as the Exxon *Valdez* spilled off the coast of Alaska—had offered a settlement worth about $12 million. In any case, the consequences had been borne most heavily by the Oriente's 150,000 indigenous people, and the surest measure of what loomed for the Huaorani could be found a hundred miles north of their territory, in the homeland of the Cofan Indians. The Cofans were a small but thriving nation when Texaco opened its first commercial well on their land, in 1972. Twenty years later, their culture was all but gone.

Moi arrived in Washington scant months before oil production was to begin in the Huaorani territory. The SCLDF petition charged that this would be ethnocide—that for the sake of enough oil to meet U.S. energy needs for thirteen days, the Huaorani way of life would be destroyed—and asked the commission to investigate. The commission has no powers of enforcement, but its moral authority is enormous, and an investigation was one of the few avenues left for the Huaorani if they were to have any chance of avoiding annihilation. The lawyers hoped that Moi's testimony would persuade the commission to act.

But the American embassy in Quito had a history of working closely with the petroleum industry, and days before Moi was scheduled to testify, it denied him a visa. The embassy argued that because Moi had no tangible assets tying him to Ecuador, there was a risk that he would disappear inside the United States as an illegal immigrant. It could be argued that, on the contrary, Moi's assets run deeper than just about anyone else's in Ecuador, for the Huaorani hold legal title to a good chunk of the territory they have always occupied. But they hold that title communally, and, the embassy maintained, this arrangement made Moi a landless peasant.

At least it did until the right question bounced onto the right desk at the State Department: Why was a plaintiff in a human-rights case being denied a visa? When I met Moi in Washington, one of the first things he did was produce his brand-new passport and show me the visa. "The embassy changed its mind," he said. "It has invited me to visit your country for five years."

As Moi saw it, he was engaged in a war, and the Huaorani were ready to fight that war with spears made from the hardest wood in the forest—"spears that can kill fifteen men without breaking," he said. Though there have probably never been more of the Huaorani than there are today—about 1,300—they have, for as long as anyone knows, roamed a territory the size of Massachusetts and fended off all comers: the Incas; the Spanish conquistadores; the rubber barons; the armies of Ecuador and Peru; modern-day colonists and prospectors; and, always, their land-hungry indigenous neighbors, the Quichua and the Shuar, who together outnumber the Huaorani by more than a hundred to one.

But fighting the Company—as the Huaorani call all interests with rights to the petroleum beneath their land—is something else again. Under Ecuadorian law, the Huaorani have no control over oil production and no share in its revenues. The Company planned to extract more than 200 million barrels of raw crude from Huaorani territory, and in its quest to exploit that oil, it had revealed itself to be an enemy far more powerful than any the Huaorani had ever known: an enemy that, as Moi saw it, killed by destroying the source of all life, the forest itself.

THOUGH IT had been almost a year since I'd last seen Moi (we'd spent months traveling together in the Amazon), when he came to my hotel room he greeted me in the Huaorani way, virtually without expression, as if only a few minutes had passed since we last spoke. "Chong," he said—that is how he pronounces "Joe"—and then he handed me his bag and his spears and walked into the room. Our relationship had been defined long ago, without words. In the forest, where I was helpless, he had watched out for me at all times; in the city, I owed him no less.

We stayed at the hotel four nights. Moi discovered televised baseball, *The Washington Post*, and modern warfare. Baseball, a game of spears and rocks, he enjoyed for its technique, but beyond that he found television useless. The *Post* he studied carefully each morning, mainly the airline ads (other than foot and canoe, small planes are the only transportation known inside the Huaorani territory) and the photographs. Of the latter he was most taken by the somewhat violent shots of an uprising in Russia. He asked me to translate the accompanying stories, and he peppered me with questions.

One morning he asked, "The United States and Russia fought a big war, did they not?"

"Yes, they did. It lasted many years."

"Which country did they fight it in? Here or there?"

"Neither."

"That is impossible."

"They fought it in other countries."

"That makes no sense. That would be like the Huaorani fighting the Shuar in Quichua territory."

"Something like that."

He laughed. "That is a very stupid way to make war."

Moi spent most of the first night working on the statement he would make to the commission. He wrote it out twice in the ten-cent notebook he always carried in his back pocket, and then he read it aloud, practicing his gestures. He would wear his shirt and tie, and over them his jaguar-tooth necklace, his string bag, and the reed tube in which he carried blowgun darts. "In the forest I wear this," he said, touching his necklace, "but your world wants me to wear this," and he tugged on his tie.

He read slowly, with little of the force or charm that came so naturally when he spoke. "Your ideas are good," I said, "but use your own words. Speak as you would without the paper."

"You mean speak like the jaguar," he said. The Huaorani consider the jaguar the most powerful force in the forest. (Moi's grandfather was a "jaguar shaman"—a shaman with the ability to transform himself into a jaguar—and, as such, one of the most revered men in the culture.)

Later, exhausted, Moi told me he wanted to clean up and go to bed. For the Huaorani, bathing is communal. In late afternoon people all head down to the river, and they hang out there for what seems forever, soaping up, swimming, gossiping, joking, and flirting. By comparison a hotel shower seemed soulless. Still, Moi disappeared into the bathroom for about an hour. I heard the water go on and off several times. When he finally emerged, he was wearing only his shorts, and his skin was red as a boiled lobster.

"Tomorrow, I would like a new hotel room," he said.

"Why?"

"I would like a room that also has cold water."

He dressed himself completely and had me tie his tie. Then, fully clothed, he got into bed. As he does at home, he would wake several times during the night—to eat, to pace our suite, to analyze the new sounds he was hearing.

He pulled the blankets up to his chin. "Chong," he said, "will we win?"

"You will try your best."

"We must win or the Huaorani will disappear forever."

Then he closed his eyes and, as always, fell asleep in seconds.

THE STRANGE JOURNEY that had brought me to Moi and Moi to the United States had begun two and a half years earlier, in March of 1991, when an odd and disturbing letter surfaced at the San Francisco headquarters of the Rainforest Action Network. The letter was tucked into an envelope that bore no postmark. No one was quite sure when it had arrived, or how it had burrowed its way into the stacks of paper crammed into the office of RAN Executive Director Randall Hayes. At first Hayes was not sure what the letter said, either, because it was written in Spanish, a language spoken neither by him nor, according to almost all of what little information was available about them, by the Huaorani, whose elected representatives the letter's authors claimed to be.

I was working at the RAN offices part-time, helping Hayes edit his publications, and he asked if I'd translate the letter and try to find out if it was authentic. It was written on plain white paper and typed on a manual typewriter, and it was addressed, simply, "General Manager, DuPont-Conoco Company, United States of North America." "The company Conoco is discussing the life of the Huaorani in meetings in which the Huaorani are not present," the letter said; on their own land, the Huaorani "are treated as if we were guests." The letter expressed absolute opposition to oil exploitation in Huaorani territory, and it warned that "the Huaorani know the problems of the whole world . . . and we will defend our land." It was signed, in flourishing script, by the officers of something called the Organization of the Huaorani Nation of the Ecuadorian Amazon. A cover note asked Hayes to forward the letter to Edgar S. Woolard, the chairman and CEO of DuPont—the corporate parent of Conoco, which held oil rights to the Huaorani lands. It advised Hayes to be careful, because "the Company has many spies."

Conoco was scheduled to begin building roads and pipelines in the Huaorani territory within a few months, but the letter had the potential to place the project in serious jeopardy. Though Conoco had already invested $90 million to explore the Huaorani land for oil, and though it predicted eventual revenues of $2 billion, DuPont had to weigh these sums against the cost of being branded as trampling on the rights of, and quite possibly destroying, rain forest natives.

But was the letter for real?

Many environmental and human-rights groups claimed to be working on behalf of the Huaorani, or the land they lived on. Letter-writing campaigns, boycotts, lawsuits, grants, and foundations were being pitched and caught by the likes of CARE, Cultural Survival, The Nature Conservancy, the Natural Resources Defense Council, Wildlife

Conservation International, the Sierra Club, the World Wildlife Fund, and a dozen other organizations, including RAN itself. In terms of both cost and reward, the money involved was substantial—tens of millions of dollars—and the infighting bitter. The positions staked out by the groups ran the gamut, from absolute opposition to Conoco to outright support (the argument being, mainly, that oil development of the Huaorani land was inevitable and that Conoco was the best of a number of bad alternatives). When I called around to the various offices, however, no one could convincingly vouch for—or produce evidence against—the letter. In fact, no one knew how to contact the Huaorani. For all the ruckus being raised, all that could be said with certainty about the Huaorani, whoever they might be, was that American oil companies coveted their land, American missionaries their souls, American environmentalists their voice. But no one knew what the Huaorani wanted. No one really knew who the Huaorani were.

HAYES AND I elected to send the mysterious letter along to Edgar Woolard, and to publish the text in RAN's quarterly newsletter, even though RAN didn't have the time or money to research it as thoroughly as it cried out to be. If it was a fraud, Conoco, or any of the forces that stood to benefit from the Conoco development (including those in the environmmental community), would find a way to expose it as such. But if it was authentic—if it was genuinely as desperate and wild and unlikely a shot in the dark as it seemed to be—then it was a voice that had to be heard. Woolard's decision on whether to allow Conoco to proceed with production development was expected within months.

So stated, our role seemed clear. But for me, at least, it was more complicated than that.

After the letter became public, it was denounced by Conoco and its supporters, who claimed, variously, that the Huaorani were illiterate and could not have written it, or that the Huaorani had written it but had done so under the coercion of "outsiders," or that the Huaorani who wrote it did not really represent all the Huaorani. But, still, no one offered hard proof of these claims, and there was no word either way from Edgar Woolard. The situation troubled me, in many ways. I had spent some time along the Amazon in Peru and Brazil, and, like a lot of people, I wanted to do something to help save the rain forest. And so after a decade as a working journalist, I'd crossed the street and tried to become an activist. But I quickly found environmental activism exhausting and bewildering, a bumper-car ride that veered from crisis to crisis without cease. There never seemed to be enough money, enough time, or enough information to do the work that had to be done. The Huaorani mystery brought it all to a head. If the letter was real, who had written it? And if it *wasn't* real, who had written it?

I decided to quit RAN and go back to South America to look for some answers. The dateline on the Huaorani letter said "Coca." That seemed as good a place as any to start.

PART ONE

East

1

THE PORT OF Coca sits on the north bank of the broad, brown Napo River, in the very heart of the Oriente, which may well be the richest biotic zone on the planet. But as I entered town for the first time, bouncing on the back of a flatbed pickup, what I smelled most strongly was raw petroleum. Coca is ringed by oil wells, and every few days its dirt streets are hosed down with waste crude. Oily mud splashed across my clothes and pack. Down along the roadside, oil had spattered chickens, mules, pigs, barefoot schoolchildren, and peasants slip-sliding along on rickety bicycles. It even slopped up onto the spanking-new four-wheel-drive trucks that now and then came blasting down the road at breakneck speed.

Some of these trucks bore the insignia of the state oil company, Petroecuador, but most of them did the work of American companies: Texaco, Occidental Petroleum, ARCO, Unocal, Conoco, Maxus Energy, Mobil, Oryx Energy, all of which have, or had, oil developments in the otherwise sylvan wilderness that surrounds Coca for hundreds of square miles. Indeed, though Coca was small, with a permanent population of less than five thousand, there were always Americans around. The truck dropped me outside a restaurant called El Buho. The menu featured such jungle fare as tapir, capybara, paca, venison, caiman, and peccary, but you could also get a cheeseburger and fries, which is what the four white men sitting across the room ordered, in English, in accents unmistakably southern. The Mission, Coca's only hot-water hotel, was booked solid with Occidental Petroleum executives in from the States, and at dawn the next day, when a squad of Ecuadorian soldiers jogged down the main street in earnest formation, what caught my attention in the sea of brown Latin skin were the blond hair and blue eyes of the man leading them: His uniform identified him as an officer in the U.S. Army.

If oil was the first thing you noticed in Coca, the second was the suggestion of Aucas, the people indigenous to the vast and mostly un-charted stretch of the Oriente that begins across the Napo and extends over a hundred miles south and east, to the Peruvian border. Trinket shops sold Auca blowguns and spears, tour guides promoted river trips to the Auca homeland to see "naked savages," and on the walls of the Hotel Auca, in the center of town, hung black-and-white photographs of Aucas dressed in, at most, bellybands and earrings, their short, power-fully muscled torsos painted and tattooed, their earlobes perforated and hugely distended. If you happened to mention that you were heading into Auca territory, you were likely to be told that the Aucas regularly killed travelers, other Indians, and their own people, and that they would not only kill you but eat your flesh. Without a doubt you would hear the story of a Capuchin missionary named Alejandro Labaca.

In the late 1970s, Labaca, then the bishop of Coca, crossed the Napo and made the first sustained contact with several Auca bands living deep in the forest. The Aucas robbed him blind. (They survive mainly by hunting and by gathering forest crops, and they regarded his belongings much as they would ripe coconuts.) But Labaca kept re-turning, and over the years he came to feel comfortable with his new friends. Then, in 1984, an oil crew succeeded in killing Taga, the notoriously fierce leader of the Tagaeri, the most reclusive of the Auca clans. The other Tagaeri managed to escape deeper into the forest, but in 1987 an oil-exploration team investigating the Auca territory by air spotted a clearing they believed to be the clan's new home. Labaca was worried that the company would track the Tagaeri down and kill them, and he asked permission to attempt friendly contact first. A helicopter crew dropped him in the clearing. It returned a few days later to find him pinned to the ground, spread-eagled, by seventeen palm-wood spears, each of them about ten feet long, which jutted like porcupine quills from his throat, chest, arms, and thighs. His corpse was punctured in eighty-nine places.

I heard the Labaca story one steamy night at the Hotel Auca, on a thatch-roofed patio where half a dozen Australian and Israeli students, young and long haired, had gathered to drink beer. The patio was lit by a single candle, and by its dim light you couldn't really tell that four dark-skinned young men who happened to be sitting on the grass a few yards away weren't of Latin blood. The tourists ignored them—not that these men would ever identify themselves as Aucas. They would call themselves Huaorani: the People. In the language of their traditional enemies, the Quichua Indians, *auca* means "savage," and the Huaorani consider it a gross insult.

The four Huaorani hardly resembled the hotel's lurid photographs. They wore spotless denim jeans, brightly shined plastic loafers, and bleached white cotton shirts. The man nearest me sometimes went by the name Eugenio, because he found it convenient to use a Latin name when he was visiting a foreign country, which is what he considered Ecuador to be. But if you looked closely when he smiled, you could catch the candlelight glinting off his left front tooth, which had been inlaid with gold in the shape of an A. This was for Amo, his Huaorani name.

The man next to him, Enqueri, had hardly any teeth at all, and he was wearing a pair of headphones that appeared to be plugged into his right hip pocket. When I asked him what he was listening to, he replied in a tone so solemn I was sure I'd committed a horrible breach of Huaorani etiquette. "I am listening," he said, "to my pants." He let that hang for a moment, and then he and Amo collapsed with laughter, rolling on the ground and cackling wildly.

"To your pants!" Amo gasped. "What do they say?"

"They say, 'Wash me, you moron!'"

The other two men, whose names were Nanto and Moi, sat with their arms around each other's shoulders. Nanto told me that to reach Coca they had traveled by foot, canoe, and truck for three days. They had been in town five days, and had not eaten since they arrived. They had come to Coca to find the Company. The Company was going to drill oil wells inside the Huaorani territory, and build new roads, and the Huaorani did not want this. Nanto was going to tell the Company to stay out. He had the authority to do so, he said, because he was president of the Huaorani federation, which was called—here he rolled his eyes up into his head, searching for the name.

"The Organization of the Huaorani Nation of the Ecuadorian Amazon," Moi said. (The acronym, ONHAE, is also the Huaorani word for "flower.") Like the others, he spoke fair Spanish. Unlike the others, he wore a crown of toucan feathers, and he didn't smile. Moi, Amo, and Enqueri were ONHAE's vice president, secretary, and treasurer, respectively. All were in their midtwenties, though there was some disagreement on just where in his midtwenties Enqueri was, and they had been elected by their people to speak to the *cowode*—the cannibals, who included the missionaries, the Company, me, and everyone else on earth.

This reaching out was an extraordinary step for the Huaorani, who until the middle of this century were almost completely isolated from the world beyond their territory. These, however, were extraordinary times. In the heart of the Huaorani homeland, the Company had found oil reserves it estimated at 216 million barrels. It was about to begin constructing a 90-mile access road, 150 miles of service roads, and a pipeline, and drilling 120 wells. None of the Company's projected $2 billion in revenues would be shared with the Huaorani, because the Ecuadorian state retains all subsurface mineral rights. But from the Huaorani point of view, money wasn't the issue. The issue was survival. Ecuador had a crippling international debt (of more than $12 billion, or about its annual gross national product), and it depended on oil production for nearly half its revenues. The government had outlawed any attempt by the Huaorani to impede the Company. In any case, from what I gathered, ONHAE had no office, no phone, and no money.

What, I asked, did the Huaorani propose to do?

It was Moi who answered, softly but without hesitation. "We will find the Company and talk to them," he said. "If they do not listen, we will attack with spears from all sides."

THE HUAORANI were not hard to spot in Coca, once you knew what to look for. They hate to travel alone—it's dangerous and boring—so they were usually in groups of two or three or more, often with their arms around one another. They are shy but keenly observant. They would stand for hours in front of the Kamikaze Disco or the Hotel Auca or a greasy spoon called Rosita's, studying the action as intently as if they were scanning the forest canopy for monkeys. If they were Huaorani making one of their first trips to town, you might see them on a street corner, mesmerized by the spectacle of cars and electric lights, or, if someone had given them shoes, by their own feet. A barefoot Huao from the far backcountry, a real tree climber, was particularly easy to spot: His big toes took off at right angles, like opposable thumbs. Sometimes you'd see a Huao walking through town innocently carrying a blowgun the length of a bazooka, while passersby froze in terror. Now and then a young Huao would come into some cash, by selling a blowgun or spear, or a harpy eagle, or a jaguar cub, or by earning slave wages as a boatman for a tour guide or a laborer for the Company, and he would bring an entourage of other Huaorani with him to Rosita's and spend everything he had buying his friends fried chicken and soft drinks. This was not profligacy: The Huaorani ideal is to be independent and self-reliant, and every effort is made to give the appearance, at least, of being so clearly in tune with the abundance of the forest that one is without fear of need. (By the time he is ten a Huao is expected to be able to survive on his own.) There is no higher manifestation of this ideal state than unqualified generosity, and no act more generous than to give away food.

You could often find Huaorani out toward the east end of Coca, at the Huaorani Hotel, as it's known—a cinder-block shack that the Capuchin mission let them use as a bunkhouse, and to which the Capuchins directed me shortly after I arrived in Coca and rang the bell at the mission gate. One morning a dozen Huaorani were sprawled across the shack's four bunk beds, draped one over another, wrestling and laughing. T-shirts, a couple of pairs of pants, and a blanket were hanging on a line outside—to dry, the Huaorani told me, although it was raining so hard you couldn't see ten feet.

"Moi, what time is it?" Enqueri yelled from beneath a pile of brown bodies.

Moi, sitting in a corner, looked at his wrist. "In Japan it is nine o'clock," he said. "In Europe it is ten. In Ecuador it is eleven. In America it is twelve."

"Twelve o'clock!" Enqueri said. "Time for the *cowode* to be hungry!"

Enqueri was the first Huao I came to know well. At five feet seven he was tall for a Huao. He had the meaty, forest walker's quadriceps that give the Huaorani an almost bowlegged lope on a city street, but his shoulders were uncharacteristically narrow, and when he laughed they shook up and down furiously, nearly touching his ears. When he laughed around *cowode*, he tried to keep his mouth closed, because he had learned to be ashamed of his bad teeth, but this was like holding a cat in a sack. Inevitably, he exploded in a steady cadence that went, quite literally, "ha-ha-ha-ha-ha." The other Huaorani called him Condorito, after a popular South American comic-book character—an avian, frenetically absentminded cross between Woody Woodpecker and Elmer Fudd. "Enqueri is like Condorito because his head has too many ideas," Amo told me. "One day he wants to be a schoolteacher, and the next day he wants to devote his life to the People, and the next day he is working for the Company, and the next day he wants to kill the Company, and the next day he is going to be a nurse, and the next day he wants to go to the sky and be with God."

Enqueri might well have been confused, but a man forced to leap from Stone Age to Petroleum Age is going to have a few things on his mind. He was perhaps the most literate of the Huaorani, able to read and write basic Spanish. These skills owed directly to the day in 1956 when his father helped kill five American evangelical missionaries who had plunged into the Huaorani territory bent on saving the "Aucas" from their heathen existence. They were "a hazard to explorers, an embarrassment to the republic of Ecuador, and a challenge to missionaries of the Gospel," one of the men, Nate Saint, wrote in his journal—a journal in which he recorded sharing dinner with the naked brown savage he called George, and which he kept right up until the moment George's friends ran him through with a spear. Nate had an older sister, Rachel, who'd raised him like a son, and when she got word of the massacre, she went after the savages. She applied herself with a holy vengeance. Within a few years, through sheer stubbornness, the intimidating magic of airplanes and bullhorns, and the seductive luxury of salt, white rice, and aluminum pots, she'd managed to establish a Christian beachhead inside the Huaorani territory, a few miles from the very spot where her brother Nate had eaten his last hamburger.

Supported by the Ecuadorian government and by legions of believers back home, Rachel built a chapel and an elementary school and set about sculpting a new model of Huao: one who spoke Spanish, saluted the flag, honored God, understood the value of a dollar (or, at least, an Ecuadorian sucre), and rejected such heathen practices as shamanism, nomadism, nudity, and "free love." The Condorito excelled in his studies and won the privilege of attending an evangelical secondary school outside the territory. Once on the outside, however, he fell under the influence of more worldly and sophisticated Indians who had begun to organize their people into federations of a decidedly leftist bent. He went home with some new ideas. When he got together with Nanto and Moi to found ONHAE, he said, Rachel branded him a Communist and his family ostracized him—and such ostracism in a clan society can be tantamount to a death sentence.

I asked Enqueri to define *Communist*. He thought about it for a moment, then said, "Someone from Cuba."

"Where is Cuba?"

"In France," he said, and added that when a Communist dies he cannot go to the sky.

I ASKED the Huaorani about the letter that had come to the Rainforest Action Network. Nanto said yes, it was from ONHAE. Why would anyone claim it wasn't? It was an official communication: It had been signed by the president, the vice president, and the secretary. What did I think of the ONHAE seal? He reached into a plastic bag, rummaged among shirts and pants, and produced a shiny black-plastic briefcase, the sole contents of which were an ink pad and a rubber stamp. He inked up the stamp and banged out a harpy eagle ringed by the name of the organization. "Isn't that beautiful?" he asked.

How had the letter reached the United States?

Nanto shrugged and said, "We gave it to a *cowode* we met here in Coca."

I asked the Huaorani what they thought of the various proposals being put forth in their name, or for their land, by environmental and human-rights groups in the United States and Europe. As it turned out, the one thing all the groups had in common was that the Huaorani didn't recognize any of them.

"How can these people speak for us," Nanto asked me, "if we have never met them?"

DuPont's Edgar Woolard had made it known that he would not

give Conoco the go-ahead for its Oriente project unless the oil company came up with some sort of "green" blessing—some stamp of approval from the nonprofit community. In secret negotiations that inadvertently had been made public two weeks before I left the United States, the Natural Resources Defense Council, an environmental group based in New York City, had indicated to Conoco that it was willing to confer such a blessing if Conoco would fund a foundation to benefit the Oriente's Indian groups. No one knew how much money that would be, though the numbers being used in the negotiations ran from $10 million to more than $200 million.

I tried to explain to the Huaorani what such numbers meant, but these were men who on the rare occasions when they worked for wages earned about a dollar a day, and whose fathers counted "one, two, one and two." Still, Moi dismissed the foundation idea outright. "You cannot put a price on our land," he said.

I asked if it was true, as I'd been told by Conoco and by the NRDC, that only ten Huaorani lived in Block Sixteen, the concession that was first in line for development.

When Moi heard this he almost exploded. "No!" he said. "That is what the Company wants people to believe, but it is not true at all. There are at least five clans in there."

"Are you sure?" I asked.

"Yes," he said. "Some live inside and some live outside, but all hunt and travel in that place."

"Can I see this?" I asked.

"Why do you want to see this?"

"I would like to see the Huaorani you have spoken about and write about what I see."

"You will write a letter to the United States of North America?"

"I will write something like a letter."

He thought this over. After a while he said, "Many people talk about the Huaorani. But they do not come to see."

Nanto proposed a deal: If I would cover the costs of the trip and a fee for Enqueri's time, Enqueri would take me to Block Sixteen. He would make a census of the area, and I would be a witness. Our optimal route would be roughly circular. In Coca we—I—would hire a small truck to haul us sixty miles south down an oil-exploration road called the Vía Auca, until we reached the Shiripuno River, which could be followed east by canoe to the Cononaco River. There Amo's grandfather, Quemperi, lived with his clan. From the Cononaco we would walk seventy-five miles north, to the Yasuní River, crossing Block Sixteen. With luck, one of the Huaorani clans on that river would take us by canoe down the Yasuní and back up the Napo, west to Coca.

Advised of this plan, Enqueri said, "The trip will take two weeks or four weeks or six weeks."

"It might even take a month," Amo said.

I WENT to the military command post. Under Ecuadorian law a foreigner could legally enter the Huaorani territory without Huaorani permission, but not without the permission of the military. This was not hard to arrange if you were an employee of the Company or a missionary, or if you were willing to hire any of the dozen or so licensed tour guides in Coca. I wasn't. Disease brought by the tourism industry had had a brutal impact on the Huaorani; competition for tourist trinkets often pit one clan against another; and despite the hefty fees charged by the professional guides, the Huaorani didn't receive a cent—except on the rare occasion that a Huao hired on as a boatman, for which he earned, at most, the equivalent of about fifty cents a day.

Entering the Huaorani territory simply as a friend of the Huaorani, however, was virtually impossible. Nominally, this was because none of the Huaorani had been licensed as a guide. Few of them could read Spanish well enough to pass the required course, and the licensing fee was far more than even the most ambitious Huao could earn in a year of hard labor. But the real reason the Huaorani could not bring outsiders into their territory was political. The military controls most of the oil-producing land, and it looks harshly on foreigners. As the captain working the command post explained to me, darkly: "They bring a mountain of bad ideas." "Outside influences" were blamed whenever the Huaorani, or any other of the Oriente's Indian groups, began to agitate against oil development, and what few human-rights workers there were in the Oriente were often threatened and sometimes jailed.

The captain was one of the Tigres, Ecuador's crack jungle troops. The Tigres receive training in the United States. "You guys really know how to make some pain," he said, in a tone of genuine appreciation. Then, grinning, he told me that if I so much as thought about trying to get inside the Huaorani territory, I'd regret it.

I FOUND Nanto and his wife, Alicia, standing in the street in front of the Huaorani Hotel, ankle deep in oily mud. Nanto was holding their one-year-old baby girl in his arms. They were silent and, as far as I could tell, going nowhere at all. I told him about the problem with the military.

"The president of Ecuador has never been to my home," he said, "but he tells me who I can bring there." He looked up and down the street. He looked at the sky. After a while he said, "There are problems on all sides." He told me to find Enqueri and give him some money. "Be ready to travel," he said. "Be careful while you are in Coca. Study the walls of your hotel room. If there is Quichua writing there, move to another room. A Quichua witch might climb out of the wall and kill you. You must protect yourself until you are in the forest, where it is safe."

Then he asked me to tell him the story of Snow White and the Seven Dwarfs. He stopped me once and asked me to explain snow, but otherwise he listened stone-faced. When I finished I said good-bye. Nanto said nothing. A few minutes later, when I reached a bend in the road, I looked back. He and his family were still standing in the mud, exactly as I had found them.

IT WAS near the dawn of a hot, sunny morning when a small truck pulled up to my hotel. Enqueri was sitting in the bed, surrounded by a fifty-five-gallon drum of gas, ten liters of oil, a hundred-pound bag of rice and another of sugar, and a plastic sack filled with cooking oil, shotgun shells, cookies, fishhooks, canned tuna, five pairs of rubber boots, three pairs of men's undershorts, and who knows what else. He handed me a fistful of cash and a piece of paper. "Your change and your receipt," he said.

As we rolled through the streets of Coca, one Huao after another materialized out of the shadows—men and women and children and babies—and by the time we reached the great brown Napo, at least fifteen of them were stuffed into the truck's bed and hanging off its sides. They screamed with delight when the truck careened around a corner and threatened to pitch them headlong into the street. When we approached the military checkpoint at the bridge, Enqueri pushed down on my shoulders, forcing me to the floor. Bodies smelling of earth and smoke swarmed over me. The truck slowed, then stopped, and I heard an exchange in Spanish; one of the voices was Enqueri's. Then we accelerated. Fifteen minutes later Enqueri hauled me to my feet. Before us the oil-soaked dirt road known as the Vía Auca snaked into low hills, and far in the distance it dropped into an arboreal quiltwork that looked to be four billion shades of green.

"*Abundancia*," Enqueri said.

2

B Y THE TIME the morning sun burst above the forest wall,
Enqueri and I and the truckload of Huaorani were a good
twenty miles out of Coca, barreling down the Vía Auca
toward the territory, sweat streaming from every pore. The
Auca is pitted and gouged and an oily mess, but the land surrounding
it is breathtaking: Behind and around us, in the undulating terrain
where the Amazon basin meets the Andes, volcanic peaks loomed above
mist-shrouded hills. It is in this region, where two distinct climate zones
join, that the Oriente is at its richest. Thirty million years ago, the
Oriente was an embayment of the Pacific Ocean. Four and a half
million years ago, the Andes thrust up from the earth, creating finely
subdivided habitats—deep valleys separated by high ridges, with micro-
climates that change radically over short distances. Plants, and the
insects and birds and other creatures that evolved with them, were
isolated, encouraging such intense speciation that in its endemism—
the presence of species that exist nowhere else—the Oriente may be the
richest place in the world. Though it is about the size of Alabama, it is
home to an estimated 8,000 to 12,000 species of plants, or up to 5
percent of all the plant species on earth. At a single research station near
the Napo River, observers have recorded 491 species of birds, or about
two-thirds as many as are found in the entire continental United States.
Four hundred seventy-three species of trees—more than are native to
all of Western Europe—have been identified in a plot of forest about
the size of two football fields.

By almost all accounts the richest section of this incredibly rich region is the land and rivers the Huaorani have inhabited for centuries. The traditional Huaorani homeland is roughly 120 miles wide, east to west, and 75 to 100 miles north to south. The ferocity with which the Huaorani defend themselves is legendary among their indigenous neighbors, which include not only nations of comparable size—the Siona, the Secoya, and the remaining Cofans—but the formidable group of interrelated peoples on their southern flank that includes the Shuar, the Achuar, and the Shiwiar, and now totals about 50,000; and, to the north, west, and south, the extraordinarily fecund Quichua, whose population is now approaching 100,000. Of all the Oriente's indigenous groups, large and small, only the Huaorani consider themselves never to have been conquered.

If there is one glaring contradiction to the Huaorani sense of sovereignty, it is the Vía Auca. From Coca the road runs due south into the territory, splitting it almost down the middle, and for four miles on each side the land has been set aside for colonization. This zone is a legacy of the symbiotic relationship between American evangelical missionaries and the Company. In the late 1960s and the 1970s, in understandings worked out with the government and with Texaco, Rachel Saint and other North American missionaries affiliated with the Summer Institute of Linguistics (a worldwide evangelical network, headquartered in Texas, that is dedicated to translating the Bible into indigenous tongues) conducted a program of pacification that, with the aid of magic and trinkets—airplanes and mirrors and salt—lured most of the Huaorani into a small protectorate on the far western edge of their traditional lands. This move helped Texaco blaze the route of the Vía Auca, which opened the Huaorani territory not only to further oil development but also, for the first time, to large-scale colonization.

The Auca is only sixty miles long, but it is the forward line of battle: It is the deepest penetration, by road, that has been made anywhere in the upper Amazonian watershed.

FOR ALMOST the entire four hours it takes to drive the length of the Vía Auca, a rusty steel pipeline runs alongside the road. In some places the pipeline rests right on the ground, and in others it is raised on stilts. Men tether their horses to it, women spread their washing on it to dry, and children play on it. On a clear day the metal soaks up so much equatorial sun that it's hot to the touch, and when you rest a hand on it you feel the oil pulsing along inside. Every few miles the line passes a separation station, where a flame as big as a house flares from a metal stack, burning off natural gas. The flames are visible for miles. They burn night and day, producing such intense heat that colonists spread their coffee harvest beneath them to dry.

Oil and oil-waste spills are common on the Auca. Trucks plow into the pipeline, trees fall on it, and in some places it is nearly rusted through. It has no check valves, and when it ruptures it can spill for days, until someone at a receiving station far down the line notices a drop in production. Sometimes the spills are deliberate. Two-thirds of the way down the road, at the Shiripuno River, there is a Texaco well inherited by Petroecuador. "The Company dug a canal from the waste pit to the river," Enqueri said, "and it drained right above a Huaorani village. Children were swimming in the river. When they came up out of the water, they had black all over their bodies. They were asking, What is this? Nanto went to the Company, but the Company said the spill had not happened. There was nothing we could do."

From beginning to end the Vía Auca is lined, in ones and twos and clumps, with the rickety wooden shacks of colonists. They come from southern Ecuador, from the coast, and from the Oriente itself—many of the new settlers are Shuar. The colonists raise cattle and coffee—neither of them well suited to the area's poor soils—but mostly they work for the Company, cutting roads, digging wells, cooking food. The colonists suffer, and their children are often hungry and sick. Still, they say that life on the Auca is better than the life they left behind. By law the land was there for the taking, free to anyone willing to cut down the trees and work it, and in Ecuador land, no matter how poor, has always been the true measure of wealth.

The mood along the road was tense. Bored with the trinkets and magic that had drawn them into the protectorate, several Huaorani clans had drifted back to the Auca, and violent confrontations with the colonists were common. In Coca Enqueri had heard that a Huao had been killed near the Shiripuno River, and when we arrived at the bridge, two dozen colonists and a handful of Huaorani were waging a heated argument in the middle of the road, their anger held in check only tenuously by a gang of nervous soldiers too preoccupied to notice me. Nobody was dead, but shots had been fired and houses burned. Enqueri defused the situation by giving the Huaorani much of the food and gas we were carrying and sending them downriver, but he said that it was only a temporary solution at best.

A little farther down the road he showed me an exploration camp that had been operated by Unocal from 1989 until 1991. When the camp was abandoned a Huaorani clan tore it apart, to prevent it from being taken over by the military, and then built huts on top of the old cement foundations. Anything the Huaorani hadn't destroyed they put to use. In one hut a wood fire burned on a linoleum floor, and the head of a wild pig had been strung on an electric cord to smoke. In another, masticated manioc fermented in a stainless-steel sink. In several homes sheets of heavy plastic had been fashioned into hammocks, and drinking water was stored in old gasoline cans. At the last home we visited I found a shelf full of drugs: erythromycin, codeine, penicillin, and half a dozen others. Next to them lay a dirt-encrusted spoon. The man of the house said that the Company had given him the medicine, and that his family took it for coughs.

"Which one do you take for coughs?" I asked.

"They are all the same," he said.

Beyond the camp the Vía Auca died into a small, muddy track that led to an exploration well operated by Petro-Canada in 1989 and 1990. Within weeks after the well was opened, three Huaorani clans occupied the site to compete for looting rights. One was led by Babae, whose father and grandfather had hunted the area tamed by the Vía Auca. The Company convinced Babae's clan to leave the well by building twelve small shacks for them on the Vía Auca. After they settled in they held a celebration feast. No other Huaorani came, but the Company did, and so did the missionaries and the military, and Babae drank his first hard liquor. Before long he was in a mission-run detox program, and the clan women were working the oil camps as prostitutes, and many Huaorani were sick with *cowode* disease. The next year the colonists who had been thrown off the land so the shacks could be built returned and burned them.

To keep Babae happy the Company built him a new house. Enqueri took me there. Babae was sitting on the front step, sipping a bottle of rum. Deep chested and broad shouldered, he radiated enormous physical strength. He was said to have a violent temper, one that inspired fear all along the Vía Auca, among Huaorani and colonists alike. Fortunately, Enqueri had brought fishhooks and rice, and at these Babae grinned hugely, flashing a mouthful of gleaming teeth—Company dentures.

Babae was proud of his new house, though it was built of planks rather than the traditional thatch, and had no windows, and was dark as a cave, and felt hot enough to bake bread. One room had a foam mattress, gnawed to shreds by rats. This, Babae said, was where tourists would stay. The family cooked in the next room, on a pile of sand that had been poured onto the wood floor, and slept in the third, which was carpeted wall to wall with Company flotsam: candy wrappers, discarded tuna tins, spent shotgun shells, a couple of car tires, a broken radio, several empty rum bottles and cigarette cartons, an empty fuel can, old magazines and newspapers. Babae pointed out the light fixtures and wall sockets. Of course, the house had no electricity. The Company, he said, had given him a generator, but someone had come in the night and stolen it.

We did not stay long. Enqueri said you never knew when Babae might explode. We left him sitting on his front step with an arm wrapped around the shoulders of his son, who looked even more powerful than his father until he stood up and exposed his withered left leg, crippled by polio.

ENQUERI AND I headed for the Shiripuno River, where ONHAE kept a funky canoe. Carved from a single tree trunk, it was about twenty feet long and two feet wide and patched with bits of tin, cloth, leather, and, directly beneath me amidships, a one-liter plastic Coke bottle butterflied and flattened and nailed over a long crack in the floor.

The green Shiripuno slips slowly east into the silt-brown Cononaco, which in turn slips into the Curaray somewhere near the Peruvian border. On even the best maps of South America this hundred-mile watershed is blank. Running with the current through a forest that grows ever richer, with parrots, turtles, caimans, monkeys, herons, the occasional harpy eagle, and, if one is lucky, the golden flash of a jaguar, a canoe takes three days to reach the clearing where Quemperi and his clan have settled. It is about as far as one can travel in the known Huaorani world, and you must skirt the northern boundary of the territory hunted by the Tagaeri, the clan that killed Alejandro Labaca. Occasionally there were rumors of a Tagaeri sighting, and though there had been no documented contact with them, it was widely believed that they watched everything that happened on the Cononaco.

Farther downriver, in the sixty or so miles between Quemperi's clan and the Peruvian border, there were said to be three more clans. In 1992 a Company seismic crew were the first to spot a group thought to be the Taromenga. ONHAE maintained that the confrontation was violent, but the Company denied this, and in any case the Taromenga were not seen again. The other groups, the Oñamenane and the Huiñatare, had never been reached; their existence was suggested only through the stories of the Huaorani elders.

Along the river Huaorani appeared out of the forest in twos and threes, bearing children, shotguns, and pots of banana juice, and after a momentary pause to twist my chest hairs or paw the stubble on my chin, and another moment to hiccup with laughter, they clambered aboard our canoe. Though it was soon filled beyond capacity, no one was refused. With earsplitting shotgun blasts a long-eared old man riding in the bow killed a paca, a couple of woolly monkeys, and several turkeys. Throughout each of these messy affairs—the game was hauled in and cleaned, and blood coursed thickly through the canoe and coated my bare feet—the other Huaorani roared so enthusiastically with advice and approval that they nearly tipped the boat over.

Enqueri released the tiller only once all day. He laced his hands on top of his head. "When a Huao sees a girl he likes," he said, "he drops one hand, like this. That means, meet me over there." Or he might point discreetly with a forefinger. "And if you think a woman wants to make love with you, you wink your right eye to say yes and your left eye to say no." He winked his left eye. "But Enqueri can't close his right eye!" he said. He tried, grimacing with effort; his lid stuck like a jammed window shade. "See? It doesn't work. So Enqueri has a hard time getting women!"

At this he laughed so hard he doubled over. The canoe ran up on a submerged boulder, and, with a sound like a gunshot, a crack five feet long opened in the floor. Water raced into the boat. Howling wildly, women reached under their skirts and ripped off their underwear and men pulled small rocks from the river. They stuffed them into the void, then bailed and kept going. Soon the stories started—the Huaorani would be telling this one for days.

3

To MY EYE the only sign that we had reached Quemperi's
settlement was the sudden appearance of a long, silent line
of Huaorani standing in a clearing on the right-hand side of
a broad bend in the Cononaco River. There might have been
thirty of them. Some held spears; some were naked. They neither waved
nor spoke; they simply stared. They stood atop a bank about fifteen feet
high, but it felt as if they were studying us from a much greater height.

After Enqueri and I climbed up through the mud, a short, pot-
bellied old man with a single tooth in the middle of his upper gum
walked over to me, indicated that I should open my mouth, then tapped
my teeth one by one. He said something in Huaorani, and a roar of
laughter went up.

"Quemperi says welcome," Enqueri said. "He wants to know if you
will give him your teeth."

At a nod from Quemperi a gaggle of small boys slid down the bank
and began hauling up our gear, which they deposited at the shaded
edge of an otherwise barren, sun-broiled stretch of open ground a few
yards from the river—an airstrip, or *pista*, as it was known. For years
Quemperi and his clan had roamed widely between the Cononaco
River and the Yasuní, to the north, changing homesites every few
months, alternating among half a dozen manioc gardens. About 1991,
however, they settled more or less permanently around the *pista*, which
the Company built during the seismic testing of the region and then
abandoned. The *pista* was intended to be temporary, but the Huaorani
were fastidious about keeping it free of brush. It was the only significant

patch of open ground for miles in any direction. From their point of view, it was a kind of trap, really, which from time to time caught missionaries, tourists, or the Company. The *cowode* didn't come often, but when they did they always brought gifts. Most Huaorani had never seen a car, a horse, or a bicycle, but the airplane had become as integral a part of their world as the blowgun, the banana, and the boa. They would have identified the make of an inbound craft long before a visitor could hear it coming ("Cessna!" they would yell, racing for the *pista*), and when the plane revved up to leave, the young Huaorani men would plant themselves behind the tail and bare their chests to the fusillade of rock and dirt blasted their way by the prop wash.

Enqueri and I spent eleven days with Quemperi, much of the time ducking in and out of the ten houses that had been built around the *pista*. Most of them were of the traditional, thatched-A-frame design, with the roofs extending to dirt floors, and they were cool and pleasant. When the Huaorani were not out hunting or gardening, or when it was raining, which was often (the first Huaorani phrase I learned was "It is wet around here"), they passed many hours in their hammocks. Some-times they were resting, but usually they were working—sharpening a spear, perhaps, or braiding palm leaf into cord, or chewing manioc, which would be left to ferment into a drink called *chicha*. They talked constantly. Their material goods were few: A typical house had a couple of machetes, a shotgun, some spears and blowguns, two or three cook-ing pots, and several hammocks.

Inside each hut a small fire burned most of the day, and there was always something for a visitor—*chicha*, banana juice, a piece of boiled manioc, a smoked monkey arm. Some of the men, many of the women, and all the children went naked, or wore a thin strap about the groin. In older times the entire clan had slept in one big house, but now each household slept around its own fire. During the night one or more of the adults would awaken and sing. The songs, rendered in a haunting three-note scale, and finished with a short, invigorating yodel, told of hunting, travel, the history of the clan, war, love. A hairy-legged can-nibal was welcome to sing his songs, too.

Despite the *pista*, in other words, Quemperi and his clan seemed to live much as the Huaorani had lived for centuries. They might drink banana juice from aluminum pots, but they still drank banana juice. They might hunt woolly monkeys with shotguns, but they still hunted woolly monkeys. Turkey, monkey, caiman, and peccary were plentiful, and so was material for spears, blowguns, hammocks, and string bags. They had long ago developed treatments for the illnesses indigenous to the area, and though scabies and skin funguses were common, and phlegm-larded, tubercular hacks often split the night air, they had only sporadic contact with the Company and had avoided many of the viral infections that in the last twenty years had become the major cause of Huaorani death.

Nevertheless, life was often brutal. At twenty-five Enqueri had already reached middle age. Typically, the body of an adult Huao displayed half a dozen major scars, from staph infection, shotgun and outboard-motor accidents, falls, animal and snake bites. Many Huaorani were missing pieces of fingers and toes and large chunks of flesh, and in the entire adult population there was probably not a single full set of teeth. Still, as Quemperi was quick to assert, life along the Cononaco was superior to life in the protectorate, which was crowded and sedentary, and it was infinitely better than life along the Vía Auca—a life of, at best, canned tuna and Coca-Cola.

Quemperi had a gentle disposition and a generous nature: When he hunted he usually brought some grandkids along for instruction, and he always chuckled to himself while doing such quotidian tasks as making blowgun darts, weaving fresh leaves into his roof, and hauling firewood. But it would have been foolish to think Quemperi anything less than a warrior. Around the fire he spoke of killing Ecuadorian soldiers for their machetes, Peruvian soldiers for their boots, oil workers for their food and T-shirts, Quichua for daring to cross the Napo into Huaorani land. Smiling, he told the story of Toña, one of the first Huaorani converted by Rachel Saint. Toña traveled to the Cononaco to preach to Quemperi, and brought with him an evil so strong that it killed a child. Quemperi asked Toña to help him make spears. When the spears were ready, Quemperi said, he and seven other Huaorani men turned on Toña and, one by one, thrust them home. Quemperi went last, using a spear that Toña himself had made.

QUEMPERI USUALLY sat beside the fire when we spoke, but when I asked his thoughts on the Conoco road, he stood up and declaimed loudly and forcefully, sometimes stamping his feet for emphasis. It was the only time I saw him angry—indeed, it was the only time I saw any Huao angry—and the display was a frightening one. The ninety-mile road that Conoco proposed to build, and along which it would develop all its 120 wells, would terminate in the heart of Quemperi's traditional hunting territory. By then it would have traversed the territory of the five or six clans that inhabit the area north of Quemperi, and it would have opened up to petroleum exploitation—by Conoco and the growing list of companies counting on the infrastructure Conoco would build—the homelands of the Tagaeri, the Taromenga, and, if they exist, the Oña-menane and the Huiñatare. The dangers the road posed for the Huao-rani were, of course, complex and immense—exposure to a simple flu, for example, could wipe out the uncontacted groups—but Quemperi's analysis was direct: A road means bad hunting. Game won't cross it. Colonists will come and cut down the forest and kill the animals. A road, in other words, meant hunger. It meant the end of abundance, and the end of the self-reliance and independence the Huaorani value above all else.

ENQUERI WENT about his work in Cononaco with diligence. He kept his census in a small spiral notebook, in a neat schoolboy script. He visited each household and, slowly and carefully, wrote down the name of each member and his or her birth date, or an approximation: "In the season of the palm fruit" became February. Many of the younger people knew what year they had been born in, but few of the elders did, and Enqueri had to dead reckon. Quemperi found this exercise hilarious. "I am eighty!" he said at one point, then, "I am forty!" and, still later, "I am six!" What these numbers actually meant to Quemperi was anybody's guess. The only number that really meant anything was "enough," which you either had or had not. The world in which he had been raised had been so contained, in fact, that a typical Huao would have lived his entire life without laying eyes on more than seventy or eighty people, almost all of whom he would know by name.

Quemperi's clan numbered about thirty-five. I knew this not from Enqueri's census but because whenever Quemperi or his daughter was preparing food for me, almost every member of the clan descended on the hut. I would see them running across the *pista*, yelling to one another. They would jam up at the door and elbow their way in, then stand along the wall, splay into hammocks, sprawl on the dirt floor. Once inside they were dead silent. The children would snuggle up next to me, and because smell and touch are still principal means by which the Huaorani gather information, I constantly felt little fingers running up my shirt or beneath my arms or along the back of my neck or, now and then, inside the waistband of my shorts.

I was allowed to eat first, using my fingers to scoop food from a small plastic bowl I had brought with me. Thirty-five pairs of eyes followed every move I made, because when I finished eating I was expected to pass along the leftovers. I was also expected to provide enough for everyone, and I quickly learned that if there is one thing a Huao can do well, it is eat. Their eating took them beyond the demands of hunger, beyond simple gluttony, into a whole other zone of engorgement the likes of which I had never seen before. They ate everything in sight. Afterward, it was all they could do to wobble back to their huts and collapse in bloated discomfort.

Enqueri and I had brought supplies that we thought would last three weeks. They were gone in four days.

"Shouldn't we save some for later?" I asked him, and he passed this along to Quemperi.

"Later?" Quemperi said. "What is 'later'?"

Fortunately, we had prepared one sack of emergency food—rice, chocolate bars, canned tuna—which Enqueri kept in his care, so that we would have something for our long trek. But once our main supplies vanished I was onto a Huaorani diet. This meant I went hungry for three days, until I learned that I had to ask to be fed. Then there was the problem of getting the food down. What is revolting about monkey, for example, isn't the taste but the smell. A good eating monkey runs twenty to thirty pounds, or roughly the size of a three-year-old child. The carcass is thrown on the fire whole. First the hair burns off; burning, it smells exactly like human hair. Then the skin chars, and as it shrinks back from the skull the lips shrivel up over the teeth. About then—if you are tired and hungry and feeling a bit out of your element—it is easy to imagine that you are watching a hideously grinning dwarf being burned alive. Later an arm is cut off and you eat it holding it by the wrist, cupping the dainty, shriveled fingers.

Of course, there is always *chicha*, which is made by wives and by elder women. They masticate raw manioc, spit it into a pot, and leave it to ferment. Later—a day, two days, or, if it is time for a fiesta and a stronger brew is required, a week or longer—it is diluted with water and drunk from a bowl in long drafts. (No matter how diluted the *chicha*, it retains a certain slobbery essence: Imagine corn kernels drenched in raw egg.) *Chicha* is said to be quite nutritious, and, carried in a damp but undiluted form and mixed with water as needed, it is often the principal sustenance during treks of a week or more. At home it is ubiquitous—it is taken with all meals and offered whenever there is a visitor. As the Huaorani term for "happiness" has it, "another serving of *chicha* we laugh happily."

Even when left to ferment completely, *chicha* never gets much stronger than very weak beer. However, like all American Indians, the Huaorani lack an enzyme critical to metabolizing alcohol, and a typical house *chicha* draped even a stalwart young buck like Enqueri in rosy good cheer. Leaning back in a hammock, sipping *chicha* steadily from a deep bowl, spinning tales of all that he had seen across the Napo, where the sky met the ground and the world was thought to end, he would hold the other Huaorani in thrall through an entire evening. Late into the night I would hear his voice drifting across the *pista*, by turns frenetic and singsong, broken up by peals of laughter.

ONE NIGHT, as Enqueri and I sat around the fire talking to Quemperi, I said, "Enqueri, please ask Quemperi if the Huaorani still kill people."

Enqueri had a long exchange with Quemperi, who punctuated his reply with much shouting and finger-pointing and deep grunting. Then Enqueri turned to me. "He says no."

"When did they stop?"

Another long exchange: shrieks, howls, stamping of feet.

"He says September."

"September of what year?"

"This year."

This conversation took place in July.

• • •

I CAME to learn that the Huaorani are highly egalitarian: Though work is divided by gender—men hunt, women garden—neither is considered more worthy than the other. I learned, too, that in their self-reliance they display a clear-eyed pragmatism, and that they strive for family harmony. But the Huaorani are not known for these qualities. What they are known for is killing.

The Huaorani kill outsiders for obvious reasons: to fend them off, or to steal their goods. But when it comes to killing their own—who, until quite recently at least, they killed as often as they killed anyone else—the Huaorani follow fairly strict rules. Almost always such killing is a matter of revenge, usually for the death of a child. The Huaorani consider all human deaths to have been caused by other humans, and require all to be avenged. A Huao does not kill alone; he must persuade other men in his clan to assist him. Each man makes a half dozen or more spears and personalizes them with carvings and feathers. Spearing is performed on moonless nights; rain is considered a good sign. The killing must be done face to face, and for several weeks afterward the killers must not hunt, eat meat, or sleep indoors.

Mercy killings of both the newborn and the aged were common in the past and probably continue today among the groups with the least exposure to missionaries. Because self-sufficiency means so much to the Huaorani, the dependency that comes with old age is unacceptable, and the aged often asked to be killed rather than become a burden on their offspring. The very young children of dying parents—the terminally ill, say, or someone mortally wounded in a raid—were sometimes buried alive with their parents, and unwanted infants were killed at birth, usually by choking. (The clan as a whole could suggest this, but the final decision was the birth mother's. However, another clan member could intervene to save the child if he or she took responsibility for raising it.)

Although it is rare today, spear killing is still practiced. In May of 1994 a Huaorani clan spear-killed a Quichua and two Shuar, and severely wounded two others, in a revenge attack triggered by the death of a Huaorani child. In any case spear killing remains a central fact of how the Huaorani see themselves. Many adults carry, and proudly display, spear scars from the battles of their youths, and the old people still chant killing songs:

You are not from here.
You are different.
I will hunt you like a wild pig.
I will plunge my spear into your body many times.
It will not break.
Down you will go.
You will never leave.
You are quick like a monkey, running through the treetops,
*   but now you will die. . . .*
I have no fear.
My enemies hunt for me.
Their spears may come tonight, or the next night.
They will pierce my body again and again.
When I die I will make no sound.
I am like the jaguar.
I have no fear.

FIRSTHAND EXPERIENCE of spear killing is rare among younger Huaorani, but it remains a source of both pride and fear—which is why Enqueri was not entirely comfortable in Cononaco. One day he told me that the Huaorani who lived there were "uncivilized."

"What do you mean?" I asked.

"They have no radio," he said, "and they do not play volleyball."

What he actually meant was that he was afraid. Raised on radio and volleyball and El Señor (the Christian God), the Condorito now found himself immersed in what the missionaries had taught him was the dark and demonic side of the Huaorani culture. As traditional as it appeared, Quemperi's clan was the most acculturated wing of what the missionary literature refers to as the "ridge group"—those Huaorani, small in number but fierce in reputation, who lived far downriver from the evangelical protectorate and who for the most part had eluded its influence. "Ridge" refers to a divide between the Cononaco and Yasuní basins, which Enqueri and I intended to cross on foot. It was said to be inhabited by three clans. While it is probably true that no Huaorani have escaped at least some influence by the missionaries—among even the most remote clans, one occasionally spots a Maidenform bra—contact with the ridge group had been minimal, and our proposed trek caused

Enqueri no small anxiety (which, in Huaorani, is the same as the word for "kill"). Visitation rights among the Huaorani are determined by a complex system of familial ties, and anyone lacking them, even a Huao, is considered an enemy.

The first clan we were likely to encounter was that of Quemperi's cousin Menga. There was no way to gauge how Menga would receive us, and as a precautionary measure, Enqueri had arranged for us to be accompanied by Quemperi's son-in-law, Miñiwa. Among the younger Cononaco men, Miñiwa had experienced the least contact with the outside, and he retained the appearance and bearing of the elders: He had drooping, perforated earlobes, long, black hair, shoulders a yard wide, and, because he spent as much time walking in the treetops as he did on the forest floor, feet deformed into crescents. He lived to hunt. Rare was the day when I did not see him striding across the *pista* with the carcass of a woolly monkey slung across his back, its arms locked around his neck in rigor mortis. Quemperi said that when Miñiwa was still a boy they had raided a military camp and butchered five soldiers for their axes.

Miñiwa spoke no Spanish, but he was, as near as I could tell, absolutely without fear. His gaze was so penetrating, so intense, that whenever it came to settle on me I felt very much as if he intended to "hunt you like a wild pig." He rifled through my pack at will, and though he took nothing, he experimented with everything—even, mimicking me, my dental floss, for which he had no apparent use. Often when I sat in Quemperi's hut making notes, Miñiwa would kneel right behind me and rest his chin on my shoulder. One day he reached down, yanked my pen out of my hand, and, gripping it like an ice pick, drew on the page. He made a series of half circles, opening first one way, then the opposite way, back and forth. When he finished he pointed to one of them and said a whole lot of things, of which I caught only one word: Menga. It would be weeks before I understood that Miñiwa had drawn a map. The half circles represented watersheds, with creeks and rivers running one way, then another. In the middle, at the biggest divide, we would find Menga: still on the ridge, still, for all intents and purposes, beyond contact.

4

ONE DAY, shortly after dawn, Enqueri appeared at Quemperi's hut and announced that he was ready to hit the trail. He was wearing only a camouflage baseball hat, a faux Yves Saint Laurent belt cinched up over his navel, a pair of men's underpants, and a pair of rubber boots. He was also wearing, proudly, the backpack he had asked me to buy for him, but it was little more than an ornament. We had almost nothing left to carry. Most of our emergency stores had been looted, along with my Swiss Army knife, my long pants, a roll of duct tape, and my extra socks. When I explained this to Enqueri, he hooted with laughter. "The Huaorani," he said, "they are the *worst*."

Still, we were to travel with Miñiwa, which meant we would find food along the way. Or so I'd thought. Standing there in his BVDs, however, Enqueri suddenly informed me that Miñiwa had decided to stay home. Instead, we would be accompanied by three boys. Two were teenagers, one a twelve-year-old. We had no radio, so we could not call a plane, and we had no gas, so we could not go back upriver to the Vía Auca by boat. The only way out was north to the Yasuní, on foot, across seventy-five miles of steaming, unmapped wilderness, and the prospect of making that journey without an experienced guide and hunter was more than I could handle, to say the least. "We need men, not children!" I shouted at Enqueri. "How will we eat? How will we find the trail?"

"The boys know the way," he said, but he would not look me in the eye. Then he added, strongly, "My people can travel ten days without food."

"Maybe they can," I said, "but *I* can't, and neither can you." Compared with the muscular young hunters in Quemperi's clan, Enqueri was a city slicker, no more likely to kill a monkey than I was.

Rummaging in my pack, however, I came up with five shotgun shells, and these gifts persuaded Miñiwa to accompany us. As for my tantrum, it hadn't lasted long, but by the time I finished we were surrounded by pretty much the whole clan. No one spoke. I had witnessed almost no public anger among the Huaorani. Surely my outburst shocked them, and it left me unsettled.

I turned and walked toward the river as calmly as I could, trying to show no fear, but when I reached the high, muddy bank I misstepped and tripped and slid down it face first and into the water, coming to a soggy stop beneath the canoe. Spitting mud, I looked up to find most of the clan standing along the bank. Some of them were pointing at me, and some were mimicking my fall. Others were so convulsed by laughter that they had to lean on one another for support.

Giggling, one of Quemperi's granddaughters knelt in the bow of the canoe and poled us across the Cononaco. One by one, we climbed the north bank and ducked into the dark forest.

WE PICKED UP a faint hunting trail and hiked all day in single file, as the Huaorani always do, and we did not stop for the lunch we did not carry. At ground level the bush was thin, but the canopy was dense as a circus tent, revealing neither sun nor sky. The forest was surprisingly quiet, and we walked in silence. The twelve-year-old, Yohue, led the way, Enqueri followed him, I followed Enqueri, and the two teenagers, Quimonca and Awa, followed me, herding me like sheepdogs ("Psssst, psssst"). Miñiwa took up the rear with his five-year-old son, who kept pace with no apparent difficulty.

As we walked I wondered whether there had been malice in the Huaorani's sudden change of plans. Having helped themselves to what valuables I carried, were they now ready to abandon me to the forest? On the other hand, I thought, the matter might well be as simple as it appeared: No one in the clan but the three boys had felt like traveling. This was an adventure for them—they intended to accompany Enqueri all the way to his home on the far side of the territory, a journey none of them had made before. It would take them at least two weeks to get there, and yet they carried nothing but the shirts on their backs, their shorts, and their cheap rubber boots. In fact, young Yohue lacked even these. His left foot was bare, and on his right he wore only a cotton sock, which slapped the soggy trail like a beaver's tail.

Suddenly, Yohue stopped short, his way blocked by a brown-and-orange snake about five feet long and thick as a man's arm.

"Boa," Enqueri said. I couldn't tell for certain what it was, and *boa* appeared to be the only Spanish word the Huaorani had for snakes. Still, fear stopped each one of us in his tracks. The Huaorani have an extraordinarily high incidence of death from snakebite. Most adults have been bitten at least once, and many have suffered multiple bites. In fact, the snake represents the most evil force in the Huaorani cosmology, and the magic of a boa *curandero*, or witch doctor, as the evangelical ministry has it, is especially feared. Killing any snake, poisonous or not, is a powerful and pragmatic taboo. Enqueri hacked a detour well away from this one, and we hustled past it as quietly as we could.

A few minutes later Miñiwa announced that his son had malaria, and that he would bring him back to the *pista*, then catch up with us on the trail. Naively, I believed him. As it turned out, I would never see him again. It would be some time before I realized that the snake had been an omen so evil that it had frightened Miñiwa away from our journey.

NOW AND THEN came the squawking of invisible parrots, and once a rustling of shrubs that Enqueri identified as peccary. Twice we flushed turkeys, two of them easy kills if we'd had a weapon.

I made this point to Enqueri.

He stopped dead and turned around and faced me with a look as cool as a river rock.

"Give me your pack," he said.

He shouldered it quickly, along with his own, and took the lead, hacking forcefully through the bush with his machete—driven, it seemed to me, by anger and wounded pride.

By now the trail had disintegrated into a slimy mess of rotting tree trunks, clotted undergrowth, thick mud, and spiny vines. Despite these obstacles Enqueri moved so swiftly that I had to jog to keep up with him. Often the only sign in what looked to me like a wall of green was a few stubby branches cut long ago. Mostly Enqueri spotted them without missing a step.

When Enqueri did lose the trail, it was Yohue who found it, again and again, without hesitation. "There," he would say, and there it was. It was soon clear that I had badly underestimated him, and the other two boys as well. Awa—handsome, dark, and disdainful—was the younger and more impulsive of the two, given to sprinting away through the forest and disappearing for an hour at a time. Quimonca was sturdier and quieter, and though, like Awa, he spoke no Spanish beyond *Sí*, any comment directed his way elicited a broad, shy smile. He refused to pass me on the trail, and once, when I pitched headlong off an improvised sapling bridge into a creek—the sort of bridge the Huaorani cross without so much as a downward glance—he sprang to my rescue, an effort that caused him to laugh so uncontrollably that both of us had to sit on the bank for a minute to collect our wits, such as they were.

By midafternoon it was clear that I had slowed us down even more than Enqueri had anticipated I would, and that night would fall long before we could reach the ridge where we expected to find Menga encamped with his clan. However, Enqueri said that we were not far from another hut. Quemperi's clan had abandoned it six months earlier, when a man and woman died there of malaria.

"Who were they?" I asked.

"They were the parents of Quimonca and Awa."

If Quimonca and Awa were at all affected by this, they did not show it. Indeed, toward dark they raced ahead of us, and when we arrived at the hut we found them gorging on sugarcane picked from the abandoned gardens. The hut itself was strikingly different from those at the *pista*. For one thing, it was ten times larger; the entire clan had lived in it. Whereas the *pista* was flat and open, and the homes exposed, here the forest was dense and the hut almost hidden. I hadn't seen it until it was three feet in front of me. There was no barren ground at all—the gardens grew right up to the thatch walls.

The hut itself was pitched on the spine of the high, narrow ridge. The Huaorani had lived in this manner—hidden, isolated, protected—

until a few decades ago, when the Company arrived and they took to settling along the rivers and traveling in canoes and raiding the oil camps. I couldn't see five feet in any direction except when I stood at the hut's entrance, which had been placed right above the ridge's steepest slope. From there, however, I could see for miles, down and across a sweeping sea of green. Without a doubt it was the most spectacular view of the Amazon that I had ever come across.

Once inside the hut I collapsed on the dirt floor. By my estimate we had walked from twelve to fourteen hours. We might have come five miles, or twenty. My clothes were in shreds, and I was covered with blood, mud, sweat, and slime. The Huaorani looked as fresh as the moment we left the river. Even their feet were clean.

We sucked on sugarcane, and Enqueri cooked up the handful of rice we had left. Each of us got about a cup. During the night it rained ferociously, and the roof leaked, and now and then rainwater splashed me awake. Once I was startled awake by the deep, constant hacking of Awa, a cough that was surely tubercular. It was so fierce and uncontrollable that it sounded as if he'd hack up his very guts, there in the place where his parents had died.

IN THE MORNING we went in search of Menga and his clan, counting on a meal when we found them. We located their hut within a couple of hours, but it was abandoned. What little was left had been neatly packed up and hung from the pole rafters, secured by lengths of electric cord pilfered from the Company. Several spears were tied to the walls, along with some shirts and blankets. A dozen aluminum pots hung from poles shoved vertically into the dirt floor. Inside one of these pots Yohue found a plastic tub of palm-oil lard, which he ate by the handful.

Menga had moved on, Enqueri said, and no one could know for certain where he had gone or when he would return. It could be days; it could be months. I began to appreciate the absurdity of conducting a census among nomads. Menga and his clan had hidden themselves so thoroughly that even their fellow Huaorani couldn't find them. They might be yards away, watching us from the trees; they might be in Peru. They were just out there, gone, independent, self-contained, unaccountable and unaccounted for.

After we raided a manioc garden near the hut, Enqueri announced that we would walk until "five minutes after five." This puzzled me—it was true that he wore a watch, but it didn't work. In any case we walked for perhaps ten hours, during which I fell, slid, and stumbled and got stung, bit, and branch-whipped so often that by the time Enqueri announced, "Five minutes after five," I had no idea of direction or distance, of where we were or even where we were going. I was aware only of my pain and fatigue. I collapsed right there on the muddy forest floor. Immediately, a line of biting ants marched up my left leg, but I was too tired to brush them off. Removing my leather hiking boots, or what was left of them, I saw that I'd broken the nails of both big toes.

Meanwhile, Enqueri built a lean-to of vines and saplings, and Yo-hue, Awa, and Quimonca fetched broad palm leaves and wove them into a roof. More palm leaves were laid to form a soft, mud-tight floor. The entire operation took about fifteen minutes.

It was raining by then—at that point, who cared?—but Enqueri found yet another palm, one with wood so hard that water couldn't penetrate its core, and succeeded in cutting and splitting several branches. Then he held a candle to them and started a fire, and the boys lay down next to the fire, curled themselves into a bundle, and went right to sleep. I managed to hang a mosquito net and wrap myself in a blanket. Enqueri watched me without saying a word.

During the night it rained furiously. I was sure the lean-to would collapse, but it didn't so much as leak. At one point, awakened by rustling near the fire, I saw Quimonca take our kitchen knife and lance a golfball-size infection on his left shoulder. It gushed pus and blood, and the pain must have been tremendous, but he betrayed no emotion at all.

Later the air turned sharply cold, and despite the blanket I shivered through what was left of the night.

WE AWOKE to silence and darkness—in that dense bush there was no "dawn" as such—and ate the last of our food, a thin gruel of rice, chocolate, and tuna. Like me, the Huaorani shook with cold.

As we set out on foot, Enqueri announced, in all sincerity, that we would reach an upper tributary of the Yasuní in "one hour and forty-two minutes." Six or seven or eight hours later, he adjusted that claim to "an hour and a half." By then he had a bewildered look in his eye, and Yohue passed him on the trail and took the lead again, the steady slapping of his muddy sock the only sound in the forest. Still later—I had by then lost all sense of time—we did in fact achieve the bank of a small river, though when I asked Enqueri whether it was the tributary we were looking for, he mumbled only an unconvincing "Of course." But there was enough light to execute a quick turn and flourish in the shallows, and to share a bar of soap. Ivory, to be specific. "It floats," Enqueri said. Time and again the little bar jiggled off downstream like a tippy canoe, a display the Huaorani found sidesplitting.

Awa had collected a small turtle on the trail. Enqueri boiled it. No sooner had the three boys inhaled their meager portions and dropped their empty bowls than they were asleep next to the fire, curled up like puppies.

Later, when I again asked Enqueri if we had reached the correct river, he launched into a long and complicated monologue that began with him fighting three soldiers in a bar in Coca, a battle he was on the verge of losing until he called "Time out" and downed a Coca-Cola, after which he prevailed. Somehow this story segued into a story of how a jaguar and an eagle mated to spawn the Huaorani. Then Enqueri said, "Last night I had a dream. We were in an airplane, and it crashed in the forest. I grabbed you right before you fell out."

"Really?"

"Yes, but we died anyway."

"That is a terrible dream."

"No, it is a very good dream. If you fall out of an airplane, it means good luck."

There was no way out of the forest except with the Huaorani. No way to call for help; no one to call if there were. My life was in Enqueri's hands. I fell asleep thinking that I liked him very much but that I did not trust him at all.

IN THE MORNING we waded the river, sinking buck naked and chest deep in the cool, slow-moving current, then dressed and shambled into the forest in search of an abandoned well called Amo Dos, one in a string of exploratory wells Conoco had drilled inside Block

Sixteen. Enqueri said that Amo Dos was near the tributary we were seeking, and that once we found the well we'd be able to set course for the Yasuní. However, after a couple of hours we had found no evidence of oil work. Even Yohue seemed confused, and we retreated back across the river. This time, wet, hungry, exhausted, and unable to see the sky, I did not bother to remove my clothes, which in any case were not going to dry out anytime soon, if ever. Enqueri, for his part, would not admit that we were lost. ("Where *are* we?" I asked, to which he replied, with an absolutely straight face, "We are in the *jungle*.")

Several hours later Enqueri stopped before a ceiba tree, affixed to which was a piece of red metal about two inches square. CONOCO, it said, and Enqueri announced, "Block Sixteen."

"GREEN WALL" is a phrase often used to describe Amazonian bush, but in all my wanderings in the Amazon I've never seen anything quiet so wall-like as what now confronted us. Two or three years earlier great chunks of the forest had been cleared for seismic lines and helicopter pads, and the new understory had grown back so densely that it was impassable even with the aid of a machete. It was a visceral demonstration of the impact, largely ignored but difficult to overstate, that seismic exploration can have on a forest. At intervals of approximately one mile, ten-foot-wide trails are cut across the concession. Dynamite is detonated every 300 yards along each of these trails, producing seismic waves that can be analyzed to determine the geological profile under the forest floor. Within a typical concession, at least 800 miles of trails are cut, as well as some 1,500 helicopter pads, deforesting up to 2,000 acres. Noise from cutting and blasting scares away much of the wildlife, and the new understory growth inhibits its return. Fructivores— toucans, monkeys, turkeys—won't move into cleared areas, and their absence means not only a loss of game but diminished regeneration of the forest, because these species distribute the seeds of the large fruiting trees.

Enqueri and I sat in front of the ceiba tree and drank water. If we were not exactly found—there was no telling just where along the Block Sixteen boundary we were—we were not quite so lost as we had thought. I expected some reaction from Enqueri—elation, righteousness, what-

ever—but he seemed completely blank. Then, after a while, he began
to speak.

Like many Huaorani men, Enqueri had once worked on a seismic
crew; he had, in fact, worked on a crew that had explored Block Sixteen.
Cutting seismic trails is the hardest, dirtiest, and worst-paying work in
the exploration process, and the Company usually hires Indians to do it.
"I needed money," Enqueri said. "When we are sick, the *evangelistas*
take us to their hospital. They make us pay them, and once when I was
gone on a trip my sister went to the hospital." When Enqueri got home
he learned that he owed the hospital the equivalent of about $180, or
roughly six months' pay at the prevailing national minimum wage. He
went to work for the Company. "I had a ninety-day contract," he said.
"I worked from six in the morning until six at night, cutting the forest.
I worked seven days a week. The Company gave us a machete and
boots, and the helicopter would drop rice and beans. After work, we cut
a clearing and put up a tarp. I worked with other Huaorani; we all slept
together. There was a lot of malaria, and someone was always getting
hurt—cutting off a finger or getting chopped by a machete or ax. But
if you didn't work you didn't get paid. When we asked for better treatment, the Company said we didn't deserve it, because we were uncivilized."

Looking around, I could see the massive sawn trunks of mahoga-
nies, ceibas, and palms littered through the forest. Awa, Quimonca, and
Yohue were sitting on a flat stump that was at least fifteen feet in
diameter. They were talking with uncharacteristic animation—angered,
I imagined, by the heedless destruction of their lands.

"What are they saying?" I asked Enqueri.

"They are saying that if the Company was still here, it might give
us something to eat."

WE THRASHED through the forest until midday, when Yohue yelled,
"Amo Dos!" and bolted ahead of us. Ten minutes later I stepped onto
the slick bank of a broad, brown river. After three and a half days under
the forest canopy, the sudden openness of the river—the long vistas
upstream and down, the vast gray sky overhead—struck me with a kind
of vertigo, and I felt dizzy and weak-kneed. Seconds later the sky burst

with a ferocity that I hadn't yet experienced in the Oriente. Despite this Enqueri and the boys waded across the river to see if they could find the well. I stood on the bank and got pounded.

After a couple of minutes it hit me that we were not necessarily lost, and in a rush of hope I ate the one candy bar I'd hidden deep in my pack. It is impossible to describe how delicious it tasted. Overall, I had eaten very little in the eleven days with Quemperi, and during our trek I had hiked perhaps seventy miles on the equivalent of two full meals. I was hungrier than I could ever remember being. It dawned on me that I might well be starving.

I sat in the rain for about an hour, staring at my feet, until I heard an ominous roar and looked up to see a fifty-foot balsa tree toppling into the river from the far bank. A few minutes later Yohue appeared on the bank dragging long coils of vine. A second tree fell, and then Awa and Quimonca scrambled from the bush and, kicking and pushing, rolled the two trunks into the water. Enqueri ran out of the forest behind them and waded into the river waist deep. Chipping frantically with his machete, the rain streaming down his body into the river, he hacked the trunks into logs about ten feet long and bound them with vine to make two rafts. Then he trimmed a couple of saplings for paddles and, wearing a serious expression, maneuvered across the river to pick me up.

"I saw where the well is," he said. "It was very far away, so we did not try to reach it." But he was mumbling and glancing up and down the river and looking everywhere but at me, and I did not believe a word of it.

In any case our next step was clear: We were going to float the river. If it did not join the Yasuní, then in all likelihood it was bound for Peru, and we had no hope of coming across help for weeks, at best. I did not think I would live that long, and after I stepped onto the raft, I was overcome with a panic so consuming that the simple act of sitting down required every bit of will I could muster.

I SHARED a raft with Quimonca. I sat amidships, facing him, and he sat at the stern and directed the raft with his paddle. If our predicament offered any saving grace, it was that we were no longer on foot. In almost no other way was it possible to see the raft as an improvement.

It was slow, drifting with the river, permanently awash, and profoundly uncomfortable—the middle log, poorly secured, bounced like a seesaw, and at the top of each arc whacked me in the tailbone. Every so often Quimonca would glance my way to be sure I was still in place, considering me with neither more nor less interest that he would, say, a turkey.

Submerged to their hips, silent, Enqueri, Awa, and Yohue drifted ahead of us. In other circumstances I probably would have appreciated the surroundings. Like most of the Amazonian rivers in Ecuador—the notable exceptions being the Napo and, farther north, the Aguarico—this one was no more than ten yards wide. Moss and vine hung like drapery from the tall trees, walling off the river. The humid air smelled of rot and mud, and aside from the occasional whistle of a bird and the gentle purling of the current, silence reigned. It was a world more concealed than exposed, all darkness and shadows. It was small wonder that the Huaorani had remained hidden for so long.

The rain let up for a few hours, until we hit a snag and had to wade into the river and work the rafts through by hand. About then the temperature suddenly dropped a good ten degrees, and seconds later the skies burst. All at once I was shivering so with cold that I could not stop—right there in the heart of the Amazon, one degree of latitude off the equator. My teeth chattered violently. If I wasn't yet hypothermic, I was getting there fast.

Enqueri, Quimonca, Awa, and Yohue appeared no better off. They were shaking with cold, their muscles jerking under the skin. There was a small plastic tarp in my pack, and we wrapped ourselves in it and stood on the bank for the next half hour, until the rain abated. We made camp right there. The business of hauling our gear up from the raft and building a shelter helped steady my nerves, but not much. The Huaorani, too, looked lost and worried, though Enqueri managed to get a fire going.

"What river is this, Enqueri?" I asked.

"I do not know."

"What does that mean?"

"It means we are lost."

"And what does that mean?"

"It means we might die."

It was a simple statement of fact, and that night, though I tried to rest, every time I dozed off I shocked myself awake. My hunger had become physically painful—my stomach burned and had begun to cramp—and it seemed to have deepened into something else entirely, a bitter stew of frustration, despair, and anger at my own foolishness. I knew, as surely as I had ever known anything, that I was going to die. I would leave behind a pregnant wife; I would never know my child. And there really wasn't a damn thing I could do about it.

IT WAS TRUE that we had a machete and could, in theory, carve hunting spears, and surely the canopy held many edible nuts and fruits. But "hunting and gathering" is not so simple as it sounds. Traveling between communities was one thing, but if our focus were to become food gathering, we would have had to make a base camp, find materials for weapons, fashion the weapons, then begin the arduous process of stalking game in unfamiliar territory. A spear for killing peccaries can be made in an afternoon, but peccaries are fast and wily, and tracking and killing them can take several days. A monkey can be killed in a day, but you need a blowgun; making a good one—straight and airtight—is a week's work. You have to make darts, too, and find and prepare poison for the tips. Usually, monkeys are high in the canopy, so you must drive a dart a hundred feet or more with enough force to pierce hair and skin. To help achieve this force, the Huaorani wrap their darts in a kind of cotton gasket, to build up pressure inside the blowgun. But only one species of tree provides this fiber, and it is not always easy to find. Likewise for the species of palm—the one among the 150 or so that grow in the forest—that provides the right wood for darts.

Once you've made your weapons, of course, you have to go and do some hunting. It takes three or four darts to kill a monkey, and even a good hunter will hit with only, say, one shot in five. Once you wound a monkey, and send it fleeing for its life along the canopy, you have to somehow keep your eyes on it while hauling your nine-foot, five-pound blowgun through more or less impenetrable forest. When, finally, you do kill the monkey, more likely than not you'll have to climb into the canopy to retrieve it.

Hunting, in other words, is very hard work, and long-term planning is not what the Huaorani do well, or, for that matter, at all. I could suggest whatever I wanted to, but they wouldn't start to think about hunting until they noticed that they were starving, which didn't appear to be anytime soon. As for what they thought of my problems—well, hey, there were plenty more *cowode* where I came from.

Far better than hunting would be to find some friends who had already been hunting and hit them up for something to eat. This, at least, was what Enqueri had in mind.

Meanwhile, I was slowly dying of hunger, and if nothing else, I was coming to understand that for the Huaorani, hunger defines life. You are hungry or you are not; all else flows from that. From this point of view, I could see why the Huaorani so value self-reliance, and why their culture revolves around food, ritual sharing, feast and famine. However illusory it might be at times, the notion of *abundancia*—of the forest as ever fruitful and providing—is absolutely critical to their ability to survive. Without such faith, one would feel terrified by the forest, terrified to the point of paralysis. It was easy to see, too, why all the money in the world could never compensate them for the destruction of their land.

LIGHT CAME early and hard to the exposed bank, raising a voracious insect hatch. The air buzzed, and mosquitoes attacked in dense thickets. But the river was up a couple of feet and moving more quickly, which had to be read as a good sign. If we were heading toward the Yasuní, we would probably find a Huaorani camp within a few days. And if we weren't? I tried not to think about that.

Soon after we put in, however, the sky turned a woolly gray, and the air suddenly chilled—signs of impending rain that were, to me, immensely frightening, for I believed that a serious rain was likely to kill me. I was not at all sure, by then, that I had the strength left to withstand even a common cold.

To the extent that I had any strategy for survival, it was to rip a hole in the plastic tarp and wear it like a poncho, and I sat athwart the stoic Quimonca looking for all the world like a human tent. Once in a while our eyes would meet and he would smile, then turn intently back to the river. He was nineteen years old. His parents were dead. He was off to the land of the cannibals armed with only a T-shirt, shorts, and boots. What did he expect, if anything at all?

The morning passed with no indication of what river we were on. The sky darkened, but the rain held off. It was probably midafternoon when I heard a sound like that of a branch snapping. It was both distant and too sharp, but only when it came a second time did I begin to think it might be something else—something manmade, perhaps; perhaps a gunshot. Yohue heard it, too, and jumped to his feet. Moments later there came the thin, low hum of an outboard motor, and then, around a bend in the river, the prow of a canoe.

Our rescuer proved to be a grinning young friend of Enqueri named Araba. He was accompanied by two clansmen, Bainca and Anaento. They had been on the river three days, and the hunting had been good. The canoe was piled high with bananas and manioc, and under a tarp in the stern were a couple of dead turkeys, a couple of monkeys, and a great pile of charred meat—hindquarters, hooves, snouts, guts. They had come upon four peccaries, that much was clear, but beyond that each man had his own story. Each version was delivered in what to my ear sounded like an absolute frenzy, high-pitched and manic, and though each man appeared to agree enthusiastically with whatever version was being told, no two versions were the same. It was at any rate a big kill, and at each telling of the tale all the Huaorani howled with delight.

As for me, I boarded Araba's canoe cautiously, not so much from fatigue—though that certainly was one reason—as from awe and disbelief. I had so convinced myself that I was going to die that for a few long moments it was difficult for me to accept without question that Araba and his friends and their canoe and their heaps of food were real.

Somebody handed me a chunk of boiled manioc. I nibbled at it; it was soft, almost tasteless, and utterly exquisite. That broke the spell, and then it was off to the races. For the next hour we ate pig like pigs, until we reached the hunting camp, where Bainca boiled up manioc and bananas and turkey and monkey and we ate some more. Toward dusk we unloaded the canoe and washed out the blood and put back into the river. The evening was unusually clear, and by the light of the setting sun Bainca motored us slowly downstream and Enqueri leaned back against the meat pile and, not for the first time, told the story of our journey. Wielding a bowl of *chicha* in one hand and a chunk of meat in the other, he pointed at me and made as if to fall out of the boat, rocking it wildly—that was me plunging off the sapling bridge. The other Huaorani were in stitches. I didn't mind at all. My belly was full, and I was thankful to be alive. I sat against my pack and stretched my legs out in front of me and stared at the sky for what seemed forever, until my reverie was broken by the sound of my own laughter.

5

THE OIL industry might well destroy the Huaorani, but the internal combustion engine had just saved my life. Its infernal roar was a happy sound. It made the droopy green forest that had once loomed threatening and unfathomable seem soft and sheltering. I leaned back in the canoe and stuck my feet up over the gunwales and set a stalk of bananas on my lap and shared them with Yohue, who sat in the bow and stared at the water and, beyond the effort required to peel and chew, did not move a muscle.

Bainca stood in the stern, working the outboard motor. He was dressed head to toe in camouflage fatigues, his hat cocked at a rakish angle. He'd been stuck in Coca when the military made one of its periodic conscription sweeps. One minute he was standing on a street corner, the next he was wearing a uniform. At first he found army life thrilling—there were a lot of guns, and he got fed every day. The thrill lasted a couple of weeks. Then he felt an urge to move. One moonless night he disappeared into the forest, uniform and all.

Bainca was the *motorista*, but Araba was the *comandante*. He was nestled amidships, an umbrella sheltering him and a bowl of *chicha* at his feet, and as the sun dropped from a sky feathered in purple, orange, and red and the moon rose over the deepening browns and greens of the forest wall, he continued to wear his sunglasses. They were the only pair I'd seen among the Huaorani. Araba wore them like an expression of rank. He sat still as a statue, except that every now and then he would point a finger in the air and wiggle it this way or that, to direct Bainca away from a sandbar or a snag. It was a gesture that looked almost whimsical, as if he were conducting an imaginary orchestra.

At one point, as we bore down on a large floating tree trunk, I turned to find Araba and Bainca fast asleep. Araba had his head on his chest. Bainca was standing at the tiller, but his eyes were shut tight and he was weaving left and right. Seconds later we rammed the log and nearly capsized. They woke up then. Araba laughed so hard his glasses fell off, and pretty soon everyone else was laughing, too. Why not? We had more food than we could possibly eat, and in the face of such *abundancia*, the notion of hunger—and of pain, suffering, danger, and death—had ceased to exist.

IT WAS well past dark when we arrived at Aucayacu. There were only three huts. They belonged to Bainca's mother and father, Camemo and Apa, and an uncle, and they appeared to be built quite differently from those in Cononaco. They were set on raised wooden platforms and had plank walls and bark flooring.

"Enqueri," I asked, "are these houses built in the Quichua style?"

"Yes."

"How are they different from Huaorani houses?"

He thought about this for a moment, then said, "They are different."

"Yes, but how?"

He paused again to give the matter thought. After a while, he said, "They are built like Quichua houses."

But by then I knew that it was fruitless to pursue such questions. Simple data would never explain the Huaorani. Such explanations as there were lay obliquely, if at all, amid snakes and hunger and mud and a forest so dense you rarely saw the sky.

In Aucayacu we ate once again, generous portions of meat and manioc and plantain. Bainca's mother was a tall, thin-faced woman, and his father was short and built like a tree trunk. Through Bainca, they told me about a time of great sickness. Judging by the number of chonta palm seasons that had passed, it would have been 1988 or 1989. "The sickness came after the heaviest rains," Camemo said— November or December. "One day the river turned black, then red, then yellow. The next day, dead fish were floating on it."

"No animals died," Apa said.

"No, no animals died," Camemo agreed. "But the manioc and the bananas did, and some of the birds, and many caimans."

"We became very sick," Apa said. "We had problems with our skin and vomiting. We were sick for a month. We could not go anywhere for help. We thought we were going to die."

Although the source of this plague dumbfounded his parents, Bainca believed he knew exactly what had happened, because he had once worked for the Company. When Conoco capped Amo Dos and its other exploratory wells, he said, it abandoned the waste pits as they were, open and exposed, and eventually—inevitably—the pits washed out into the Yasuní.

"What did the Company do about the spill?" I asked.

"Nothing," Bainca said.

What did Apa and Camemo think of the road the Company was going to build?

"What road?" Apa asked.

Once the road was built, of course, Aucayacu—so remote that not even the missionaries went there—would suddenly find itself within a few hours' canoe ride of the Company, and of everyone who would follow the Company into the forest.

I explained the Company's plan. They were appalled.

"Everything will die," Camemo said.

"I do not want to be sick in that way again," Apa said.

A sudden gloom enveloped me, and I changed the subject. Bainca had told me that his father was a healer, and that had given me hope. For most *cowode*, skin problems—fungus, staph infection—are an almost unavoidable hazard of rain forest travel. Anyone who goes into the forest for more than a few days comes out covered with itching, open sores. Dealing with such problems is a major topic of conversation in the bars of Coca. Everybody has a system. I was trying one recommended by a friend: wash with antibacterial soap twice a day, carry a separate set of clothing to sleep in, go naked whenever possible. But I was losing the battle. My skin was itchy and inflamed across my chest, down both arms, around my waist, down both legs. The toes on my right foot were so swollen and crusted they looked webbed.

Apa examined my foot carefully, then said something to Bainca.

"He says there is a cure for this," Bainca told me.

"How can I obtain this cure?"

After a second consultation, Bainca said, solemnly, "Go to a pharmacy in Coca."

In the morning we drank *chicha* and set off for Garzacocha, two more hours downriver.

Garza IS SPANISH for "heron" and *cocha* is Quichua for "lake": The village of Garzacocha stands at a wide bend in the Yasuní opposite a black lagoon rich not only in herons but in hawks, toucans, macaws, eagles, caimans, freshwater dolphins, manatees, and an impossible number of fish. In its prospect on a high, muddy bank, Garzacocha is situated much like Cononaco, with a commanding view of the river and a strategic location: When the *cowode* started to invade the Huaorani homeland, they came by canoe, and the Huaorani waited for them in the river's big bends, where strong currents pushed the canoes toward the bank and exposed them to a hail of Huaorani spears.

"Do tourists come here?" I asked Araba.

"Not anymore!" he said, and cackled with glee. "At one time many tourists came here, but they brought bad things with them, coughs and diseases that made us sick. I told them that they would have to pay us, and they stopped coming." However, the year before, two canoes of *cowode* had come to Garzacocha without asking his permission. (Later I learned that they were American college students on a study-abroad program.) "They had already come once," Araba said. "We told them to stay away, but they came back. So I took their boats and tied them up, and then I took everything they had with them and put it in my house, and then I put all the *cowode* in another house and locked them in there and held them for two days. That was the last time we had any tourists!"

Owing to the great kill Araba had brought home—to which, somehow, I was attached—I found the Garzacochans receptive and friendly. There were about fifty of them. It was in the Garzacocha region that the doomed Capuchin Alejandro Labaca had made most of his forays, and his legacy is a village far more domesticated than Cononaco. I spotted several fruit trees—lemon, orange, papaya—a number of pigs and chickens, and, with them, a swarm of blackflies, gnats, and the small biting mosquitoes known elsewhere in the Amazon as *pium*. The Capuchins encouraged the Huaorani to pursue work with the Company, in the belief that they had to learn to deal with a cash economy, and loaned Araba money to buy the outboard motor that had now made him, at twenty-nine, the king of Garzacocha. His home, which he shared with two wives and six children, as well as with Bainca and his family, displayed material wealth far beyond the Huaorani norm: half a dozen muskets and shotguns, a tattered Ecuadorian flag, a Nike day pack, four bras.

"Araba is so rich he has two wives," Enqueri said. This was permitted if the wives were sisters. But there were problems. One wife was always favored over the other, and so did less work, but to keep them happy there were certain ways in which they had to be treated as equals.

"How is that?" I asked, and Enqueri made a sawing motion with a banana.

WHILE WE WERE in Garzacocha Araba held a community meeting to discuss the Company's plans. His was the lone voice raised in favor of the Conoco road. He figured that once the road was in, he would grow pigs and herd them to market. But everyone else was against it, and one of his wives shouted him down. Holding up their infant son, she said, "A road will bring sickness. It will kill our children. We do not want it. No, no, no."

Enqueri completed his census, and the morning after the meeting we left Garzacocha for the town of Nuevo Rocafuerte, which stands at the confluence of the Yasuní and the Napo, near the Peruvian border. Into two canoes we stuffed seventeen Huaorani adults, ten children (including three nursing babies), a shotgun, two pots of *chicha* almost as wide as the canoes, three stalks of bananas, and one monkey tied to a leash. Garzacocha is in Yasuní National Park, which the Huaorani consider their land, and late in the day we crossed the park's eastern boundary, where we passed a sign prohibiting hunting, fishing, logging, and colonization. There was a guardhouse next to the sign, and it bore, in large bold letters, the logo of The Nature Conservancy. In 1989, funded by Conoco, The Nature Conservancy helped the Ecuadorian government draft a management plan for Yasuní. The plan zoned half the park for industrial use. It was condemned by most Ecuadorian environmental and indigenous groups, but a few months later, using this plan as a base, the U.S. Agency for International Development selected The Nature Conservancy, Wildlife Conservation International, and CARE to administer a $15 million program of park management, tourism, and "sustainable" resource extraction in Yasuní and two ecological reserves. (In 1990 Ecuador's Tribunal of Constitutional Guarantees ruled that it was illegal to extract oil in a national park; foreign oil companies then threatened to freeze further investment in the country, and the tribunal abruptly reversed itself.)

Though it was midday and the height of tourist season when our canoes reached the park boundary, the guardhouse was empty. "The guard is on vacation," Araba said. "He doesn't come here very often." Did Araba recognize the name of the group on the sign? "Yes," he said. "It is part of the Company."

We beached the canoe and the Huaorani broke into the house. They ate all the food they could find, drank a bottle of rum, and threw the refuse in the river. Then they walked around the exterior, ripping at the siding lumber to see if any of it would be worth taking home.

THERE WAS so little to mark the point at which the Yasuní flows into the Napo—to the right, half hidden in bush, was a sign the size of a case of beer that said PERU in square, plain letters hand-painted in black and white, and to the left a similar sign that said ECUADOR—that it was hard to believe that a war was fought there, in 1941, and that the border is still in dispute. (In fact, in early 1995 Ecuadorian and Peruvian forces battled for more than a week in a valley about two hundred miles to the southwest.) Nothing beyond the border signs suggests that this stretch of the Napo has changed in the slightest since 1542, when Francisco de Orellana inadvertently became the first white man to follow the river into the main trunk of the Amazon, and from there across the continent to the Atlantic.

And to call the conflict of 1941 a war is to seriously overstate the case. By all accounts but those Ecuadorian, and by many of those, the Peruvians simply overran the border and took all the land they could hold—at that time more than half of the Oriente. It was land believed even then to be rich in oil, but in the face of the invasion the Ecuadorian soldiers dropped their guns and fled. Although no one knows for certain, a strong case has been made that the only thing that stopped the Peruvians from advancing farther was the Huaorani.

Now, looking out across the Napo, I could see whitecaps kicking and bucking and sheets of rain slashing the distant shore beneath a low and slowly shifting ceiling of gray-black sky. Araba pointed a finger in the air and the canoes beached right there at the mouth of the Yasuní and the Huaorani men put on clean shirts and the women skirts and dresses. Bainca jammed Araba's ragged Ecuadorian flag down into a crack of wood at the bow of the lead canoe. Then we entered the Napo and the wind and the rain beat at the canoes and tossed them roughly on the river-sea. The Huaorani sat silent and brooding.

We turned upstream and in a while came to a wooden pier with some of the wood falling into the river and above the pier a small wooden house that had settled unevenly on its wood pilings. An officer came out wearing boots and fatigues and a pistol and a T-shirt that read, in Spanish, MURDER BEFORE DISHONOR. He snapped his fingers and I handed him my passport and Bainca handed him a card that said he was trained as a *motorista*. The other Huaorani looked out across the river or up at the sky or down at the floor of the canoe. A baby cried and a breast was quickly offered.

The officer nodded and handed back the papers.

We pushed on upriver for another hour, pitching all the while in the storm-torn Napo. Water collected in the floor ankle and then shin deep but the Huaorani did not bail or shelter themselves or move at all except for some whose teeth chattered with cold.

NUEVO ROCAFUERTE was a handful of tiny shops and one-table cantinas and mud streets and at one end the Capuchin mission, and in the mission was an empty, doorless building the size of a small warehouse that the Huaorani entered as if they owned it. The wood floor was covered with a thin film of dried mud. They put down the *chicha* bowls and the monkey and lit candles and set them on the floor. Some of them sat and some disappeared into other rooms and some took their machetes and made carvings on the walls. The candlelight danced in the dark emptiness as if in a cave.

Araba said, "Welcome to my house."

"We have no food," Enqueri said to me. "What will we eat?"

"What did you bring?" I asked.

"Nothing," he said. "*Chicha,* but that is gone now."

"What did you expect to eat?"

"What will we eat?" he asked.

In a cottage behind the building I found a priest. He was a Spaniard, placid and laconic, but he had been in Nuevo Rocafuerte for twenty-one years. He had known Alejandro Labaca very well. He would not come down to say hello to the Huaorani that night, but perhaps in the morning. "It is a delicate situation," he said. "Until a few years ago some of them came here to school, but they stole paint and food and other things, and we could no longer allow them to attend. They kept coming here anyway. Our mission became like one of the garden sites they visit during their migrations. We let them use the building so they will not have to sleep in the street." The Capuchins maintained the building only minimally, and did not otherwise help the Huaorani except at their medical clinic. "We do not feed them, we do not give them gasoline," he said. "There is no other way. They have to learn this world. The lessons are hard, but they must be learned. If they are to survive, they must learn to plan, to understand the value of things in this world."

"Why?" I asked.

He took off his glasses and cleaned them slowly and slowly put them back on. "Because the petroleum companies will end their life as they know it," he said. "Of that there is no doubt. The companies are here already and many more are coming. They are going to take the oil and they are going to destroy the forest. All we can do is try to prepare the Huaorani. Last year one of the women in Garzacocha had malaria and a flu at the same time, and she was so sick I thought surely she would die. It was the *petroleros* who made her that way. But when the Company comes to me and asks me to vaccinate the Huaorani in Garzacocha and they pay for the medicines and the gasoline, of course I must do it."

I said good night and walked down the street in the rain and mud and sat on the covered porch of a cantina and ordered beans and eggs. While I was waiting for my plate I looked out across the street, and in the darkness of the storm I saw a pair of glinting eyes and then another and then many more, a long, silent line of Huaorani standing in the rain and the dark and the mud waiting to be fed.

WE LEFT the women and children in Nuevo Rocafuerte and set off in a single canoe and for two days sat in the canoe from dawn to dusk in the sun and the rain and the wind and beat upriver, weaving back and forth around snags and bars and now and then running aground and more than once twisting sideways in the flooding river and losing all control but somehow never quite going over. In the long stretches between these dramas I bent my head down between my legs and pulled my parka over my head and slowly went numb, though when it rained I shook with cold and when the skies cleared and the equatorial sun blazed down I thought I would go blind. From time to time I would give in to a wild impulse and raise up and look around. The Huaorani seemed never to move, holding like statues against sun, wind, water, hunger, heat, and cold.

We made camp at an abandoned *chacra*, or small farm, on the north bank of the Napo. A Quichua man spotted our fire and invited us to his home, explaining that the *chacra*'s owner had died of malaria, and that his ghost still haunted the land. "And you are Huaorani," he said nervously, shining his flashlight on Enqueri and Araba. They said nothing. "You used to kill." Turning to me, he said, "One day when I was a child the Huaorani came with their spears and killed everyone in my family—the men, the women, even the children. There was blood everywhere. It was a slaughter. I hid in a hole, and they didn't find me. I was the only one who survived." He turned back to Enqueri. "But now you are civilized," he said. He reached out and patted Enqueri lightly on the arm, as if he were an apparition. "You are civilized, aren't you?" The Huaorani said nothing.

There were a dozen Quichua men and some women and children. The men were drunk and wore leather shoes. The house, raised high on stilts, was spacious and dry and light-years beyond anything the Huaorani knew how to build, and it was surrounded by fruit and nut orchards and fields of coffee and manioc. The Quichua had a radio. They listened to Voice of America. "There is a bomb that can destroy entire countries," one man told me. "It might even destroy the Napo River."

Another said that he was going to start growing marijuana. A Colombian had promised him seeds.

The Quichua cooked rice and gave each of us a piece of boiled peccary and passed around a bowl of *chicha*. For all their sophistication they moved as delicately among the Huaorani as small dogs would among stallions. The Huaorani sat silently in one long line. They answered questions politely but without elaboration and volunteered nothing and accepted what was offered as if it was rightfully theirs and by their very bearing made the Quichua seem not like people of the forest but like pale impostors.

WE ARRIVED in Coca late in the day and docked the canoe at the cement ramp that rises from the river near the bridge that connects the town with the Vía Auca. One by one the Huaorani climbed the ramp and along the bank mestizo women looked up from their wash and children stopped swimming.

Young Yohue followed me up the ramp. As we reached the street I turned to see how he would enter this new world. His face registered neither shock nor surprise nor joy nor fear. It was blank: a hunter's face, frozen in concentration on some prey or predator he had spotted. Turning back to the street I saw what he saw, a truck, a battered, muddy, yellow pickup bearing down on us with a speed and force that by all he had seen and known and learned in his life Yohue had no way to comprehend. No way to gauge power or intent or consequence. So he waited as he would in the forest, still as stone, searching the beast for some clue, some signal, that would suggest to him how best to act.

I stepped quickly to the side of the road and yanked Yohue out of the way and the truck blasted by, kicking up mud and oil.

THE ENTRANCE to the Capuchin mission was blocked by a military patrol, four men in mirrored sunglasses. They leaned against the wall and cradled their Belgian rifles like kittens. Father José Miguel Goldáraz came to the gate. He said that the Company and the military had requisitioned the mission school to discuss the Rio Napo Foundation, as the project being proposed by the Natural Resources Defense Council and Conoco was being called. As we spoke, representatives from the military and Conoco and Petroecuador were meeting with Nanto and Moi, and with Valerio Grefa, the Quichua who was president of the Confederation of the Indigenous People of the Ecuadorian Amazon (CONFENIAE), under whose auspices the Huaorani federation was incorporated, at least in theory. The Capuchins had refused to participate in the meeting; José Miguel believed the plan held nothing for the Huaorani. He did suggest that Araba sit in. "After all," he said, "it is your home they are trying to buy."

Enqueri and Yohue and Awa and Quimonca and Bainca went to the Huaorani Hotel and I went to the Hotel Auca and got a room with a single bed and a single bare lightbulb. Night had fallen by the time I returned to the street. Out in front of the Auca the Huaorani had gathered beneath a streetlamp, standing with their arms around one another and staring this way or that. They seemed transformed. They were scrubbed down, it was true, and they were wearing their city clothes—clean jeans and T-shirts—but it was more than that. Each one of them was also wearing a sort of goofy grin, the shy, dazed, and deferential face of the lost at sea. The look of confidence and stoic self-reliance that I had grown so accustomed to in the forest had been replaced or hidden by one that pleaded for direction, instruction, help. A look, I was sure, that matched the one I had worn in the forest every single day.

I invited them to sit down at the hotel cantina, and soon a dozen more Huaorani materialized beneath the light and found their way to us. While they ate, Enqueri and I went to my room. I had agreed to pay him a salary for the time we had spent together in the forest—he had, after all, been my guide. When I asked him what I owed him, he named an extravagant sum and launched into a complicated rationale that included the medical bills he owed the evangelists and a plane ticket for his sister and the new boots he would need for the trip back to Toñampare. When he finished I counted out the sum he had asked for and put it on the bed and put my hand over it.

"You must promise me one thing," I said. "You must buy food and passage for Quimonca and Awa and Yohue. You must see to it that they arrive safely in Toñampare." If I gave money directly to the boys, the other Huaorani would have it in minutes.

"Of course," he said. "We will take the bus to a place where we can cross the Napo and walk into the forest."

"When will you leave?"

"Tonight or tomorrow morning."

"That is a good idea."

"And when will you come to Toñampare?"

"I do not know," I said. "In a few months, if I can get inside the territory somehow. First I must go to the United States of North America. My wife is going to have a baby."

"It would please me very much if you would come to visit my home."

"I would enjoy that. Thank you."

He handed me a sheaf of papers—his census, which documented 141 Huaorani living in or around Block Sixteen, roughly 10 percent of the total Huaorani population. He asked me to hold on to it and make copies and bring the original back to him when I came to Toñampare. "This will show the People that I am working hard for them," he said. He said to tell the whole world that the Huaorani lived well and that many Huaorani lived where the Company said they did not and that the Company must not go there. Then he said, "It was a good trip. And you thought you were going to die!"

"Yes."

"But the Condor knows the forest!"

"Yes, he does!"

Then we laughed—*ha-ha-ha-ha-ha*—and as I watched his bony shoulders shaking up and down I thought, again, that I liked him very much and trusted him very little. Yet here we were, alive, in Coca, which for at least one long night I had believed would never come to pass.

6

A FTER I said good night to Enqueri I sat on the patio and drank a bottle of beer and then I took my first shower in a month. I stood under the cold water and tried not to begin to sort or interpret what I had seen but I was in a dark and exhausted mood and the questions arose on their own, like bones spit up by a swamp. In the morning I went back to the Capuchin mission to talk to José Miguel Goldáraz.

José Miguel led me to a cement bench in a cool courtyard one high fence and a stone's throw from the Huaorani Hotel. He brought two cups of coffee. He is tall and lean, and he wore a beret, a cotton T-shirt, khaki pants that were frayed at the edges, and cheap tennis shoes. He had been in the Oriente for more than twenty years—or close to half his adult life—and he no longer returned to Spain for his vacations, preferring instead to walk in the mountains above Coca. José Miguel had accompanied Alejandro Labaca on many of his exploratory visits into the Huaorani lands. He still had the seventeen spears that were taken from Labaca's body. And he had traveled a long way down a risky path that Labaca had only begun to explore: Eschewing religious conversion for political activism, he had become a quiet but tireless, and often solitary, advocate of those, colonists and Indians alike, who suffered most from the consequences of oil development.

DuPont's Edgar Woolard had yet to decide whether he would allow Conoco to proceed with developing Block Sixteen, and the meeting held at the Capuchin mission the day before had been another bid by Conoco to win the stamp of approval Woolard required. I asked José

Miguel how the meeting had turned out. After a moment or two, he said, "How much of the story do you know?"

I knew enough to know that the future of the Huaorani hung in the balance. I knew this:

In 1967 Texaco discovered commercial oil in the Oriente. In 1972 it completed a 312-mile pipeline from the Oriente to Ecuador's Pacific coast. During the next seventeen years—until Petroecuador assumed operational control of the pipeline—the Texaco consortium shipped 1.4 billion barrels of oil over the Andes and accounted for 88 percent of the oil taken from the Oriente. Ecuador had no environmental regulations for oil production, and almost no attempt was made to assess its environmental impact until 1989, when an American named Judith Kimerling came to the country and began to stick her nose into things. Traveling by foot, canoe, and truck, sleeping in the homes of Indians and colonists, she visited producing wells, exploratory sites, seismic trails. She combed government reports. A former environmental litigator in the office of the New York State attorney general, she learned that the Texaco pipeline had ruptured at least twenty-seven times, spilling 16.8 million gallons of raw crude (the Exxon *Valdez* spilled 10.8 million off the coast of Alaska), most of it into the Oriente's delicate web of rivers, creeks, and lagoons. Little of it had been cleaned up, and the pipeline was all but worn out and rupturing with increasing frequency. She calculated that the petroleum industry was spilling an additional 10,000 gallons of oil from secondary flow lines every week and dumping 4.3 million gallons of untreated toxic waste directly into the watershed every day. Malnutrition rates near oil-producing areas were as high as 98 percent. Health workers reported exceptionally high rates of spontaneous abortion, neurological disorders, birth defects, and other problems linked to contaminants and predicted an epidemic of cancer.

After Kimerling wrote up her initial findings (they eventually appeared as a book entitled *Amazon Crude*), Petroecuador tried to have her deported. It was dissuaded by the American embassy, which argued that making an international incident of Kimerling's investigation would draw further attention to it, but the military arrested her, in Coca. She was released only when José Miguel Goldáraz and the local Quichua federation intervened on her behalf.

I had met Kimerling in Coca. She is a compact, intense woman with wide, green eyes, thick, curly, black hair, and a voice that carries hints of her native Alabama. She had set up a pilot legal-aid program in several Indian communities, and she was teaching the residents how to document contamination for a lawsuit against Texaco. She had received so many threats that she no longer traveled in the Oriente without an escort. She had also spent weeks bedridden with shigellosis, a rare bacteriological infection she picked up in the field, and funding for her work was so scarce that she often lived hand to mouth in one of the poorest countries in the hemisphere. But she said that she had suffered most at the hands of two men she once considered her allies— Robert F. Kennedy, Jr., a staff attorney for the Natural Resources Defense Council, and S. Jacob Scherr, the director of the organization's international program.

In July of 1990, Kennedy and Scherr had asked Kimerling to show them the Oriente, which neither man had ever seen. She took them on a five-day tour. They canoed through an oil spill in the Cuyabeno Wildlife Reserve and helicoptered over Yasuní National Park. Moved and impressed, Kennedy and Scherr hired Kimerling to work in their organization's Manhattan headquarters, and that October they announced that they intended to pressure Texaco for $50 million to start a cleanup fund for the Oriente. At the same time they wrote to Edgar Woolard to condemn Conoco's plans. Though Conoco would be the first company ever to produce oil inside the titled Huaorani homeland, it represented something even larger: Beneath the virgin rain forest inhabited by the Huaorani Conoco had discovered substantial deposits of heavy crude, the production of which had only recently been made profitable by technical advances, and which the Oriente has in abundance. The Ecuadorian government was counting on Conoco to launch "the era of heavy crude," for which it predicted $3 billion in foreign investment through the end of the century and tens of billions more in revenues. Conoco, in other words, was the key to opening up huge tracts of the Oriente to oil exploitation.

The NRDC was by no means alone in its opposition to Conoco. Because Conoco's concessions fell within Yasuní National Park, the Sierra Club and its Ecuadorian partner, a nonprofit law firm called La Corporación de Defensa de la Vida, had promised DuPont a "brawl." The Sierra Club Legal Defense Fund (which is not part of the Sierra

Club) had petitioned the OAS on behalf of the Huaorani. CON-
FENIAE, the Amazonian Indian confederation, was demanding a ten-
year moratorium on oil development, and in a groundbreaking alliance
with the Indians, Ecuador's Latin environmentalists had endorsed the
moratorium, driving their point home with a three-day occupation of
Conoco's offices in Quito, the nation's capital. At least two dozen
groups in the United States and Europe sympathized with or formally
supported the moratorium. By late 1990 Woolard was facing serious talk
of an international boycott against DuPont.

When the NRDC entered the battle, Conoco requested a meeting.
It took place in the NRDC's Manhattan office in November 1990. In an
abrupt about-face, Kennedy and Scherr left the meeting convinced that
forcing Conoco out of the Oriente would be a mistake—that Conoco
would do a cleaner job than the companies that would move in if
Conoco pulled out—and they scheduled a second meeting with the
company to explore a settlement that would allow it to proceed. Kimerling was aghast: "If a deal was going to be made, that decision had to
be made in Ecuador." She was fired, and the NRDC withheld some
$8,000 in severance pay in an attempt to force her to sign an agreement
not to publicly criticize Kennedy and Scherr. She refused.

Kennedy and Scherr met again with Conoco, in New York in
February 1991, under a veil of confidentiality. Conoco told them that
without the NRDC's endorsement it stood a less than even chance of
being able to proceed with development. Kennedy and Scherr proposed
that Conoco fund a nonprofit foundation for the Oriente, with the
NRDC allowed to nominate representatives to the board of trustees.
They gave Conoco a strategic analysis of how groups involved in the
region would react to the deal—they said, for example, that neither The
Nature Conservancy nor the World Wildlife Fund would pose a problem, and that the deal would compromise the Sierra Club Legal Defense Fund's petition before the OAS. Conoco offered to put up
$10 million.

In March, Kennedy and Scherr returned to Ecuador to pitch the
deal to Valerio Grefa and Angel Zamarenda, the newly elected president and vice president, respectively, of CONFENIAE, the umbrella
under which the political leaders of the Oriente's eight indigenous
nations come together. Grefa is a Quichua and Zamarenda a Shuar.

The Quichua and the Shuar are the Oriente's largest nations, and its most acculturated politically and economically, and they had controlled CONFENIAE since its founding, in 1980. In the past they had done so with a spirit of inclusion—in fact, CONFENIAE had helped the Huaorani gain official title to part of their traditional territory, and it had been instrumental in the founding of ONHAE.

But Grefa and Zamarenda had been in office less than two months when Kennedy and Scherr arrived, and the two Americans did not understand the change their election represented. Grefa, known in the Amazon as El Vaselino, had ruthlessly set about rekindling the centuries-old enmity between the Huaorani and the larger nations. (Among other things, he was involved in a controversial deal in which his family land in Coca was sold to become offices for a company that was exploring the Huaorani territory for oil.) The Shuar, meanwhile, were moving more aggressively than anyone else to take land from the Huaorani—a quest the Conoco road could only enhance. Grefa and Zamarenda were more than willing to go along with what was, in essence, the sale of the Huaorani homeland. The only real question was the price: They wanted not $10 million but $211 million, or about a dollar a barrel for all the oil in Block Sixteen.

Kennedy and Scherr flew home and relayed the counteroffer to Conoco. About then, however, confidential notes of their second meeting with Conoco were leaked to every nonprofit group in the world with an interest in the Oriente, and they found themselves under wide attack. People who had devoted years to saving the Oriente felt betrayed by those they had considered their own. "Robert Kennedy and Jacob Scherr are what we call environmental imperialists," Esperanza Martínez, at that time the coordinator of a coalition of thirteen Ecuadorian environmental groups, had told me in Quito. "They came to Ecuador for five days, and then they went home and sat down with an oil company and decided they knew what was best for us. What on earth gave them that right?"

The Ecuadorians were outraged at what they saw as a double standard—if the NRDC was opposed to oil drilling in national parks in the United States, why was it willing to promote such activity in Latin America?—and by what they saw as the callous way Kennedy and Scherr had quashed the fledgling alliance then developing between

Ecuador's urban environmentalists and Amazonian Indians. The alliance had produced only one major piece of work, a joint letter to the World Bank opposing a proposed $100 million oil-development loan to Ecuador. But given the enormous cultural gulf that has always existed between Latins and Indians in Ecuador, the letter represented an important step forward. Alone, neither group had the power to influence the Company, but combined they were a force that had to be reckoned with—a fact underscored when the World Bank subsequently shelved the loan. However, when Kennedy and Scherr showed up and put millions of dollars on the table, the Indians and the Latins found themselves divided by old feelings of suspicion and mistrust, and the alliance disintegrated.

Meanwhile, seemingly out of nowhere, the mysterious Huaorani letter surfaced in San Francisco. Suddenly, Conoco wasn't sure who spoke for the Huaorani. It went directly to Valerio Grefa and Angel Zamarenda: What if Conoco were to accept their counterproposal? Would the Huaorani go along with the deal?

The meeting in Coca was arranged. Valerio Grefa vowed that if Nanto and Moi blocked the deal, he would destroy ONHAE and start his own Huaorani organization.

"I BELIEVE the Huaorani said no," José Miguel said when I asked him about the meeting. "I am not sure what the Company heard." He smiled—a small smile. Were the Rio Napo Foundation to become a reality, he said, it would make it easier for the Company to develop the Huaorani territory, and the Huaorani would almost surely receive nothing of value from it. The American "politicians" who had come up with the deal did not understand the Oriente. But it was not accurate to say simply that CONFENIAE was corrupt—one had to consider the enormity of the temptations facing its leaders.

That led me to a harder question, one I had found myself struggling with more and more of late. What right did the Huaorani have to be protected from change?

José Miguel sipped his coffee and thought for a while before he answered. "The forest is relentless," he said. "It shows no mercy. When the Huaorani deviate from the rules they have developed over time, they perish. But on your travels, did you observe their joy? They are joyful in a way that is complete and without self-consciousness. You and I are condemned to live our joy knowing in each moment of that joy that it must end, but in the moment when the Huaorani experience joy it lasts forever."

Again he was silent. Then he said, "Change is inevitable. The Huaorani cannot avoid change. The real question is, on what terms will change occur? The right the Huaorani have—a basic moral right that all people have—is to be allowed to evolve their own cultural tools for dealing with change, rather than having that change imposed upon them."

He said, too, that he thought violence probable when the Conoco road went in. "You see it already on the Vía Auca, and the Huaorani who live around Block Sixteen are much more traditional—they are much more likely to kill."

He had a question for me. "When the Huaorani kill, there is a spiritual discipline to it," he said. "Americans kill without knowing they are doing it. You don't *want* to know you are doing it. And yet you are going to destroy an entire way of life. So you tell me: Who are the savages?"

THAT AFTERNOON I found Enqueri walking the streets of Coca. He had spent every cent I paid him. I took him to the bus station and bought tickets for him, Awa, Quimonca, and Yohue, and then I bought him some food for the trip and gave him a bit more cash and walked him back to the Huaorani Hotel.

"José, come back soon!" he called out as I left. I promised I would.

NOW AND THEN on the flight to California I awoke startled and sweating, and when I got home I had violent dreams. I immersed myself in elemental tasks—gardening and carpentry—and for two and three days at a stretch I did not leave the house except to take solitary walks in the rain. I had been in South America for three months, and I needed time to adjust, but it was more than that. In a world of television and freeways, I needed to feel soil, wood, water. Direct experience is the fabric of Huaorani life, and I sought it out as if it were the only way to remain connected to what I had seen.

A month after I got home Conoco announced that it was pulling out of the Oriente. It would concentrate its energies about as far from the Amazon as it could get—the oil fields of Siberia—and it would sell its share of the Block Sixteen consortium to one of its partners, Dallas-based Maxus Energy, about whom this much was generally known: Back when it had been called the Diamond Shamrock Corporation, it had been one of the two principal producers of Agent Orange, and it had dumped so much dioxin into New Jersey's Passaic River that in 1983 it was forced to undertake one of the most expensive cleanups in the history of the state, if not the nation. The cleanup was so big, in fact, that it was still going on eight years later, even as Maxus rolled up its sleeves and headed for Huaorani territory.

I went to New York to speak with Robert Kennedy about the Conoco-NRDC deal. We met at his office at Pace University. He has piercing blue eyes, and though taller and leaner, he looks very much his father's son. He was dividing his time between directing an environmental-law clinic at Pace and working for the NRDC, at which, after his felony conviction for heroin possession, in 1984, he was sentenced to serve two years of "community service." The NRDC is one of the wealthiest environmental groups in the country, with a core of Ivy League lawyers and scientists who operate at the highest levels of governmental and corporate power, and Kennedy went on to become a fund-raiser and staff attorney. It was a desire to do something "substantive," he said, that had drawn him to the Oriente.

"Do you know what [$10 million] would mean down there?" Kennedy asked me. "We saw a hospital in the Oriente that was operating on a budget of three thousand dollars a year. If you had that kind of money, and you had it in a framework where the Indians couldn't steal it, which has happened in the past, you could make a vast difference. And you would have a model. The Indians could then go to any oil company that came into the Oriente and say, 'You have to match this.' They'd be getting a way to ratchet themselves into the corridors of power. They'd be able to stand up to the military, and the government would have no choice but to deal with them. Conoco was the ideal place to start that process."

He was befuddled, if not shocked, when the deal fell apart. He blamed American environmentalists. He had been impressed by the commitment of Valerio Grefa and, even more so, of Angel Zamarenda, who struck him as "no nonsense, no bullshit, very aggressive." Kennedy seemed surprised when I described the conflict between the Huaorani and the two larger nations, but he shrugged off the suggestion that the Rio Napo Foundation would have been a sellout of the Huaorani, and that it was stopped not so much by environmentalists as by the Huaorani themselves. "I have no idea what happened, or what the internal politics were," he said. "Who *are* the Huaorani?" In retrospect, he had concluded that there was "almost an anthropological question" of whether the Indians of the Oriente "have the capacity to negotiate." They were, he said, "essentially inept at government." He wouldn't say why Judith Kimerling had been fired but insisted that it had nothing to do with her opposition to making a deal with Conoco. There was one thing he would do differently: "Make sure that at that meeting we had with Conoco nobody was taking notes."

What, he asked, would I have done in his place?

I said that I really didn't know. I felt that so long as oil companies dominated the Oriente, groups such as the NRDC had a legitimate, even obligatory, role to play there. But the Oriente was a political snake pit—there were a hundred ways to make mistakes, and if you figured out fifty of them, you were a genius. There were no simple solutions, and no substitutes for spending real time on the ground. And I believed that before you sat down with an oil company to negotiate a deal for Huaorani land, you should, at the least, get to know the Huaorani.

While I was home I talked to quite a few people who had taken up the cause of the Huaorani, or their land. But none of them had a relationship with the Huaorani that was anything more than tangential, because working with the Huaorani was a high-risk, low-reward proposition: Travel to the territory was expensive, dangerous, and time-consuming (and, often, illegal); communication was nearly impossible; the cultural gulf was enormous; the Company was all-powerful; and the Huaorani themselves were utterly unpredictable. So it seemed inevitable when, in the wake of victory, the international coalition of environmental and human-rights groups that had stared down mighty DuPont collapsed, worn out by betrayal, meager resources, the enormity of the challenge. Though people continued to discuss the Huaorani, little of substance was being done.

If there was any consolation to be found, it was that the Huaorani didn't miss such support—they hadn't known it existed. As they saw it, they had never been conquered and never would be, because they were "the bravest people in the Amazon."

PART TWO

West

7

WHEN MY DAUGHTER was three months old I packed up the family and we moved to Ecuador. On my travels with Enqueri I had seen a lot of the remote eastern half of the Huaorani territory, but I knew little about the area west of the Vía Auca, where 80 percent of the Huaorani lived. I decided to go first to Toñampare, if I could get in. It was the largest of their villages. And I wanted to find the Condorito—I'd promised him I'd come back.

In time I would grow skilled at sneaking into the Huaorani territory, but my first trip into Toñampare was a simple matter of dumb luck. I flew in from the town of Shell, which sits at the eastern foot of the Andes a hundred miles southwest of Coca. Most of the Oriente's small-plane traffic originates at the Shell airport, and Huaorani were always lurking about. Alas de Socorro (Wings of Help), an affiliate of the Missionary Aviation Fellowship, charges them a discount rate for their flights. Of course, for the Huaorani, "discount" is as illusory as any other financial concept, and some of them have run up accounts their grandchildren will be paying off. Still, they invariably leave the territory whenever there's an empty seat to be had on an outbound Alas flight. It's too much fun. Later, they collect in Shell waiting for a ride home, or to anywhere else on earth.

When I walked into the Alas hangar, Huaorani were climbing over the desk and laughing at the pilots and poking into bags and snatching the sunglasses off the red-eyed dispatcher, a white man who looked as if he'd dropped in from Kansas. Rain was blasting the hangar roof like buckshot, and the radio was screeching, and planes were roaring down the runway one after another. As in almost every collision between *cowode* and Huaorani, the chaos was colossal. It was so colossal, in fact, that the harried dispatcher mistook me for a Christian. He hustled me out the door toward a six-seater bound right then for Toñampare. "Praise the Lord!" he said, waving me aboard.

The blue-eyed, cleft-chinned young pilot, Brian, rested his hand on the steering shaft and bowed his head.

"O Lord," he prayed, "guide me in my decisions."

"Amen," I said.

Then he taxied through fog and mist and lifted us through gray into a sky of bright blue. Bouncing like a hobbyhorse, we banked east. Soon we picked up the twisty, coffee-and-cream line of the Curaray River— the same line that Nate Saint had followed thirty-six years earlier. When a bone disease disqualified Nate from flying for the air force, he elected to fly for the Lord, and he opened up the Huaorani territory with a clever but dangerous technique called the bucket drop, hand-lowering a bucket of goodies—salt and an aluminum pot—into the green hell below so precisely, and so steadily, that the Huaorani could loot it: Contact.

Brian was seven years old when he first heard the story of Nate Saint. "Ever since that day," he said, "the only thing I wanted to do in my life was to be a missionary pilot and bring the opportunity of know- ing Jesus Christ to these people." He said this quietly, and then he didn't say much at all unless I asked. He was from Minnesota, from farmland, and looked it. He wore blue jeans and a blue cotton work shirt with epaulets. They were starched and crisply pressed. He had been in Ecuador for four years, and had two kids, nine and five. His family lived in a missionary compound in Shell. Brian said that he found the Huaorani "childlike." He was reluctant to give his opinion about the oil industry, though after some thought he allowed that "I heard before oil development started here, Ecuador had a pretty stable economy." For him, that was almost a speech, and he took a moment to catch his wind.

He followed the Curaray for half an hour, until a patch of bare ground opened like a dun wound in green skin and we landed skidding on mud. Along one edge of the strip stood five Huaorani elders. They wore toucan crowns and their earlobes were stuffed with brightly painted wooden plugs and their arms and legs were adorned with feathers and bracelets. What made me catch my breath, however, were their spears: They were the long, hard, red-painted spears used only for killing people.

But not meant for me, as it turned out. The cocaine industry has taken to flying its product to Ecuadorian ports, and many of the planes pass right over the Huaorani territory. Mainly they fly at night. It seemed that one such plane had crashed, and the Huaorani had found it. They had assumed the white powder was salt—which, after all, they had first come to know when an airplane dropped it from the heavens—and they had tested it as they test everything: by smell and by taste. Disappointed (though no doubt excited), they had then given the plane and its contents to the military in exchange for a promise of gifts. In due time the military sent a note saying that it didn't have the money to buy gifts, but thanks for the help. Now the Huaorani warriors wanted a ride to the military post in Shell—they intended to settle accounts.

Toñampare looks nothing like the small clan settlements east of the Vía Auca. It is more of a shantytown, really, tin-roofed shacks clustered around a muddy clearing next to the humongous airstrip. You could say Toñampare was built around the voice of God. In the middle of the village was a radio transceiver strapped onto a tall tree stump and encased in a crude, open-walled wooden box that was surrounded by wire mesh, so the Huaorani couldn't steal it. It was powered by a solar panel mounted high in a nearby tree, and except when a local condor took up an extended stay on the panel and decommissioned the system, the radio squawked all day long. Each day started with a Bible story. (*"Pan y pescado,"* about an *abundancia* of loaves and fishes so great it never ends, was a local favorite.) The pitiful shacks of Toñampare seemed to huddle under the radio, as if its magic could somehow ward off the forest's heathen evils—as if life were a choice between the forest and God.

You could also say Toñampare was built around a toilet. Next to the transceiver was a tiny porcelain crapper tucked into a tiny shed. The Huaorani never used it. The only other flush toilet in the entire 2,600 square miles of the territory was about twenty feet away, hidden inside a mesh-enclosed wooden house that looked as if it could have been lifted directly from the Pennsylvania farmlands that had given birth to its inhabitant, Rachel Saint. The radio, of course, was Rachel's work, as were the toilets, and the chapel next to her house, and the small bronze plaque beside the chapel. The plaque commemorated her brother Nate, who was killed on the banks of the Curaray, within shouting distance of the only real home Rachel Saint had known since 1968.

A young man named Salomón invited me stay with him. He said that Enqueri wasn't around. He had taken off down the Curaray, in a canoe—he was going to elope. His bride-to-be was thirteen years old. It was, Salomón said, Enqueri's fifth attempt at marriage.

I slept on the floor of Salomón's shack, which had all the ambience of a henhouse, including hens. But we prepared our meals in the home of his mother, Dayuma—the first Huaorani Rachel Saint had met, and the first she "saved." Rachel and Dayuma were so close that the Huaorani considered them sisters. Dayuma herself was a pleasant woman, with a wide, open face. She smiled a lot, and she had the sort of glazed expression that some might describe as beatific and others, perhaps, as vacant. In any case, the Christian life had been good to her. Compared with the other Huaorani, she lived like a queen. Her house had an electric light and wood floors and a propane stove. On a wall hung a poster advertising a Quito nightclub owned by Samuel Caento Padilla—her son from her first marriage, to a Quichua. The poster had been placed between a photograph of a snowcapped mountain peak and another of a Huao dressed only in the traditional penis strap. The man's groin had been marked out with blue ink. There were no religious posters on the walls, and in the several hours I spent with Dayuma, she did not mention Jesus. In fact, she didn't say much at all. Salomón did most of the talking, and mostly he talked about sex. Sex with women, sex with chickens, sex with rocks.

I was staying within a stone's throw of Rachel Saint's house, but it was three days before I saw her. Every day, however, I heard her voice ringing out over the radio speaker in the center of the village, and every day she sent me a note via a Huaorani runner. One note accompanied a chunk of venison: "The Aucas killed this for you. I'm sorry you'll have to eat it their way. I prefer it fried." "Their way" meant boiled.

Finally, late one afternoon, I looked across the clearing in the center of the village and saw an immense, and immensely white, figure staring fixedly in my direction. Rachel Saint was a tall woman. She was taller than any Huaorani, stooped not at all by her seventy-nine years, and not only tall but wide. Her size was surely an advantage in a culture that so values physical prowess, and she was made larger still by the soft lines of the pastel blouses and skirts she favored. Her white hair was pulled back in a tight bun, and she peered from behind her glasses with eyes that seemed as pale blue as ice. To the Huaorani, certainly, they were every bit as rare.

Our eyes met, briefly; hers betrayed no emotion. Then she turned slowly, and slowly climbed the steps back into her house and shut the door.

I went over and knocked.

"Would you like some tapioca pudding?" she asked.

RACHEL SAINT CAME to Ecuador in 1955. She had been "saved" at age fifteen, gone to Bible college, and spent twelve years working with alcoholics in New Jersey and five more translating the Word for Piro and Shapra Indians in Peru. She was forty-two years old when she took up her true calling among the Aucas, through Dayuma, whom she discovered "living like a slave" at a plantation in the Oriente—most of Dayuma's clan had been slaughtered by other Huaorani, and Dayuma had fled the territory. In their grief over the loss of their loved ones, the two women found a bond. Dayuma taught Rachel Huaorani; Rachel taught Dayuma about the Lord. In 1957 she brought Dayuma to the United States. They went onstage with Billy Graham; they appeared on *This Is Your Life*; they raised gobs of money. By the time they returned to Ecuador, Rachel was the most famous missionary in the world.

In October of 1958—twelve years after Dayuma had fled the Huaorani—the two women set off into the territory on foot, hacking their way through the forest for four days until they found what was left of Dayuma's clan. Rachel became the first missionary to sleep in the territory and live to tell about it. She and Dayuma established a settlement, and with radios and airplanes Rachel conjured machetes and shirts and pants and candy and rice. Lured by these riches, Huaorani clans came calling, and Rachel and Dayuma tried to persuade them to give up their heathen ways. Taboos were the Devil's work, so hunting, once limited to birds, monkeys, and peccaries, was expanded to include all the beasts of the forest and all the fish in the rivers. Nomadism was evil; the Lord's way dictated that the Huaorani must settle down, build permanent villages, and raise garden crops and barnyard animals. Sexual license, polygamy, and chanting were strictly forbidden.

Rachel became Dayuma's clan sister: Nemo, she was called, Huaorani for "star." They built their homes side by side, and to the *cowode* world Rachel presented Dayuma as the leader of the Huaorani. The Company showed them where it wanted to explore for oil; Rachel and Dayuma moved the clans out and brought them into the tiny "protectorate" they persuaded the government to create in 1969. Desperate to colonize the Oriente as rapidly as possible, the government put Rachel's sponsor, the Summer Institute of Linguistics, in charge of Huaorani health and education, and Rachel bent herself to her contracted task of making the Aucas "useful citizens."

But things began to unravel in 1973, when the SIL sent James Yost, an evangelical anthropologist, to study the Huaorani. He came away profoundly dismayed. Rachel Saint, he said, was trying to turn the culture upside down—trying to convert it to a matriarchy, with Dayuma as its queen. (Rachel Saint usually referred to the protectorate as "Dayuma's Land.") The SIL asked Rachel to leave the Huaorani; instead, she left the SIL. She moved out of the territory in 1979, but she returned within two years, with ten dollars to her name and the backing only of a small church in Oklahoma. Although she kept an apartment in Quito, and went there every few months, she never really left the Huaorani territory again.

Inside Rachel's house were another radio transceiver, a kitchen sink and counter, dishes drying in a rack, a propane stove. A solar panel provided electricity. A small bookcase held copies of the Bible, wrapped in plastic against the humidity, and five copies of the French translation of her biography. A blowgun and a fishnet hung on one wall; on another were aging black-and-white photographs of the Huaorani. She waved me toward a rocking chair and brought pudding, then collapsed into a hammock slung across the middle of the house and stretched out her long, pale legs, which were covered with insect bites. Scratching at the bites, she apologized for seeming tired: She had spent the last twelve hours in a malarial fever. Around her throat she wore a necklace with a single jaguar tooth. The roundness of the tooth, she said, indicated that it came from an old cat. "It was so old it couldn't kill anymore," she said. "Just like me."

Dayuma had fled the Huaorani in 1946 in the face of a wave of intertribal killing that has never really been explained, though it probably had something to do with the outbreak of incurable disease brought by the Company, and by the Huaorani custom of avenging all deaths. By most accounts, it was extraordinarily bloody—some estimates have placed the mortality rate as high as 60 percent of the population—and when Dayuma returned to the territory with Rachel, only forty of her clan's two hundred or so members were still alive. "They were committing ethnic suicide," Rachel said. "When a child died, they'd go to their witch doctors to find out who to blame, and there would be reprisal killings. They stopped the killings when we showed them the way of peace. So when an anthropologist accuses me of destroying the culture—well, if I told you how mad that made me, you'd have to write it on asbestos paper. *Destroying* the culture? I'm the one who saved it!"

She had been told by the Huaorani—"by my sources on the inside," as she liked to put it—that I'd been to see Quemperi. "You were lucky to get out alive," she said. "You go there at the wrong time, your life isn't worth a plugged nickel. The only Auca you can trust is a Christian Auca. The ones over on the Catholic side are all savages. Pure savages. I can't think of any other word for people who kill their own kind." She added, "Of course, you can't help but like them. They're the most charming killers there ever was."

To her critics, the nature of Rachel Saint's work is exemplified by the fate of one of the first bands of "wild Aucas" she brought into the protectorate, in 1969. Almost immediately all 104 contracted polio. Sixteen died; another 16 were crippled. "You have to ask how many more would have been killed if we hadn't brought them here," she told me. "How can you let your brother die without giving him a chance at peace? The tribal dictates—you might as well call them the Devil's dictates. When you put aside the Ten Commandments, you have pure chaos, and that's what we had here with the Aucas. You had husbands marrying two sisters. You had brothers sleeping with their brothers' wives. Sometimes a man would marry a mother and a daughter. You had your free-love fiestas, where anybody slept with anybody. Pretty soon, a father has kids in five places. A boy grows up, he wants to marry a girl, and he finds out she's his sister! If you don't think that's chaos, you haven't read your Old Testament."

Several Huaorani were hovering at the foot of the steps outside her house, talking quietly among themselves. A man shouted at us from what was now the inky darkness of the forest night. I recognized the terms "Auca" and "Huaorani." Rachel shouted back to him in his own tongue. "He's saying they're Huaorani, not Aucas," she said. "But they're Aucas. Always have been. I told him he should be proud of that—there's a soccer team in Quito named the Aucas." She got up and tossed a bar of soap in the direction of the voice. "That *Huaorani*"—she arched her eyebrows— "wants to wash his Auca clothes."

Rachel struck me as kind—kind and lonely and touched with regret. It seemed painfully obvious that by any measure—emotional, physical, material—her remaking of the culture in her own image had been a net loss for the Huaorani. The people of Toñampare were visibly less healthy than those who lived in more traditional ways. So many Huaorani had crowded into the village, and, with the loss of the old taboos, so many of the native animals had disappeared from the surrounding forest, that there was virtually no hunting. The people were dependent on goods brought in from outside, and many of them had become wage slaves to a culture they could never hope to be truly a part of—to a culture that, in fact, considered them little more than animals.

Rachel Saint conceded that it may have been a mistake to trust the Oil. (She used "the Oil" the way the Huaorani used "the Company.") The Oil flew Dayuma into Shell to sign a contract to work the Auca lands, but "they lied to her," Rachel explained. "They told her they'd crossed out the parts giving them permission to build roads, but they hadn't really, and she can't read Spanish." The Oil brought alcohol and prostitution, which made the Huaorani "demon-possessed"; worse, it brought roads and colonists and epidemics. "Sometimes I wish the Oil had never come," she said, and added that once development began in Block Sixteen, "the killings will start again, mark my word."

Yet she was in favor of that development, in no small part because it would further what had to be seen as her final great quest: the conversion of the Tagaeri, the most notorious of the last uncontacted Huaorani bands. She was going to meet with Maxus just as soon as she could, she said. She hoped to reach the Tagaeri before anyone else, particularly the Capuchins, and the opening up of Block Sixteen would greatly increase her chances of access. Alejandro Labaca had had his chance, and he had blown it: "I think he wanted to be a martyr." She ridiculed the Capuchins for their political activism ("They say they're trying to save the land for the Indians—I say save the Indians for the land!"), and she chose to ignore the fact that Labaca's death had led to the sort of victory that had always eluded her: Temporarily, at least, the government suspended oil development in the Tagaeri zone. What seemed to bother her most about the Capuchins, though, was a much-reproduced photograph of a young nun, Sister Inés, who was killed with Labaca. In the photograph, Inés is cooking soup for several Huaorani. "The Catholics claim that the Aucas liked Inés, that they were friendly with her," Rachel said, "but I happen to know that's not true." Although no one else in a hundred miles spoke English, she leaned over and whispered in my ear: "My sources on the inside say they peed in her soup pot!"

ON SUNDAY, at Rachel's invitation, I went to services. Of the roughly 250 Huaorani living in Toñampare, 11 had made it to chapel. One man was in a wheelchair, another on crutches, their legs crippled by polio. Four decades of tilling the Huaorani field had yielded a slim crop; Rachel Saint's relationship with the Huaorani was one not of shared faith but of power and reward. For years she controlled Huaorani dealings with the government and the Company, and, to a great extent, she continued to control the radio, the air traffic, and the entry of outside goods and services, including what few health workers and medical supplies found their way to Toñampare. (Later I asked one of the worshipers what Rachel did, and he said, "She asks God for things.") Rachel had battled off many attempts by CONFENIAE to introduce a school curriculum that, in theory, would help preserve some elements of traditional Huaorani culture, and she showed no signs of giving in. "I have warned the people to stay away from such dangerous organizations," she said. "They're Communists."

At the front of the chapel stood a young Huao preaching the Gospel. He spoke mainly in Huaorani but slipped into Spanish to deliver admonitions against drinking and dancing. Rachel sat to one side, impassive, but the man was clearly nervous, stuttering occasionally and shooting her sidelong glances. He was an odd-looking Huao. It wasn't simply that he wore dentures. No, what was strange was that he also wore glasses: I had never seen them on a Huao.

Suddenly, I realized that the man I was watching was Enqueri.

"Credit!" he told me later, gleefully, by way of explanation. He had gone to the Christian hospital in Shell for the choppers and specs. "Now maybe Enqueri will get a woman!" he said. He grinned broadly, and held the grin. What about his marriage? There had been problems—on the second day of the elopement he'd accidentally tipped the canoe and dumped his young fiancée and all his shotgun shells. He'd left her there on the bank, camping with her brothers.

Enqueri seemed genuinely excited to see me. It had been months since we parted in Coca, and I had not been sure, then, what he had thought of our trip. "Come to my house," he said. "You must meet my family. But first we will hide your things in a safe place."

We left my pack there in the center of the village, with a friend Enqueri said we could trust. ("Not like in Cononaco!" he said, laughing. "They are barbarians over there!") Then we set off across the *pista* and down a long trail that led away from the village and across a creek and ended at a small clearing, where Enqueri's family had built their home. As we walked, he said that Quimonca and Awa and Yohue had not made it to Toñampare. Instead, in Coca, they had hooked up with a tour group seeking to visit Cononaco. With the three Huaorani onboard their canoe, the tourists were guaranteed safe passage into the territory.

"Were Quimonca and Awa and Yohue hired as guides?" I asked.

"Yes."

"Were they paid?"

"Yes."

"How much?"

"Food, and some new boots."

Enqueri told me the name of the tour company. Each client—he thought there were six of them—would have paid at least $50 a day for the ten-day trip.

For his part, Enqueri had managed to save a little of the money I'd given him in Coca—that is, the money I'd given him the second time.

But in Shell he had run into a Quichua man he knew and loaned the man everything he had left. The man was supposed to have met Enqueri at the airport to pay him back, but he hadn't shown. Now Enqueri planned to fly back to Shell and find him—even though, as I pointed out, the trip back would cost five times the money he hoped to collect.

In the morning Enqueri told me that he had to return to the river to join his fiancée. Meanwhile, a missionary plane was on the way.

"Hurry to the *pista*," he said. "I will bring your *mochila*."

I went to the *pista* and a few minutes later Enqueri brought my pack.

"Come back soon to the land of the People," he said. "I will wait for you."

Then, uncharacteristically for a Huao, he gave me a hug, and then he turned and was gone.

Soon a fog settled over the *pista* through which no pilot, no matter how strong his faith in the hereafter, would attempt a descent. I went back up into the village and sat by Salomón's house. When I reached into my pack for something to eat, I found that many of my supplies were missing—cans of powdered milk, rice, candy bars. I had no further need of these things and had intended to leave them in Toñampare, but in the rush to the plane I had forgotten to do it. Still, the idea of the loss—the feeling of violation—saddened me, and while I was brooding about it I happened to spot Enqueri hustling across the far side of the central clearing. He was perhaps twenty yards away, but even at that distance I could see that his hands were filled with the goods from my pack. He saw me, too, and for the briefest instant our eyes connected and held, and then he disappeared into the forest.

It occurred to me then that he had also stolen the food in Cononaco, and that he was not only a liar but a thief, and that despite this I was still very fond of him. Even so I found myself troubled, perhaps by his cleverness. Potentially, Enqueri was the most capable leader I had met among the Huaorani, at least in terms of the political skills demanded by the *cowode* world. He was able to move among the disparate Huaorani communities with relative ease, and when he spoke he held the ear of all he met, because he understood far more about life outside the territory than did almost any other Huao.

It was impossible, of course, to know what Enqueri truly thought.

It was hard even to guess. Did he believe in the Christian God? He seemed unfettered by any *cowode* concept of sin. He lied, cheated, and stole, and then he stood up in church and translated Bible stories. But he had told me, in what seemed like all sincerity, that he intended to help Rachel Saint find the Tagaeri. He was not afraid to die in this quest—he believed that if he did, he would go right to the sky. Clearly, El Señor held an appeal for Enqueri beyond material gain.

Meanwhile, though Enqueri knew in some way that the Company would destroy the Huaorani, his dissatisfaction with the Company seemed personal—it hadn't paid him well on the seismic crews. How then to explain his work for ONHAE? Among other things, working with ONHAE enabled him to hang out with a whole new type of *cowode*. But he had compiled his census with great diligence and care, and at no small risk. However cynical or opportunistic, his participation in ONHAE contained a vein of altruism.

The other Huaorani called Enqueri the Condorito because he could never make up his mind. But he had learned to play all the angles: ONHAE, the church, the Company, *cowode* like me. If Enqueri was in any way lost, it may have been because he was so far out in front of the rest of the Huaorani that he had no real idea of where to go, and no one to show him the way.

8

EVERYTHING'S GONE *wrong*," Ali Sharif says. He's walking in circles with his eyes pinned to the sky, his expression that of a man hoping for a miracle. For a hundred yards all around him lie felled trees the size of wrecking cranes, and at one edge of the clearing trunks tilt into the Tihuano River like giant matchsticks. Surrounded by forest, the clearing looks like the epicenter of an enormous blast.

"We can't *possibly* succeed," Sharif says.

"Relax, Ali," Moi says. "Everything is arranged."

Suddenly, a chorus of urgent voices erupts from the bush:

"Watch out, Ali!"

"Ali, protect yourself!"

"Ali-Ali-Ali-*hold on to your ass!*"

Then: madhouse laughter, followed by a cacophony of excited shrieking, and, finally, a faint yawing, like a door swinging on a tight hinge. A flock of parrots bolts for the sky. Ali Sharif stands dead still. The yawing swells to a tremendous roar as an eighty-foot ceiba crashes to earth, pushing a dozen lesser trees before it. They explode into the Tihuano, their thunder resonating for long seconds. Ali sighs and lights a cigarette and surveys the wreckage. "The Huaorani love to cut down trees," he says, "but they *really* love to fuck up rivers." He inhales deeply. "Well, maybe it's coming together after all."

Ali stands in the glare of a sun so bright it burns the skin in seconds. Moi, though nearby, is buried in the dark shadows of the forest, and is almost invisible. He is sitting on a log, trying to set a machine-gun bullet in a spent shotgun shell, into the metal base of which he has carved a small hole.

"Moi, what time is it?" Ali asks, once again searching the heavens.

"In Japan it is twenty-two minutes past three."

"I mean, what time is it in *Ecuador*?"

"I do not know."

"But I gave you my watch."

"My brother's wife likes it very much, Ali."

"Of course."

"Ali, gift me your pants."

"You'll just give them away, Moi."

"Ali, gift me something."

We are deep in the forest west of the Vía Auca, waiting for a military helicopter that is long overdue with supplies for a weeklong *jornada*, or work session, during which Ali, Moi, and a team of eighteen other Huaorani men hope to mark seven kilometers of their territorial border. This sun is the first break in the rain in four days. The rivers are in full flood, and back in Coca a military airlift—far-fetched as the idea seemed—had been judged the only possible way to bring in sufficient supplies. How had Moi coaxed this assistance from the Tigres, who were hardly known for their fondness of the Huaorani, let alone their generosity?

Moi shrugs. "They are afraid of our spears."

Ali is now pacing the rude clearing. He is a horticulturalist by trade, and he knows nothing at all about building helicopter pads. "It will never come together," he says. "Help from the military? *Impossible.*" He lights another cigarette. "This is a *disaster*. We've no money left. The food we brought? The Huaorani ate it all in one meal. We'll have to walk out of here—*swim* out is more like it—and it will be *months* before we can get it together to come back and why the *hell* are we wasting our time?"

Ali Sharif is thirty-nine years old, slim and fit, professorial. In height he is so like a typical Huao that in a crowd it is sometimes difficult to pick him out. But he wears wire-rimmed glasses, and though Iranian by birth he speaks fluent English in a crisp British accent, and his hair is auburn and his coloring fair. In other words, "I look white, don't I? Well, not that it matters, but I *am* white, except in your country." He spent his youth in British boarding schools—"which is paradoxical, because my father hated the British, and I hated their schools"—his adolescence in Italy—"Paradise! *I could eat again!*"—and an unfortunate stretch of his young adulthood in Iran, where he was imprisoned for what he will describe only as a "political crime." He was in the second year of a thirteen-year sentence when one day the prison yard was full of talk that the shah had been overthrown. "I looked around and I couldn't see any guards," he says. "I went right over the wall." An uncle living nearby arranged a flight to Italy. From there Ali made his way to Mexico, crossed the Rio Grande, picked grapes in California's Napa Valley, and eventually settled in Santa Fe, New Mexico. One evening he attended a lecture about the Huaorani, presented by a small and somewhat ragged Australian environmental group called the Rainforest Information Centre. He sent a donation to RIC's Quito office, with a note asking if it needed any further help. "When I didn't hear back I wrote them this really nasty letter—I mean *nasty*—but I got a sweet reply inviting me down. That was four years ago. I've been here ever since. The government has given me a *missionary* visa, of all things. I don't even believe in God."

This is Ali's sixth session "on the line," but it will be the first session to enjoy the luxury of a helicopter lift, should it come to pass. "Usually we carry all the supplies on our backs," he says. A horrible thought. The hike in had been eight wretched miles, uphill and down, through mud, thorns, bees, fire ants, and mosquitoes, all of which had paled beside the nightmare of crossing the Tihuano on a bridge made of a single log about two feet wide and forty feet long—thirty-six feet of which I negotiated successfully before following my backpack headfirst into the roiling brown river, emerging, after some time, to the vision of a placid, pistonlike Huao named Omaca poised stork-still on the log above. "*Not die,*" he counseled.

"It is coming, Ali," Moi says, and though I can hear nothing but the sounds of the forest itself, a dozen Huaorani men have gathered in the clearing and are gesticulating skyward. They are still doing so twenty minutes later as the chopper descends, flattening what little bush remains and whipping up a frightening hail of debris. The Huaorani don't give way until the blades are beating right over them, and they race back into the clearing almost as soon as the helicopter touches down. With

Moi directing operations, they quickly extract machetes, axes, rubber boots, mosquito nets, flashlights, pots and pans, bags of rice and oatmeal and noodles and bubble gum.

Ali is grinning from ear to ear. "Moi makes magic happen," he says. "He pulls rabbits out of hats. I love him. I mean, I just *love* the guy."

THE HUAORANI cut vines and palm leaves and fashion them into baskets and shoulder racks and divide up the supplies and set off into the forest carrying loads of an impossible weight. Moi, I estimate when I try to heft the mound balanced on his head, is hauling close to a hundred pounds. Still, as he walks he points toward the canopy, and, straining my eyes, I can just make out six dark, furry balls that seem to swing like yo-yos a hundred feet above us: a troupe of howler monkeys. Every once in a while Moi hacks down a section of a vine called *omeica* and passes it to me. When one end is tilted up, it emits a thin but refreshing stream of sweet water.

The Huaorani move rapidly through the forest, almost trotting, yet silently as ducks swimming a pond. A wiry elder named Pego is a mile ahead of us, hacking a path through the bush. "He's unbelievable," Ali says from behind me. "Last time, we hiked all day like this and it wasn't until we made camp that I realized I'd forgotten my pack. Old Pego told one of the boys something like 'It's next to the nine hundred and twenty-sixth tree behind us, on the left,' and three hours later the kid shows up with the pack."

Within minutes Ali and I are plastered with bits of everything that grows in this forest and some things that do not. The Huaorani remain spotless. "And on we plunge into the savage heart of this dark continent," Ali intones in a mock basso profundo, "going where no white man has gone before." Then he adds, in his normal voice, "Well, I guess if *you* weren't here that would still be true, wouldn't it?"

Several hours later we quit the trail, collapse against a ceiba, and sit there oblivious to an onslaught of mosquitoes. "I've had malaria so many times that one more bite can hardly make a difference," Ali says, slapping absentmindedly at his arms and legs. Lightning fast, the Huaorani chop saplings and build a village of snug little watertight lean-tos, laying a mattress of palm leaves on the floor of the hut Ali and I will share. "El Palacio

Gringo," Moi announces, and Ali rolls out an air mattress and falls asleep.

Throughout the afternoon and most of the night Huaorani men continue to filter into camp in ones and twos and threes. The ancient Dawe has been two weeks on the trail; the six-toed deaf-mute, Merca, has traveled even farther, from Quemperi's settlement. Nanto arrives from Toñampare with two beefy brothers, excellent axmen both. Right behind them, having jogged all the way from Tzapino, a two-day journey, come Amo, the ONHAE secretary with the gold-inlaid front tooth, and his young cousin Yahue. Toward dusk, gentle Euhue, an elder said to have been in on the killing of Nate Saint, pads into camp so quietly I don't see him until he's standing right next to me, cutting his jet black hair straight across his forehead with the shells of two river mollusks. He reaches up and twists my chest hairs and laughs out loud. As for the ball of coiled muscle that is crazy young Pego, we could hear him booming his way along the bush for more than an hour, wielding his machete as easily as a penknife, toppling trees for the hell of it. His voice barreled through the forest: "Let's go to work, Huaoranis!" Then, leaping into the camp, laughing hysterically, his shorts bulging with an erection, *"Suck this!"*

At dusk old Pego purses his lips and makes a sound like a soft kiss: A toucan appears, and Moi fires his reconstructed shotgun shell. To Pego go the feathers, to Moi the bill, and to our cook, Omaca, the rest, dumped into a stew of woolly monkey, tree rat, frog, oatmeal, rice, sugar, salt, cinnamon sticks, an onion, and two dozen lollipops.

"Weird eating habits," says Ali, sniffing the pot, then loads up his bowl. "Dig in, mate."

IN THE LAST LIGHT I follow a faint trail away from camp and down a short ridge to a small creek and wade shin deep a few yards upstream to a boulder. I climb up on the slick rock and peel off my shorts and lower myself naked into the creek. I paddle about for a moment and then wash up. The forest is quiet and cool and peaceful, and my exhaustion fades to a pleasant fatigue. Then, quite abruptly, I realize that I can no longer find the trail I descended. The forest is so thick I can't see but a few yards in any direction. Above me, I can't see through the canopy to the sky.

Then I hear "Hoooo—hooo!": Downstream, old Pego stands in the creek, watching me. Quickly, I pull on my shorts and follow him back through the forest and up the ridge to camp. It is the last time that I let myself get beyond sight of another human being.

IN CAMP the young men sleep in bunches—Moi and Amo and Nanto curled up together, young Pego with Merca and Omaca—but the old men sleep alone, in tiny shelters of a single broad-leafed sapling bent low and tied with vine to a short pole. It pours all night. Beneath his tree, bone dry, Euhue nurses a bed of coals, waking now and then to cook a bit of monkey or a plantain. He chants, almost to himself, and Moi translates for me:

> Today I killed a monkey;
> Three darts tipped with poison.
> I brought it to the People.
> We ate and sang.
> Yesterday I killed a deer,
> Today I work the skin.
> I know how to hunt the pig.
> My spears are hard,
> They will not break.
> Some have not yet learned to make good spears.
> They have no meat. . . .
> I killed the cowode, many cowode,
> They had guns but they could not kill us. . . .
> I am an old man.
> I know many songs.
> Now you must learn to sing,
> You young men,
> You Huaorani,
> You strong young Huaorani.
> aaaaoooooAAAH!

But the young Huaorani do not chant, preferring to take their tunes by cassette. Someone has carried in a tape player and a single tape, a collection of urban Quichua songs, electric guitar, drums, ooohhh,

Juanita. Muy civilizado. Throughout the night snatches of this din blast me awake, and each time I see different men sitting around the fire—eating, shaping spears over the flames, fiddling with the music box. In the morning, paralyzed by fatigue, I ask Ali how long the batteries will last.

He laughs. "No batteries, mate," he says. "It's a windup box. One of the boys wakes up, he wants some music, he cranks the box. No day and night here, mate. No asleep, no awake. No dreams, no reality. No past, no future. It's a continuum: Huaorani time. *It's all right now.*"

AT DAWN Ali and old Pego and Amo and I are working the front line, clearing out the underbrush with our machetes. Behind us come heavier machetes, downing small trees and big brush, and behind them the axmen, felling skyscrapers. Within an hour my hands are blistered and swollen and embedded with thorns, and my arms and legs are pocked with insect bites. Sweat runs in sheets. The Huaorani never take a break and never cease to screech with delight at every substantial piece of falling timber—the bigger the better. Ali works slowly but steadily, stopping now and then to light a cigarette or to remark, "Now isn't *that* a lovely tree?" and wander off into the bush. Moi has assigned old Pego to keep an eye on Ali—the Huaorani consider it but a matter of luck that he hasn't been crushed to pulp. (Such courtesies are extended to me, as well; though a stranger, I am regarded as part of Ali's clan.)

Ali collects seeds as we go, and Amo sees to it that as we go we eat: seeds and nuts and sappy vines. And once, hidden in a ceiba, liberated by a hundred frenzied ax blows, a beehive the size of a basketball. It's a free-for-all, twenty pairs of hands ripping at the comb, honey dripping down chins and across chests and bellies. Ali eats as wildly as the Huaorani. Thrusting a gob of comb at me, he exclaims, "Bee pollen! *Nature's orgasm!*" His nostrils flare. "This is *everything!* The essence of *all immunization!* Eat it—there! Now you're immunized! Immunized against *everything!*"

This immunization does not appear to work against jungle rot. The fungus starts about day three. Everyone gets it, and, says Ali, you get it every time you go on the line. You feel it first in the joints—a burning in the crook of an arm or behind a knee—and then it spreads, on a *cowode*, to the hairy places, belly and chest, and to anywhere that gets friction: I soon have a trail of scabs along my waist. At night the Huaorani line up to be treated by Ali, not only for fungus but for colds, sprains, cuts, toothaches, headaches, and staph infection, the boils of which are ubiquitous.

"Most Huaorani have never seen a doctor," Ali says. "Wouldn't it be nice if we could find someone to come in and treat them, even just for onetime stuff like scabies?" Ali himself stumbled out of the last *jornada* with malaria; this time he will bring with him amoebas and an intestinal fungus. But none of this quite rivals what I saw at the RIC house in Quito, on a young volunteer named Nils. Two months after a *jornada*, his entire stomach was still flaming red and horribly swollen, and right under the skin it was crosshatched with what looked like the sorts of markings ants make in sand. "Nematodes," Ali says. "There's not much you can do about them. Another friend of mine had them, and he had to burn all his clothes and his mattress and towels. Thank God, Nils's doctor said just boil them. I mean, we only make a hundred dollars a month, and we can't really afford to buy new clothes, you know?"

IT'S AN ODD thing, this cutting the forest to save it.

In 1990 the Ecuadorian government granted the Huaorani title to a territory of some 2,600 square miles. It was an act of apparent, but deceptive, generosity: The contract granted the Huaorani only a third of what they consider their traditional homeland, and it stipulated that they could not attempt to impede the extraction of oil or any other mineral or resource. Whatever its shortcomings, title was title, and soon after the contract was signed the Huaorani identified the job of marking the territorial boundary as the most important work facing them as a unified nation. Some sections of the boundary were formed by rivers, but almost a hundred miles of it were simply lines drawn on paper. To mark it, they must hack a fifteen-foot-wide trail through the forest and replant it with palm trees to make a discernible border. Until the territory could be delineated, there would be no practical way to keep colonists from moving in, and once in place they would be impossible to dislodge.

At first, CONFENIAE (the confederation that encompasses all the Oriente's indigenous nations) oversaw the job of marking the boundary, but its surveyors made serious mistakes, and the Rainforest Information Centre was asked to step in and help. As Douglas Ferguson, a Briton who is RIC's director, had told me in Quito, "We know the forest and we happen to like Indians, and we're the only people crazy enough to do it." The Ecuadorian government endorsed the idea, and RIC went to work side by side with the Huaorani out in the bush, chopping the line with machetes and axes at the rate of about half a mile a day. It also raised funding for the project, including money for supplies, survey crews, and equipment.

Despite all the noise being made about the Huaorani, RIC was the only organization that could be said to be working with them in any real way, though "work" hardly describes the relationship. When the ONHAE officers were in Quito, as they had to be from time to time to deal with the Company and the government, they slept at the house RIC used for its home and headquarters. The RIC staff fed them, helped them buy clothes ("They pick the most *bizarre* colors," Ali says, "like, you know, *neon*"), arranged classes in such *cowode* skills as banking and small-motor repair, and took them to karate movies, for which the Huaorani had developed a passion.

"Once when Nanto and Amo came to town they got it into their heads that they wanted to speak to the president of the country," Ali says. "So they went to the presidential palace and just walked up and knocked on the door and said, you know, 'Hi, we're the Huaorani, let us in.' Sure enough, in they go. They can do that, you know. They're innocent—they charm everyone they meet. So in they went and they sat down and they chatted with the president. I'd loaned Amo these pants"—Ali indicates the pair of surfer's baggies he's been wearing on the line—"and the president said, 'Where did you get *those?*' Afterward, Amo talked me into buying him a dress shirt and long pants, and a dress for his wife. She'd never been in a department store. So there I was in this weird situation"—he makes as if he's holding up a dress—" 'Is this *waponi?*' But, you know, it's all part of the work."

Clearly, whatever protection Ali affords the Huaorani when they're in the city, they return it here in the forest. On day two we start well, cutting a full kilometer of trail in the morning, but at midday a howling rainstorm descends. Amo makes a shelter by building a log rail about waist high and bending palm fronds over it, and Ali, old Pego, and I huddle under it, our heads between our knees. The forest grows black with the tempest, and above its roar one hears the greater roar of crashing trees. Winds soon rip the shelter to shreds. The abrupt fury of the forest is quite frightening, and I find myself counting my breaths to try to steady my nerves. The other Huaorani hustle past us, jamming their machetes and axes into tree trunks as they bolt for the camp. But Moi searches us out, and we race off with him in the lead and Amo behind us and Pego in between. As we run and slip and slide through the forest, I can see massive trees falling on all sides.

"Ali, be careful!" Moi yells. "Watch out for the trees!"

Not comprehending, his glasses fogging up, Ali yells back, "That's great!" Old Pego laughs loudly. We cross a small creek; as usual, I fall in. Pego fishes me out, but that is the only time he strays more than a few feet from Ali.

Twenty minutes later we are safely in camp. Omaca, the cook, has kindly bundled up our gear to keep it dry, and he brings us cups filled with hot oatmeal and something the Huaorani call *yupi*, which I assume to be the extract of some rain forest plant.

"Nope," says Ali. "It's Ecuadorian Kool-Aid. Used by astronauts, or so it says right on the envelope. Used by so-called Stone Age tribal peoples, too. The Huaorani think it's the best thing about Western civilization."

In gratitude I give Omaca my bandanna, which he ties over his head like a little old lady wrapping her curlers, and Pego tells the story of our flight through the forest. *"Bueno!"* he says, imitating Ali. The Huaorani roar with laughter, as does Ali himself.

WE CUT half a kilometer on day one, a kilometer on day two, and considerably less than that on day three, when it rains all morning and we spend hours huddled under tiny shelters. In midday a small, squat fellow named Jonas comes sprinting through the forest with two pots half his size hanging from either end of a machete slung across his shoulders: lentils and rice. Moi shows me how to fashion a palm leaf into a bowl. We eat with our fingers.

On day four, Ali plunges inadvertently into a nest of fire ants. I'd already been bitten once, on my right index finger. For about ten minutes it felt as if someone were holding a match to my skin. Multiply that by two hundred, and—well, as Ali screams, "I'm on fire!" Though he yells in English, the Huaorani know at once what has happened: The ants are trapped beneath his clothes, next to his skin. Immediately, Moi and Pego rip off Ali's shirt and shorts. But there is nothing else that can be done, and the Huaorani stand about somberly as Ali sits on the ground grunting with pain. Finally, he raises his head and lights a cigarette. "That's the forest," he says with a sigh. "It gives you the best and it gives you the worst."

ALTHOUGH NANTO is the president of ONHAE, Moi is the natural leader out here on the line. This is only the second time Nanto has been on the line, and he's given to quitting work early some days. Amo works hard, but he has participated in only three *jornadas*. One he fled in fear, because he thought the Tagaeri were nearby. Enqueri has never been on a *jornada*. "But that's typical of him," Ali says. "Enqueri's just a really weird bird. When he's with you he's right there, very intelligent and cool, yes and yes and yes and I'm going to do this and this and this. And then he just disappears."

Moi, however, has been on all seven *jornadas*. "He's all heart," Ali says. "He just goes and goes and goes. He's the spritual force behind the organization. One day he's directing the *jornada*, then he's traveling to Quito to meet with the other Indian groups or the government, then he's crossing the territory to tell the other Huaorani what he's seen and heard. The only way I can explain his energy is that his vision is true. But they all work hard, you know?"

Nanto was elected president of ONHAE in part because he's from Toñampare, which has the largest population. Tall and strong, with high cheekbones and wide, brown eyes, he would be considered handsome in almost any culture. So far, he had not struck me as a politician; he had no heart for posturing. But he was, by reputation, a superior hunter and fisherman—unlike Moi, he was a husband and father, and what mattered to him above all else was a safe home and food to eat—and in a culture that is still closely attuned to the often harsh life of the rain forest, these skills commanded respect. At the same time, having spent four years in a missionary secondary school, he had a *cowode* education that rivaled Enqueri's.

Moreover, says Ali, "Nanto can be downright regal when he wants to be." The year before, the local Quichua federation had staged a strike in Coca, shutting down restaurants and shops and sealing off the roads. They were demonstrating against Occidental Petroleum, protesting abuses on Quichua land, but they had made themselves up to look like Huaorani. Ali had been there. "The Quichua were running around, waving their spears and doing this sort of semimarch, like the *carabinieri* in Italy," he says. "They were threatening people in the shops, going into restaurants and eating the food off their plates. They came marching along the main street and ran right into Nanto. They didn't know he was in town. He was just standing there with his arms folded, staring them down in this bulldog stance. The Quichua got this sheepish look and put down their spears and wanted to shake hands and Nanto just shook his head no. Wouldn't even talk to them. Made them look damn foolish. That was the end of the strike."

As for Moi, on the line he is one of the best axmen, working the forest with a machinelike perseverance, and when he isn't cutting he's walking the line like a coach, checking to see how everyone is doing. Moi talks constantly with Ali, but compared with the other Huaorani he seems subdued and introspective. Now and then he walks off the line and stands to the side of the action, staring into the forest, lost in thought. At night, when I sit down to write my notes, he lashes a candle to a twig to give me light, and when I have finished he practices writing in my notebook. He writes love letters to women in his village, Quehueire Ono. He writes letters of defiance to the Ecuadorian government.

It is this spirit of defiance that most distinguishes Moi from Nanto, Amo, and Enqueri. Like them, Moi attended elementary school when he lived inside the protectorate, but his higher education was carried out in the forest itself. One night I am startled awake by a flashlight playing across my eyes. "Chong," I hear Moi whisper. "Tiger—in the bush." I squint into the darkness, but I can see nothing. "Maybe Mengatohue," he says. Mengatohue is his grandfather, his teacher—The Captain, Moi sometimes calls him—and the last of the true Huaorani shamans. Confronted with strange new *cowode* diseases brought in by the missionaries and the Company, branded as devils by the missionaries, the shamans were driven out of the culture and often killed, in accord with the vengeance code. Only Mengatohue survives—a jaguar shaman, able, Moi says, to *become* a jaguar, and so to travel great distances telepathically and communicate with other Huaorani.

"Yeah, I thought it was bullshit, too," Ali says the next day. "Until I saw Mengatohue go into his trance." It happened before the first *jornada*, which was being held near the Tagaeri land, "and even the Huaorani were shit-scared. So Mengatohue said he'd talk to the Tagaeri. He laid down on the ground and curled himself up into a ball and went into this *frenzy*. He was clawing the air and snarling like a big cat. Not like you or I would do it—he was an *animal*. It was *frenetic*. When he came out of it, he said we'd be safe, and he gave me a jaguar chant to use if I got in trouble.

"So we go in, we do the *jornada*, and basically everything goes okay except for some malaria. We don't see any Tagaeri, but toward the end we do meet some Huaorani from the far side of the territory, and they say, 'Mengatohue told us you were coming.'

"Now *that* scared me."

SOMETIME NEAR dawn on our seventh day, I am awakened by Moi, who says, softly, "Pack your things." Then, with no more planning than that, we break camp.

"They just sort of reached a mutual decision that it was time to go," Ali says as we set out. "It's all consensus, you know? We had enough food to stay a few more days, but they were ready to leave. If I'd tried to keep them around, they'd just have drifted off one by one." Later, at a fork in the trail, there is a brief debate between Moi and Amo on which route to take. Their voices rise slightly, the only time all week that I have heard anything close to a disagreement.

We hike out nearly twenty miles, no less brutal than those coming in, but the march is uneventful save for my execution of yet another headlong fall off a one-log bridge and into the Tihuano. This fall is short—about eight feet—and painless, and, I believe, possessed of a certain grace. Or so Ali suggests when I come up. "You didn't make a sound until you hit the water," he says.

Late in the day we burst out of the dense, cool forest into harsh sunlight and a desiccated landscape of ribby cattle and coffee fields baked to clay. I've hardly seen sun all week, and the tropical glare blasts my eyes so sharply I give an involuntary gasp. "What wonderful agriculture," Ali says, indicating the acres of seboya grass that have been planted for cattle forage. The knife-edged grass rips at clothing and slices any skin it touches, and it is a fertile environment for hard-biting, fingernail-size blackflies. "Once this grass is in the ground it just takes over," Ali says. "You can't get rid of it, and you get eaten alive walking through it. It's just awful, miserable stuff. Why don't the *colonos* plant fruit trees? They have the worst nutrition of anyone in Ecuador. If they planted a papaya today they'd be feeding fruit to their kids in six months."

A little farther on, he says, "Ah, I should stop bitching. The colonists are everybody's scapegoat, you know? The oil companies love to have them around so they can blame them for whatever goes wrong, an oil spill, whatever. The timber companies, too—they always point to the colonists. No, what I should do is I should just come back here and get a nursery going for them." Over the last week he has collected seeds from half a dozen kinds of wild fruit trees, although when I ask him their names he shrugs. "I can tell you the Huaorani name," he says, "but that doesn't mean I know what kind of tree it is. I'm often coming out of here with seeds the botanists can't identify." (One year later Ali will return and not only start a nursery but, with the support of the Capuchin mission, teach a weeklong class in permaculture: to greatly oversimplify, a system of organic agriculture that produces edible crops by mimicking the natural structure of the forest. He will prove so successful a teacher that in time he will be asked to conduct such courses throughout Ecuador and in Colombia, Brazil, and Chile.)

With Moi in the lead, we cross the wretched *colono* lands in single file. The two mud-drenched *cowode* marching in the middle of the line are less than imposing, but the Huaorani brandish their spears and hold their heads high and wear on their faces looks of grim but confident defiance. If any *colonos* are about, they have wisely chosen not to reveal themselves.

Finally, abruptly, we step through a wall of coffee bushes onto a slick of mud and oil. Once I see the road I realize that for quite some time I've been smelling it, too, and that my throat has grown parched and tight from the heavy fumes. "It's a scar is what it is," says Ali, and he is right: the Vía Auca looks like nothing so much as a gray-brown scar slicing through green skin. Alongside it, riding waist high on trestles, the pipe-line shadows the road's dips and curves like a black, rusting snake.

We march down the road toward a small *tienda*. An earthen berm rises on one side of the road, and beyond it, listing dangerously, stands a tiny schoolhouse. As we pass it a pack of *colono* children, barefoot and sunken cheeked, scurry forward through the mud, and the braver among them advance to the edge of the berm. They stare down at us in silence. The Huaorani ignore them until the bravest and smallest child, a little girl, whispers "*Waponi*," the catchall Huaorani salutation. Moi cracks a smile. "*Waponi!*" he roars back. Squealing with fear and success, the children bolt for the schoolhouse.

At the *tienda* itself—one room, plank-board walls, no windows—Ali buys soda and crackers for all and we sit on the stoop and sweat in the immense silence of this not-forest, waiting for a ride to Coca, which we hope will materialize in the form of an empty truck. Over the next two hours, however, the only vehicle that passes is a drilling rig, and the two burly mestizos hanging off the back glare at the Huaorani. "Wimps," Ali says as the the rig passes. "Oil, beer, and whores, that's their life. They're so arrogant when they're on their trucks. Put them in the forest for an hour and they'd be blubbering babies." The Huaorani study the truck intently, as if trying to assay its essence, but show no sign of emotion whatsoever. In fact, they say almost nothing for the rest of the afternoon. The boisterous high spirits they displayed in the forest now seem hidden away.

As we wait Ali and Moi calculate that we have cut six and a half kilometers of trail, leaving forty-two still to mark. Finishing that work will depend on many things, not the least of which is funding. Follow-ing the Conoco–Natural Resources Defense Council affair, funds sup-posedly being held by CONFENIAE for the Huaorani line cutting mysteriously disappeared; Nanto and Moi released an open letter ac-cusing Valerio Grefa of thievery. Meanwhile, at precisely the time Conoco and Grefa were making their final push for the Rio Napo Foundation, Ali, Douglas Ferguson, and three RIC volunteers were arrested at the Vía Auca checkpoint.

"We were on our way to a *jornada*, and we had all our papers in order," Ali says, "but, hey, this is Ecuador." The military turned them over to the Coca police, "who didn't know what to do with us, so they decided to send us to Quito through Lago Agrio. But the cops didn't have a car, so we said, Let's go in our car. So we did, the five of us and two cops.

"It was dark when we got to Lago Agrio. Douglas offered to buy the two Coca cops a beer. So we had a few beers, and then we said, Well, where are you guys going to sleep? And the cops said, We don't know. So we bought them a hotel room.

"The next day, the Lago police put everyone—us and the Coca cops—on a bus for Quito, and when we got to Quito we got thrown in jail. A hundred guys in a room fifteen meters by fifteen meters with no windows. You don't get any exercise, and you don't get out. Prisoners were bashing one another senseless. I spent three fucking days in there. That's when I used my jaguar chant. I just stuck my head through the bars and chanted the way Mengatohue taught me. Chanted for my life, I tell you."

The military tried to have the RIC staff deported, but the British embassy intervened, pointing out that they had done nothing illegal. Nanto and Moi traveled to Quito to vouch for them. Still, RIC was more or less banned from the Oriente until the deadline Conoco had given itself to work out a deal with the Huaorani.

"My God," says Ali, shaking his head. "An enormous amount of money is spent on 'saving the rain forest,' isn't it? And so much of it is being wasted. You have all these wealthy groups just sitting around in New York or Washington or wherever talking about things, and meanwhile we lose more and more of the forest. You just can't do it from the top down. There has to be some kind of real communication between here and there."

Finally, at dusk, an empty dump truck lumbers up the Vía Auca. Moi waves it over. I toss my pack up into the bed, climb the tailgate, and land in a thin film of oil. Then I give a hand up to Nanto and a shy young Huao named Gaba, who are also bound for Coca. From here the other Huaorani will disperse across the territory, while Ali will accompany Moi to Quehueire Ono, two days by foot and canoe. "I haven't visited Moi's family in months," Ali says. "It's about time."

"We have to find Ali a wife," Moi says.

"*Waponi*, Moi."

"*Waponi*, Chong."

"Take care of yourself, Ali."

"That's not really the point, is it?"

9

M Y FAMILY and I rented an apartment in the new section of Quito, much of which had been built during the twenty-year course of the oil boom. Most of the American *petroleros* lived there. We were nine thousand feet in the Andes in a city of a million people, and I felt closer to California than to the Amazon. From our apartment I could see the gleaming towers of steel and glass that held the offices of Texaco, ARCO, Occidental, Oryx, Maxus, and Mobil, their dozens of smaller partners, and their suppliers of parts, services, and bodies. These buildings rose higher into the thin Andean air than anything in sight save the great snow-capped volcanoes that ring the city like white diamond sentries. Beyond the office towers, up along the valley walls, were lavish new condominiums and golf courses and tennis clubs. A good French dinner ran about fifteen dollars, a full-time, live-in house servant about twenty-five dollars a month.

I called them servants; one of my neighbors, Alex, called them slaves. Alex lived a few blocks from me. He was a petroleum engineer. He fled Communist Europe in 1978, crossed the oceans in a rusty freighter, ate crackers and sardines for six weeks, and landed in Ecuador with the proverbial shirt on his back. But he knew petroleum technology, and before long he was importing American field equipment. Fourteen years later he owned a house with six bedrooms and six bathrooms and a guest bungalow, on a tree-lined street of stone mansions hidden behind high stone walls. He paid cash for the house. He had three slaves and land in the mountains and land on the coast. He had bank accounts in Switzerland, Miami, and Oklahoma. The highest officials in the American embassy dropped by for cocktails. There were seldom any Ecuadorians at his parties—unless you counted the slaves.

"Slaves" may have been an exaggeration, but not much of one. In terms of material goods, a monthly salary of twenty-five dollars—about the national minimum wage—didn't buy a whole lot more in Ecuador than it did in the United States. But the slaves were always free to quit and rejoin the desperate bulk of the population that had it even worse: According to UNICEF, 79 percent of Ecuadorians are considered poor and 39 percent of the children under five are malnourished.

I took a lot of long walks in Quito—the Andean sky was a stunning blue and the light extraordinarily clear—and often I strapped the baby on my back and headed south, passing out of the new part of town into the old, poor, colonial half of the city, where the slaves lived. The streets were narrow and cobbled and jammed with Andean Indians and smelled of roasting meat, kerosene, sewage. Somewhere on almost every street appeared the same graffito: *Más petróleo = más pobreza.* More petroleum equals more poverty.

In 1970, just before the oil boom started, Ecuador's national debt stood at less than $300 million. It wasn't exactly solvency, but it was more or less manageable. Twenty "boom" years later, after the Company had extracted some 1.5 billion barrels of crude—about half of the country's estimated total reserves—Ecuador had a national debt of more than $12 *billion*, or roughly its annual gross national product. The story of how that debt was incurred is hopelessly complicated—administrations of the left, right, and center share the blame equally with the Company—but from it emerges at least one simple and undeniable fact: The more oil Ecuador produces, the further in debt it goes. Today its poverty ranks with the worst in Latin America and its programs for economic development are moribund, because more than a quarter of every dollar earned from exports must go toward paying and servicing the debt.

Ecuador has no choice but to continue to produce oil as quickly and cheaply as it can, and to continue to borrow money. To remain eligible for credit, every year or two, and sometimes more often, the government enacts one or another of the draconian "austerity programs" mandated by the International Monetary Fund, the World Bank, or the host of private institutions to which the country is indebted. Overnight the price of staples—cooking and heating fuel, flour, rice, sugar, milk—doubles or triples. Increasingly, there were strikes and bombings to protest the austerity programs. In response, the government was calling out the troops.

So what happened to those $12 billion?

"Twenty-four-hour dollars" is what Alex called them. "The money comes in from the United States, you sign some papers, and twenty-four hours later it goes right back to the United States," he told me. A lot of it paid for petroleum equipment, supplies, and services. Most of what was left—and Alex was testimony to the fact that this was a goodly sum—went to Miami, where it was deposited into the personal bank accounts of petroleum executives, government officials, and the small Latin elite that owns most of Ecuador. Not that all the money wound up in Miami. Like Alex, many oil people squirreled their profits in Swiss bank accounts, and German deutsche marks were also popular. But only a fool would keep his money in Ecuador. The IMF has decreed that the sucre must be regularly devalued, and from 1987 through 1993 it fell against the dollar at a rate of more than 50 percent a year.

For someone like Alex—that is, for anyone, American or Ecuadorian, who works in the white-collar end of the petroleum business, and whose income is tied more closely to the dollar than to the sucre—Ecuador's ever-increasing poverty was a windfall. The price of slaves kept dropping. "The debt?" Alex said. "I *love* the debt."

ONE NIGHT a few weeks after I'd left him at the Vía Auca, Ali Sharif called me in Quito. "The boys are with me," he said. "Come for breakfast. Come early—we're on Huaorani time. Bring some jackets and blankets."

I went to the RIC office at 5:00 a.m. and rang the bell. Curtains parted and in the window loomed the startled face of Tementa, the Huaorani secretary of land. Tementa had been in charge of planting the palm trees on the line. He is a hard worker, and immensely kind. His kindness is exceeded only by his shyness. Many of the Huaorani are shy, but Tementa may be the shyest person I have ever met. He rarely speaks. When he does, you feel as if you are cutting the words out of his mouth with a knife.

Tementa looked me dead in the eye and closed the curtains.

Fifteen minutes later I rang the bell again.

Moi opened the door. "Tementa told me there was a ghost here," he said.

Moi led me to a room off the hallway. Nanto, Tementa, and three Huaorani I didn't recognize were piled onto two beds. A small radio was tuned to a station blasting Bible stories. Tementa was awake, but the others were asleep. They were fully dressed. No matter how nice the weather in Quito, they were always cold. Moi took the jackets and blankets I had brought and draped them over Nanto and the others. For himself he kept a bright blue nylon parka, and after he put it on, he said, "Gift me your sunglasses."

"Sunglasses?"

"When *cowode* wear such jackets they also wear sunglasses."

I gave him my glasses, and he put them on and went to the window and looked out.

"With these glasses I can see for many kilometers," he said.

"No, you cannot," I said. "They are only for the sun."

He frowned, but he kept the glasses on.

"We are hungry," he said.

We went out into the street. The sharp, cold light of dawn was racing over the mountaintops. Moi walked behind me and Tementa walked behind Moi and we walked as if we were following a hunting trail. We reached an intersection and waited for the cars to pass. Then I started across and Moi followed me and Tementa froze in place as though he'd seen a snake. It was his first time in Quito. "He does not know when the cars will come again," Moi explained. He went back and spoke softly to Tementa and put his hand gently on his shoulder and guided him across the street.

We walked to a produce stand. Moi selected one of every kind of fruit and two large bottles of Coca-Cola. Tementa picked up six loaves of sliced bread and hugged them to his chest. He'd discovered sliced bread the day before, and he'd fallen in love with it. But that wasn't all he'd fallen in love with. By the time we got back to the street, Quito had begun to stir and pedestrians were scurrying up and down the sidewalk.

Tementa stopped outside the produce stand and studied each face as it passed.

"What is he looking for?" I asked Moi.

"Ali took us to a karate movie last night," Moi said. Tementa had lost his heart to a Chinese actress who could kick like a mule. He was filled with shy and silent longing and yet believed with all of his strong soul that he would meet her there on the streets of Quito.

Back at the house we found Ali awake, drinking instant coffee and smoking a cigarette. Nanto and the others were in the kitchen with him, trying to con him out of his shoes. "Had a close one," Ali said by way of greeting. Coming out of the territory he and Moi and old Pego had dumped their canoe twice on the Shiripuno and walked the last half of the trip in the dark in a torrential rain. "Walked all night," Ali said. "Had the shakes from the cold. Stepped in a hole, and I turned to Pego and said, 'Watch out for this . . .' and then I fell into a *bigger* hole! Things *biting* me, you know? All night like that." He paused a moment, and then said, in a tone of scientific objectivity, "I was pretty sure I was going to die." They reached the Vía Auca near dawn and slept in the *tienda* with a dozen peasants waiting for the jitney into Coca and a fight broke out between a mestizo and a Shuar. "The Shuar grabbed a machete and cut off the guy's ear," Ali said. "Just sliced it clean through! Bloody ugly. Moi and I were cowering in the corner, you know, and I said as quietly as I could, 'Do we have shells for the shotgun?' And he said, in this tiny little voice, 'No.' So we just curled ourselves up in the dark like a couple of bloody slugs."

We ate papayas and bananas and bread. Tementa cleaned up the dishes, and when he finished he turned to Ali and said *"Gracias"* and left the room.

"He's a sweetheart, isn't he?" Ali said. "He did that yesterday, too. It's like he hasn't learned to leave common courtesy in the forest." He lit another cigarette. "We have a problem," he said. Moi and Nanto had come to town to talk to the Company, and to Valerio Grefa. They had written a letter denouncing Grefa and sent it to all the various organizations they knew of in Quito. The letter charged that Grefa had stolen funds that a European environmental group had donated to CONFENIAE for the Huaorani line cutting. Grefa had done this, the letter claimed, because the Huaorani turned down his deal with Conoco. "CONFENIAE thinks that when ONHAE has no money they can control ONHAE," the letter said, but it declared that the Huaorani would continue to fight for their right to "*autodeterminación.*"

Nanto and Moi had come to Quito to confront Grefa. They were going to go to his office. They wanted Ali to be a witness. Nanto said that the last time he had gone to CONFENIAE the Quichua had gotten him drunk and tricked him into signing papers.

Ali was in a bind. "It all gets back to oil, and I just can't have anything to do with it," he said. "I'll bloody well get thrown out of the country."

"Chong," Moi said, "you will come with us."

"If I go with you," I said, "I will write about everything I see, good or bad. But I cannot speak for you. It is not my place. Do you understand that?"

"Writing is a very good way to get things without doing work."

"Some people think so."

"Write everything you see. Tell everything to the whole world."

We went out to the street again. Nanto and Moi wore their toucan-feather crowns and carried their spears and their plastic briefcases. They took turns wearing my sunglasses. Heads turned and crowds parted. Six empty cabs passed us up, the drivers slowing down, checking out the Huaorani, then fleeing wild-eyed in a cloud of exhaust. In the cab that stopped we rode with the spears thrust out the window like jousting lances.

"Who are they?" the driver asked me.

"They call themselves Huaorani," I said.

"Jesus Christ," he said. "They're Aucas. They kill people with those things."

"They have been known to."

"Wait till I tell my wife!"

We cruised south, into the colonial quarter. As ever it was jammed with Indians and poor mestizos, all of them on foot, and most of them carrying on their backs immense loads of children, wood, potatoes. At times, trapped amid the old city's squat mud-brick buildings and squat brown people and the intense fecundity of its street life, you could well imagine that you'd gone back a century or more. But the illusion dissolved at the building that housed Valerio Grefa's office, where an elevator lifted us away from the masses.

Grefa's secretary confirmed that Nanto and Moi had an appointment but said that Grefa wasn't around.

"We will wait," Moi said.

We sat down. Moi and Nanto took turns trying on my shoes.

"Gift me your shoes," Moi said.

"How will I get home?"

"Taxi."

I wore their crowns. They laughed and collapsed one against the other. Nanto told me the story of the karate movie. He fixed his gaze on the wall in front of him and spoke in an uninterrupted monotone for nearly twenty-five minutes. It was a stunning exhibition: He appeared to leave no detail unaddressed. When he finished he stood up and wandered over to the window to watch the people in the street.

We waited for an hour and a half.

Finally, Moi spoke to the secretary again. She said that Valerio Grefa was still not available.

"Come," Moi said. We went out into the street and walked up and down until Moi spotted Grefa sitting in a restaurant, bent over a plate of fried chicken, a bottle of beer on the table.

"My friends," Grefa said, and flashed a wide mouthful of teeth. He was wearing a starched white dress shirt, black slacks, a black leather jacket that said, in Spanish, MADE IN ENGLAND, and black leather shoes polished to a spit shine. He was a tall man, but sallow faced and bony, and he appeared frail next to the thickly muscled Huaorani. "How can I help you?"

"We can speak here or there," Moi said. In silence he and Nanto followed Grefa back to his office and sat down across from him at a large desk.

"What do you want?" Grefa asked them.

"There are problems," Nanto said. He hesitated. He crossed his eyes to study a forelock of hair that had flopped down over his forehead. Then he rolled his eyes up beneath their lids, as he often did when, as he put it, "my head is too full of ideas."

Moi spoke right up.

"You have stolen our money," he said. "We want it."

Grefa put his elbows on his desk and rested his chin on his hands and for one long minute stared at Moi and said nothing at all. Both men were Indians, but they could not have looked more different. Moi, clearly, was a man of the forest. In one hand he held a man-killing Huaorani spear—the longest and heaviest spears used by anyone in the forest, spears that take real muscle to wield. He wore his crown, of course, and, strapped across his chest, twin quivers for his blowgun darts. Around his neck hung a single jaguar tooth. As for the look in his eyes—if, at that moment, you'd run across Moi in the bush, you'd have had only one thought: May the end be swift.

Grefa, on the other hand, was a schoolteacher and a professional politician—a civilized man, a man of the city. He may have seemed wan and slightly effete compared with Moi, but that impression was misleading. In his own way he, too, was a warrior. He had risen to power on the sort of political boldness and sophistication that no leader coming out of the Oriente had shown before. "Valerio Grefa can sit down with the president of the country and argue with him face to face and win something from him," the head of one of the local Quichua federations had told me. "It is true that he is out of touch with the people, but maybe that is the price you pay to have an impact at a national level." Earlier that year, for example, when ten thousand Quichua Indians marched from the Oriente to Quito to demand title to their traditional lands, Grefa was instrumental in pushing their demands through the Ecuadorian government and having them signed into law—a huge and unlikely victory. (Grefa would continue to rise: Later that year he would become the head of the Coordinating Council of the Indigenous Nations of the Amazon Basin, under which the Indian confederations of every Amazonian country come together. As such, he would be the most powerful Indian politician on the continent.)

Now Grefa took a deep breath, and, with his eyes still fixed on Moi, launched into an oration that lasted twenty minutes. He stood up, paced, sat down, leaned across his desk, leaned back, pounded his fists on his desk, pointed in the air. "Every day I am faced with thieves!" he shouted. "I am sure you are not thieves, but there are others who say you are. How do I know what you would do with that money? How do I know you are really cutting your line? You have no proof. Where are your documents? You say the money is for machetes and axes and food, but how do I know this is true?"

Moi opened his briefcase and handed Grefa a pile of receipts.

"Receipts?" Grefa said. He grabbed the papers and shook them and threw them down on his desk. He laughed a big, horsey laugh. "You call this *accounting*? Are these all the documents you have?"

"Yes," Moi said.

"You are simply not being clear. How can I be expected to give you funds? You say you have all these congresses, all these meetings, but still you are not organized. Why should I give you anything at all?"

"We are organized," Moi said. "We are cutting our line. We work hard. We are doing it ourselves. It is not easy for me to sit here and listen to these things."

"It is our money," Nanto said. "It came in our name."

Grefa leaned back and smiled broadly. "I have not received anything in your name," he said. "Now, it may be true that the previous administration did, but how would I know where they put it?"

Disgusted, Moi stood up to leave. Nanto followed suit.

"CONFENIAE would like to help you," Grefa said. "When you are willing to work with us, let me know. In some of the Quichua communities we have had to accept the fact that the Company is there, and work from that."

On the way out, I asked Grefa whether CONFENIAE had an official position on Maxus's plans to develop oil on Huaorani land.

"We are completely opposed to it," he said. But if Maxus went ahead, CONFENIAE would demand a dollar a barrel for all the oil Maxus extracted. Then he made a chilling point. "The Quichua and the Shuar have had fifty years in which to learn how to deal with the *petrolero* world," he said. "The Huaorani have what, maybe two or three years? And the technology and the forces they must face are much more severe than what we faced. Now the Company has satellites and computers and fast helicopters. The Huaorani have their feet and their spears. It will be harder for them to survive than it was for any group before them." He laughed again, that horsey laugh. "They will never make it on their own. *Never.*"

He told me to feel free to call him at any time. "Here," he said, and scribbled a number on a card. "This is my fax."

IN THEIR LETTER Moi and Nanto had also denounced the road that Maxus was going to build in the Huaorani land, and they stated unequivocally that the Huaorani people were opposed to the Maxus development. Now, in Quito, Nanto and Moi were determined to find the head of Maxus, the *gerente*, and make sure he understood exactly what they were saying. But the *gerente* was an American, and they wanted someone who could speak to him in English. They wanted no misunderstandings. Ali, of course, couldn't do it, and neither could I. In desperation, Ali tracked down Samuel Caento Padilla.

Samuel was the son of Rachel Saint's protégé, Dayuma, and a Quichua man, and he had spent so much time with Rachel that she was "like a mother for me," as he told reporters when he toured the United States with Rachel and Dayuma in 1971. He was called Sammy then, and he wore long hair and bell-bottoms, and he spoke English so well that he was the advance man for the tour, captivating the Bible Belt press corps with tales of savages and spears and the healing powers of the Lord. As a boy Samuel had spent a year in the United States and seven years in Quito; he spoke fluent Quichua, Spanish, and English. He didn't learn to speak Huaorani until he was seventeen, when he went to live full-time in his mother's village. Later he worked as a translator for the oil companies. But he preferred life on the "outside," as he called it—he'd developed a taste for American girls—and eventually he moved back to Quito. For a while he had a nightclub called Caento's, in the *petrolero* district, and later, describing himself as a "native" Huao, he went into "ecotourism," bringing tourists to a compound he built near Toñampare—where, as Dayuma's son, he enjoyed all the rights of a prince.

Pushed and pulled by wildly disparate cultures, Samuel had learned to think fast and to cover whatever bases were available. He was more than happy to speak for Nanto and Moi.

Moi, learning on the fly, asked to borrow my tape recorder—"So the whole world will know."

AT THE MEETING, with Nanto and Moi and Tementa sitting next to him, Samuel spoke with William Hutton, the general manager of Maxus's Ecuadorian operations. Hutton is a Texan, and a big man, with a broad, round head, close-cropped white hair, and thick glasses. He was new to the Oriente; he had taken on an exceedingly difficult job in

an industry that is exceedingly difficult even in the best of circumstances. Maxus was an independent company, without the financial resources of a Texaco or an ARCO, and its high-risk strategy of signing
up unexplored mineral rights around the world had led it into deep
trouble. Though it was less than five years old, Maxus was already
close to a billion dollars in debt—well more than the company was
worth—and it was losing tens of millions a year. Its best hope, it appeared, was to be bought by a larger oil company, but for that to
happen Maxus had to develop proven assets, and develop them
quickly. It was betting on Block Sixteen. However, the price of Ecuadorian oil was dropping steadily, and it wouldn't take much to
make the concession yet another economic disaster. So, while Maxus
had no legal requirement to make a deal with the Huaorani, confrontations with them—or, God forbid, a wave of killing—would im-
peril the entire company. And if Maxus could get the Huaorani to
sign, it would go a long way toward undermining the critics that had
helped drive Conoco out of the Oriente.

But Hutton is a devout evangelical Baptist, and he didn't see Block
Sixteen as simply an oil operation. It was also an opportunity to save the
Huaorani. Hutton believed that those who thought the Huaorani should
be allowed to live as they always had—what he called "the pressure
groups"—were "cruel," that they wanted to treat the Huaorani "like
people in a zoo." The way he saw it, the best route for the Huaorani was
through the word of the good Lord Jesus. He was going to work with the
evangelical missionaries to enhance their "education" of the Huaorani.
It would be, he was convinced, the greatest gift Maxus could give them.

But when he sat down to talk to Nanto and Moi and Samuel, he
kept such thoughts to himself.

Samuel spoke to Hutton in English. Nanto and Moi spoke to Samuel in Huaorani. Samuel told Hutton that ONHAE wanted copies of
the Block Sixteen management plan, and that it wanted Maxus to stay
away from the Huaorani. He told Hutton that the Huaorani especially
"don't want to see and hear, know about, anything, *nothing* with this
lady called Rossana Faieta," a Maxus staff sociologist, whose job it was
to secure a contract with the Huaorani—and who, the Huaorani
charged, had been conspiring with Valerio Grefa.

Hutton said, "Okay."

Samuel said, "They would only like to deal with the general manager of Maxus, or the guy who was vice president, and the translator from English to Spanish . . ."

"That would be you," Hutton said.

"Could be," Samuel said, and the tone of his voice seemed to shift, as if he had suddenly come awake. "I didn't even know I was in this thing," he said. "I just walked in today. But I'd be more than willing to do anything and help."

"We appreciate that," Hutton said.

"Anything you want," Samuel said. "I don't want anybody to get hurt, I don't want anybody to be cheated. I don't want you guys to stop the whole operation because of this and that. If my service could be good to you, and good to the people, and good to everybody else, I'd be more than happy. I know how you guys think, I know how these guys think, I know how the preachers think, I know how the Ecuadorians think, all that. I grew up in those cultures. So if my service is useful, for translation or whatever you guys may need, count on me. I'm not hard to reach."

"Good," Hutton said. "That's good to know."

Hutton went on to tell Samuel that "anyone who promises them that there won't be changes in their lives is not being truthful. There will be changes. Our plan is to try to keep them away from as much of that as possible . . . the only commitment I can make is we can start right now and they can learn more about who I am, about who this company is, and maybe to ease the pain and to equip them to deal with what people call civilization, which is very, very difficult."

While Hutton and Samuel spoke, Nanto and Moi and Tementa were talking heatedly among themselves in Huaorani. Then they got up and left. As they walked out Hutton's door they passed Dayuma and Rachel Saint, who were on their way in.

THAT EVENING I returned to Ali Sharif's house to speak with Moi and Nanto and Tementa. When I opened the door Moi stuck his crown on my head. Ali wasn't there, but Nanto went to the refrigerator and pulled out a liter of Coca-Cola and a loaf of sliced bread and a jar of peanut butter and put them on the dining table. They were feeling pretty good, Moi said. They had gone to the Company and told the Company to leave the Huaorani alone. They were especially pleased that they had brought Samuel, because Samuel had told the *gerente* in English. Now the Company knew exactly where the Huaorani stood. "They are afraid of our spears," Moi said. Nanto nodded in agreement.

One by one they lathered each piece of bread with peanut butter. Then they ate each piece, one after the other, in a rhythm as steady as an assembly line. They didn't say a word, and they didn't stop until they'd eaten the entire loaf of bread. When they finished, I asked, "Did Samuel help you speak?"

"Yes. It is all on the machine," Moi said. But we couldn't listen to the tape—they had taken turns singing into the machine, and now the batteries were dead. I offered to bring the tape home and type up a transcript ("write what is on the machine"), and Nanto considered that an excellent idea. All the Huaorani would have a record of what had happened.

Soon there would be an *asamblea*—a gathering of the clans—in Moi's village, Quehueire Ono. Nanto and Moi would tell everyone about their trip. "All the Huaorani will be there," Moi said. "We will discuss the problems of the whole world." He added, in a serious tone, "We will drink a lot of *chicha*. You must come, Chong." I said I would try, and then I went home.

They left Quito the next morning, on a bus bound for Coca. It would take Moi longer to reach Quehueire Ono than it would have taken me to travel from Quito to California and back.

I SAW Ali Sharif a few days later. He was carrying a newspaper, and he was in a deep funk. The RIC office had received yet another hostile letter from the Ecuadorian government, a thinly veiled threat to throw them out of the country, written by an official who had been a key figure in the Conoco–Natural Resources Defense Council deal. Meanwhile, the front page of the day's newspaper reported the discovery of 250 million barrels of petroleum in a field downriver from Coca, near a lagoon called Pañacocha. "Pañacocha is the most beautiful place in the Oriente," Ali said. "Black-water lagoon, every kind of bird. You can swim with dolphins."

In addition, the government had announced plans to license a new series of oil concessions. A map showed a string of oil fields stretching chockablock across the east side of the Huaorani territory. The Maxus concession was the centerpiece, the linchpin. "It's totally out of control," Ali said. "The powers that be know that, and they're taking full advantage of it. There's this mythology that somebody has a plan and everything's being developed according to a schedule and somebody's *paying attention*. But it's all bullshit." He lit a cigarette and inhaled deeply. "It's funny," he said. "As individuals, the Company people are really polite. But on a corporate level they refuse to develop any sense of humanity at all. In twenty years the Oriente will be dead, and they'll all be saying, 'It wasn't my fault.' "

He was about to leave Ecuador for a few months, to raise money in the United States. He wasn't sure just when he'd return, or what he'd do when he got back. He had planned to help the Huaorani build their own radio network, but now it seemed unlikely he'd be able to continue working with them. "Would you like to see Quehueire Ono?" he asked. He wanted to make one last trip, for the *asamblea*.

I said I would. And I gave him a copy of the transcript of Moi's tape. He read it through. "Oh, my," he said when he had finished. "Oh, *my*."

10

FROM QUITO I flew into Coca, white knuckled, aboard an old twin-engine Fokker that strained mightily to burst free from the jagged Andes. It grunted up over treeless sawtooth peaks capped with snow white Chinese hats and shuddered down into the preposterously green Amazon in a kind of free fall that left my stomach in my ears. In Coca itself oil washing off the road and puddling up in rainbows of blue and gold and big trucks sliding through narrow streets throwing up sheets of black mud and over all of it the hot, wet, oleaginous air of the Oriente draped like a blanket of bug pudding. At the Hotel Auca, Ali Sharif sitting in the cantina calmly sipping a glass of babaco juice. Smoking a hand-rolled cigarette, staring into the rain. Sweat rolling down his forehead and along his arms and dripping off his elbows onto the floor.

I bought a bag of chicken and rice and waded over to the Capuchin mission and stood outside the Huaorani Hotel and watched a suitcase and a pair of rubber boots smolder in a fire near the door. "Life is good!" I shouted to the door. "Are you still alive?"

"Yes, we are still alive!" someone shouted from the other side. "Are you coming here?"

"I am coming here," I said and I pushed open the door and saw the Garzacocha gang holed up on the bunks, eating bananas and playing Colombian rock and roll on a boom box cranked to stun. I recognized Araba and Bainca, and there were three others, thick-shouldered young men named Yacata and Gabamo and Dahue.

"Do you remember when we shot the four *sahino*?" Araba asked.

He sat up and took the bag of food without acknowledgment and told the story of the four peccaries and a story about me falling out of his canoe. To make his point he fell off his bed onto the floor. Laughter ensued. We went outside and he gave the suitcase a turn.

"Why are you burning that?" I asked.

"It is old."

"How does it go in Garzacocha? Are you living well?"

"We are living well," Araba said. "But there is confusion everywhere." The Company was opening a well east of the village and another to the northwest, and it had started to construct its road. To keep peace it had built a soccer field for the people of Garzacocha, but in the process it had destroyed their orchard. Meanwhile, there had been a visit from the Taromenga. Three men had come to Garzacocha for one night. They had spoken of their own clan, and of the Oñamenane. This was startling news. It lent substance to the earlier report of the Taromenga skirmish with the Company's seismic crew, and to the notion of the Oñamenane and the Huiñatare, and it suggested that there might be some truth to the speculation, advanced by many of the Huaorani themselves, that anywhere from a few dozen to a thousand or more uncontacted Huaorani were hidden in the remote forest that straddles the border between Ecuador and Peru. Yet Araba presented this bombshell with all the urgency that, say, I would have confirmed the existence of a city south of San Francisco called Los Angeles.

"Everything is bad and getting worse," he said just as matter-of-factly. He said that Nanto had come to Coca that morning, after an all-night bus ride, and had immediately been hustled away by Maxus personnel and flown to Cononaco, where he was supposed to convince Quemperi to accept the new road. Araba, meanwhile, said that he had changed his own thinking about the road. He didn't want it, not any part of it. He said this once, and then he said it again. "It will kill us," he said. The men from Garzacocha were on their way to Quehueire Ono, to the *asamblea,* to make a plan.

What did he think about Nanto going to visit Quemperi?

Araba turned the suitcase one more time. "Maybe the Company will give Nanto some gasoline," he said. The men from Garzacocha had used all their gas to get to Coca and had no money to buy more.

• • •

ABOUT EIGHT O'CLOCK that evening the power went off in Coca. It happened every night, sometimes early, sometimes late. Despite all the oil being pumped out of the Oriente, Coca couldn't afford enough fuel to keep its generators running.

I was sitting alone at a table in front of the Hotel Auca, sipping a beer by candlelight, when a man naked but for a pair of shorts walked up with a carcass the size of a mountain goat slung over his shoulder. The animal had been skinned, and in the pale light its hairless pink body gleamed like gelatin. Grunting, the man flopped it to the ground. The cook came out.

"I'll have some of that," I said.

I was eating a fried greasy hunk of that tapir calf, spitting out shotgun pellets, when Nanto loomed out of the darkness and sat down next to me. "I have many problems," he said. He looked tired and drawn. He had indeed gone to see Quemperi, with Rossana Faieta, the Maxus sociologist, and two people he didn't know.

"I thought you told the *gerente* you did not want Rossana Faieta to bother you," I said.

"Yes," he said. "That is what we told him."

"Then why did you go with her?"

He looked around, as if studying the darkness for ghosts, and then he surveyed my plate with great purpose. "That is very beautiful," he said.

"When did you last eat?"

"It has been two days."

I gave him my plate and ordered another and asked what had happened at Quemperi's.

"It was very difficult," he said. "The Company said they want Quemperi and Penti to want the road, but Quemperi does not want the road and Penti gave me this to read at the *asamblea.*"

He handed me a rumpled piece of paper torn from a schoolchild's notebook and signed with a flourish by Penti, the only Huao in Cononaco literate in Spanish. It said, in part, "Our ancestors lived well and without sickness, but now the petroleum companies and the tourists are coming . . . the Huaorani people must fight against the damage to our forest." The Company, Nanto said, had been pouring big cans of dark liquid into the Cononaco River above Quemperi's settlement, and many people in the community were sick. "The children especially are not healthy," he said. "There are many skin infections, and funguses, and problems with the skin on the head, and some people with hair falling out. I believe it is because the river has been made very dirty."

"What are you going to do, Nanto?"

He stared out into the blackness of the night, into sheets of slashing rain.

"I am going to ask Ali to buy me a good plastic poncho," he said. "In Quito they cost twelve thousand sucres, but here they are only eight thousand."

I offered to get him a room at the hotel, or let him stay with me, but he said he would go to the mission and sleep with the other Huaorani. It would be safe there. "There are *ladrones* here," he said. "Quichuas— and Negroes! They are so big, those Negroes. They will kill you in your sleep."

I walked him to the mission and returned to my room at the Auca. A bargain: two dollars, cold shower, worth every penny in the ninety-degree midnight heat. One thin trickle of foul-smelling liquid tumbling into the stall, flushing roaches the size of my big toes. Exquisite. Two minutes later I started to sweat again. I drifted off to sleep with the room rumbling, massive diesel rigs barreling through town four feet away on the other side of the paper-thin wall. I woke up sometime later, in the dark, to two men arguing in front of the brothel across the street.

"Go ahead, kill me!" one yelled. "Kill me, you asshole!"

Then four gunshots and a cry of pain or shock and the slap of feet running in puddles, and later the sound of something being hauled away, a slack weight sliding through mud and oil. I went to the window then, but all I could see was blackness. I fell back asleep and dreamed of a hairless, slick-skinned tapir racing through the forest, racing for its life.

IN THE MORNING the Huaorani said that they needed rice and sugar for their *asamblea* and gas for the canoe but that they had no money. "Well, they do have some funds," Ali said, "maybe fifty dollars or so. But it's in the bank, and since Enqueri is the treasurer they can't get it out without him. But he didn't come to Coca. I haven't seen him in months and months. He's strange, you know?"

"Ali, the bank is robbing our money!" Nanto said.

"No, no, no," Ali said. "They're just *holding* your money. But Enqueri has to be here to take it out. Remember?"

"How will we buy rice, Ali? How will we buy Yupi?"

Ali spoke with the bank manager, and the funds were released. But Ali emerged shaking his head. "These guys can't even get money out of the bank," he said. "How are they going to protect themselves against oil?"

Then: slithering along the Vía Auca in the back of a truck laden with rice, potatoes, onions, sugar, machetes, a drum of gas. And Yupi. Bags and bags of Yupi. My head nestled against Araba's outboard motor. Araba and Nanto and Yacata high over the cab, shirts off, laughing into the rain and the wind. Counting on Moi to meet us at the Shiripuno bridge with a canoe. "He'll be there," Ali said. "He told me he would, and he's always where he says he'll be." Three hours in the rain, rain running down across my poncho onto bare legs, running across the truck bed, across treetops, across the world. Pouring, driving, relentless rain. Hard rain, soft rain, sideways rain, rain that seemed to explode from the ground itself. "Just have to accept it," Ali said. "Fight it and you'll lose your mind."

It had been only two months since my last trip down the Auca, but new roads snaked off in all directions, and I saw dozens of new colonist houses. We splashed past the compound operated by Elf Aquitaine, a French oil company. Inside its barbed-wire fence: a satellite dish, neatly trimmed lawns, a volleyball court. Outside the fence: an oil-blackened pond. On the bank three workers in yellow rain slickers, staring into the muck. At the far end of the pond, black muck overflowing into a creek. Farther on, two bulldozers driving trees and mud down into a pit of oil. On a red-clay hillside shaved as clean as a basketball, a third bulldozer stuck in the clay, tilting on its side like a breaching whale. The driver oblivious to the deluge, yelling something, beating the machine with his hat.

Then the great flames of the oil field and separating station known as Cononaco, named after the river. It was the biggest of the thirty or so

Texaco-built sites on the Auca and had the dimensions of a factory—
acres of tubes and stacks and ladders and pumps—and, day and night,
night and day, through rain and wind and flood, while the price of
kerosene tripled and the lights went out in Coca and the slaves in Quito
slept shivering in the Andean cold, its separating station burned the
massive volumes of natural gas that the wells spit up with raw crude.
Burned it without cessation or reflection or application, burned it for
the simple and solitary reason that it had to be gotten rid of and there
was no cheaper way to do the ridding. The bright yellow flames leaped
higher into the purple sky than any other manmade object in the forest.

Nearby, the Shiripuno bridge. The truck erupted in cheers: Moi
was waiting in the river below, shrouded in mist, standing like a statue
in the bow of a canoe.

Down to the river, slipping and sliding on the mud bank, the
Huaorani laughing in the rain, hauling hundred-pound sacks of rice on
their shoulders as casually as if the bags were parrots. Araba one-handing
his forty-horse off the truck and down to the canoe. One *cowode* butt-
skiing down the bank. Nanto stopping in the rain to mix a pot of Yupi.
The rain thinning, lifting, and as the rain abated the forest slowly
coming to life with sounds so subtle that at first one did not notice
them. Then, suddenly, a roaring in the ears: bird, bug, frog.

Then, more suddenly, the roar of an outboard, drowning out all
else. Nanto at the tiller, nosing the long canoe into the current, upstream. Around the first bend and the flames of the Cononaco cluster
disappeared. Gone the road, gone the bridge. All became forest and
water. Later, after I had been to Quehueire Ono often enough that I no
longer believed I was pursuing something new and alien but returning
to something familiar, I would realize that if there was any single point
in the long journey when I most felt I had left one world and entered
another, this was it.

EACH BEND in the Shiripuno revealed rolling, forested hills, and as
we ascended the river these grew steep, a prelude to the Andes. I hadn't
been in a canoe since the Napo. The Napo had spread before us like a
sea, but the upper Shiripuno felt close, hidden, private. It was typical of
the rivers in the western side of the territory: about forty feet across, the

banks walled with trees twice as high as the river's width. Trees had tumbled down into the water, creating an obstacle course of bony snags. In the rosy late-afternoon light we bumped and prodded our way ever deeper into wildness. Now and then Nanto gunned the engine to hurdle a half-submerged trunk and twenty feet of canoe vaulted into the air like a jumping horse and the Huaorani urged Nanto on with excited cries. The *cowode* held on for dear life. At one point, sure we were about to flip, Ali lunged from the bow to a tree stump and hung there in the middle of the river, hugging the stump like a koala bear. As we bucked past him Nanto yelled, "Jump, Ali!" and Ali dropped into the stern. Cheered by all. Ali without expression, one hand on his glasses.

A fog rose from the bush, and on its heels nightfall, chasing what little visibility remained. Three hours groping along in the dark. Now and then the canoe ramming a shadow head-on. Abrupt, shuddering stops. Splintering sounds.

And the wild men from Garzacocha—how did they react to such imminent disaster?

Araba pointed a finger in the air, Bainca turned on the boom box. Cranked it. "Ohhh, Juanita. . . ." *Crash.*

Cranked it louder.

Then, off to the left, a pinprick of light. A voice, hooting: Amo. Nanto gunned the engine, turned the canoe ninety degrees. Rammed the bow right through what proved to be another canoe tied up along shore. Smashed it broadside, amidships. Splintered its hull half the length of the boat. Inspired the loudest laughter of the day.

"That's okay," Amo whispered down through the black night. "I took it from a colonist."

The rapid-fire nasal monotone of Huaorani voices sliced through the surprising chill of the night air. Dark, glistening bodies hurried down the steep mud bank and lifted backpacks and bags of rice and sugar and Yupi. Up on high ground a huge fire burned beneath a high thatch roof. Around the fire fifty pairs of Huaorani eyes, long, droopy ears, strong arms holding spears, blowguns, children. Roasting on the fire chunks of caiman, and on the ground nearby, a caiman head, its jaws singed into a death rictus.

"This is Quehueire Ono?" I asked. I could see only a few small cabins and a single large building.

"No," Amo said. He smiled, the firelight glinting off the gold A embedded in his left front tooth, and handed me a piece of caiman tail. In fact, we had arrived at the Shiripuno Center, as it was known, a kind of headquarters built for ONHAE with the help of RIC. The center was one large platform, forty feet by fifteen, raised on stilts and divided into four cabins. I threw my bedding down in one of them and collapsed in sleep. I awoke during the night and wandered outside. The fire was still blazing, and the Huaorani were still crowded around it, laughing and talking and eating. They were still there at dawn. Meanwhile, the damaged canoe had sunk, its engine was waterlogged, and a barrel of gas had floated away. No one seemed concerned, even though the *asamblea* was scheduled to begin that afternoon and we had, from what I could gather, at least eight hours of travel ahead of us. "We will get there Huaorani style," Moi said. "Bit by bit."

After a breakfast of manioc and piranha, they raised the canoe and fished out the gas tank and took the engine apart and put it back together. Amo gave me a tour of the center. Next to the platform were three smaller cabins. He, Moi, and Nanto each had one, to use as an office and as a rest stop on their journeys. Behind the cabins they had cleared two large fields and with Ali's help planted chili pepper bushes and hundreds of fruit trees—tree peanut, guava, papaya, tree grape, orange, lemon, grapefruit, guanabana. There were manioc gardens as well. As we walked, the gentle sounds of communal life drifted across the fields: wood being chopped; two women singing while they did wash in the river; around the fire pit, some older men gumming monkey bones and telling stories. The cry of a monkey, and every eye focused on the forest canopy. But for the moment there was food enough, and peace reigned.

"Our idea was to show our strength here on the river, near the edge of the territory," Amo said. Despite the boldness of his gilted dentition, he was the most soft-spoken of the ONHAE officers—to hear him, I often had to stick my ear within inches of his mouth—but he was also the one most vulnerable to the Shuar aggression. Because, as secretary, he had the job of walking among the villages to deliver messages, and of traveling to Coca with correspondence, he was constantly exposed to attack. "The Shuar keep pushing up the river from the road, taking our land," he said. "When I walk out to the road from here, they threaten me. They demand that we give them some of our territory. The elders do not want to fight the Shuar. They remember the spearing days, and they do not want war. But Nanto and Moi and I and many of the younger men are ready to fight. The Shuar have to be stopped, now. If we can create a community here, we can confront them." Amo was particularly proud of how well the fruit trees were doing. "If there is food at the center, then the Huaorani will always be here," he said.

Indeed. One of the cabins held supplies for the line-cutting project—or at least it had at one time. "Most of the rice is gone, and the sugar, too, and all the boots," Ali reported later. "The stuff was locked up, but the Huaorani managed to pinch it."

"Stole it from themselves?"

"You can't really say they stole it. One of them was guarding it, in fact. ONHAE pays him a small salary to live here and protect the place, but I'm sure he just opened the door for whoever wanted the stuff. To them it's not stealing. It's more like, This stuff is here, let's use it. No tomorrow, you know? Huaorani time."

By midmorning the sky was a shifting palate of gray—slate gray, pearl gray, ash gray. Half of the Huaorani headed out for Quehueire Ono on foot, and the rest of us put into the Shiripuno again, in the two canoes, the vessel so spectacularly rammed the night before having been repaired with sticks, stones, mud, and underwear. Moi took the tiller. Ticking like metronomes, two of the passengers bailed with my rubber boots. Meanwhile, I set myself up in the bow, leaning back on what remained of the commissary. If the forest seemed less rich here than in the lower rivers—no wild turkeys lurking for an easy kill, for example—it was no less peaceful. I read and dozed and ate bananas ("Savagely fighting his way through green hell," Ali noted at one point), my idyll broken every hour or so by complete panic as the boat listed violently left or right or came to a grinding halt on a trunk. Then it was into the river to push and pull until afloat once more.

Once, standing at the tiller, Nanto simply fell out of his canoe and hit his head on a rock, a performance greatly appreciated by all. He climbed back into the canoe and took up his position, and as the second canoe approached he called out, as if to reaffirm his command of the fleet, "Moi, what time is it?"

Dead serious, Moi said, "In Japan it is two o'clock." Nanto nodded, just as seriously, and onward we pushed.

We stopped at a sandy beach to swim and drink Yupi and nap. From there we proceeded in utter tranquillity until sometime late in the day, when a shout went up and the canoe rocked wildly and the Huaorani poured out of it and went diving and thrashing through the river screaming for all they were worth.

"Guanta!" Moi yelled, and pointed to the bank.

It took me a moment to spot the guanta. It was covered in mud and looked like a slimy rock and had the shape of a rodent and the size of a very large rabbit. It slithered into the water, surfaced, disappeared. The Huaorani made a circle, standing waist deep in the shallow river, and Nanto dove at the spot where the guanta had last been seen and it surfaced paddling frantically toward Araba and Bainca and they bombarded it with rocks. Araba caught it once in the head. It disappeared again. The Huaorani waited in silence. The guanta surfaced on the far bank, and a cry went up, and Moi launched a spear that appeared to shatter the guanta's left leg and it gushed black blood and Bainca beaned it with a rock and Araba flushed it back toward Nanto. Nanto reached into the river and grabbed it by its hind legs and raised it over his head like a trophy and the guanta clawed and twitched desperately and Nanto slapped it against the water and the guanta burst free. Araba snagged it by the tail, twirled it like a lariat, and beat its head against the canoe until blood burst out its ears.

As soon as we returned to the canoe, the Huaorani started in on the hunting story, like ballplayers dissecting a victory.

About an hour later, I asked Nanto, "How much further?"

"Half an hour."

Four hours later Moi took to cupping his hands over his mouth and shouting into the bush: "Come to the *asamblea* tomorrow! Lots of *chicha!*" I could see no sign of human habitation. We stopped to kill a capybara and a small caiman. Six hours later, triumphantly awash in blood and meat, we motored into Quehueire Ono.

11

OVER TIME I would make several visits to Quehueire
Ono, but my first impression of the village would endure:
secluded, independent, remarkably self-reliant even by the
exacting standards of the Huaorani. For all practical purposes, Quehueire Ono was hidden on the Shiripuno. It had no radio,
no airstrip, no access at all beyond foot or canoe. It lies at the extreme
northwestern corner of the territory—at the opposite end from Cononaco and Garzacocha, from which it is separated by a journey of at least
a week—and it is a three-day walk from the nearest village inside Rachel
Saint's protectorate, directly south. This distancing is quite deliberate:
Quehueire Ono (a Huaorani phrase that means "the river where it is
good to live") was founded by Moi's father, Ñame, in what amounted
to an act of rebellion against the evangelical missionary influence.

Moi's family had once lived inside the protectorate. In 1973, led by
an aunt and uncle of Moi's, a group of Huaorani opposed to the Summer Institute of Linguistics left the original evangelical station on the
Tihueno River and created a new village, Dayuno. But Moi's aunt had
watched Dayuma prosper under the wing of Rachel Saint and the
evangelistas, and she permitted a rival group of American fundamen-
talists to establish a presence in Dayuno. They built a school and an
airstrip, and the settlement quickly grew into a large village. Beads and
trinkets appeared, and the children were taught that the ways of their
parents were uncivilized. The Huaorani stopped chanting. The hunting
got bad.

The years passed. A decade later, Moi's father began to hunt far to the north, in the area once occupied by his wife's grandparents. It was a rich and wild land, and one day in 1989, having returned from a hunt laden with monkey and pig, Ñame decided he would go there to live. And so, as is the custom, he and his wife and children abandoned all that they had in Dayuno (house, canoes, machetes, axes, pots) and went into the forest to build a new life. Their exodus caused bitter feelings in Dayuno — inciting, in particular, a blood rage on the part of Ñame's brothers — but some sixty relatives, or more than half the old village, soon followed them. They erected palm-thatch houses in the old style: The walls went right down to the earth floor, and the forest came right up to the walls, and birds and monkeys came right to the edge of the camp. They established hunting trails and planted gardens, and while they waited for the gardens to produce they raided banana and manoic from Quichua and Shuar colonists living near the Napo and Shiripuno rivers. At times they ate so much meat that they made themselves sick, and they spent days lying in their hammocks. They chanted, often for hours on end. They taught their children to climb the trees to retrieve monkey carcasses and ungarawa nuts, to make curare for blowgun darts, to carve spears and weave palm-string bags.

By almost all measures Quehueire Ono offered "good life," and by the time I got there, three years later, the population had more than doubled. What had begun as a nomadic camp had become something more permanent, larger and more organized than, say, Garzacocha and Cononaco. Even so, there was a sense of privacy and seclusion not only without but within Quehueire Ono — the homes were tucked so deftly into the forested hillsides that it was rare to see one from another. It may well have been the prettiest of all the Huaorani settlements. Although the river itself was shallow, only knee deep in some places, it ran clear green over rock, and its water was sweet and far more translucent than the mud red of the lower river. In the center of the village stood a communal hall, and beyond it lay a broad green clearing that was often filled with children heaving spears at imaginary game. However, this pastoral setting belied the mood of Quehueire Ono, which continued to be one of independence and defiance: It was not unusual to hear people plotting against the missionaries, the Shuar, the Quichua, the president of Ecuador.

We arrived in Quehueire Ono late on a sunny afternoon, and Moi invited Ali and me to stay with his family, who considered Ali kin. Their homesite was well removed from the village center, down a long path and across the river and two hundred yards up the far bank. The land rolled and dipped. We strolled past banana and papaya trees and into a clearing that held three small huts and a sleeping platform raised off the forest floor on stilts. Each hut was about ten feet square, and behind them rose a steep hill crowned with tall trees. "Did you bring Yupi?" Moi's mother asked, and Moi gave her Yupi and a guanta haunch and a bandanna I had brought from Quito, and she tied the bandanna around her head and threw the guanta into a battered pot and the pot onto the fire and hauled another pot down to the river and filled it with water for Yupi. Moi's father and an uncle were up on the hillside, clearing a field for manoic. Their work chant drifted down to us in a gentle lilt.

At twilight Ali and I and Moi and his parents and his uncle sat in hammocks around the cook fire and ate guanta and boiled manoic and ungarawa nuts and drank *chicha* and Yupi. An afternoon thunderstorm had left the air cool and pleasant, and smoke from the fire kept the mosquitoes at bay, and birdsong drifted from the trees. It was not at all hard to see why the Huaorani considered lying in a hammock doing next to nothing the highest state of grace a human being can achieve. (Until the missionaries came, the Huaorani had no word for "lazy," and no concept of sloth.)

"Chong," Moi said, "the forest is very peaceful, no?"

"Yes, it is very peaceful."

"Look," he said. He stood up and pointed to the ground and stamped his feet in a kind of jig.

"Yes?"

"No cement!"

Later I unrolled my blanket and stretched out on the sleeping platform and felt as if I was on a raft floating through the forest. Voices continued to rise quietly from around the fire, and somewhere in the dark an owl hooted. I was drifting off to sleep when Moi's uncle sat down next to me and began to chant. Moi came, too, and translated: Songs of his skill as a hunter, songs of how the People had come to Quehueire Ono, a song about the field he had cleared that day. But only when Moi told me his uncle's name—Dabo—did I understand the significance of his presence: Dabo had been livid when Moi's father left Dayuno. That peace had now been made was a reminder that despite their talk of killing, despite the ferocity of their reputation, despite their high regard for autonomy and independence, the Huaorani value harmony above all else and will spare no effort to achieve it. In terms of respect, a Huao can earn no higher title than *ahuene*—"the one who makes peace."

And so Dabo sat with Moi, delivering his three notes in endless variation and by all appearances effortlessly. It was night music of the finest sort. I soon fell into a deep and extraordinarily restful sleep, there by "the river that is good for living."

ALI AND I and Moi and his entire family slept on the big platform. Nanto and his brother Juan stayed there, too. They slept with Moi, all three of them piled onto a ratty mattress stolen years before from an oil camp. Slept? They spent most of the night telling stories and laughing and knocking one another off the bed, and sometime before dawn they went down to the river to hunt monkeys. Moi's parents, Zhiro and Ñame, got up a couple of times to eat nuts around the fire. Dabo chanted on and off throughout the night. At some point Ali woke up and read a book by candlelight. I think I was the only one who actually did much sleeping.

Moi's mattress was on a frame, of sorts, and under the frame, in his plastic briefcase, he kept copies of most of the written documents ONHAE had generated in the two years since it had been formed. "Here is ONHAE," he said in the morning, and handed me the brief-case. There were proclamations, denunciations, invitations, announcements, newspaper clippings, a copy of the agreement the Huaorani had signed with the government when they were given title to their territory. Many of the papers were smeared with mud, or torn, or crumpled. Some were written in longhand, some were neatly typed and stamped with the ONHAE seal. But taken as a whole, they were extraordinary: They suggested that while it would be tempting to see Quehueire Ono as a return to tradition, that would be innaccurate. If anything, Quehueire Ono represented a Huaorani synthesis: a traditional way of living enhanced by certain modern tools that offered access to an *abundancia* not found in the forest and on which, increasingly, they had come to depend. That is, *cowode* abundance. And in what must be considered a rat's nest of paradox and irony, one of the most valued of these new tools was literacy.

The Huaorani, of course, had been subjected to Western-style education, of one sort or another, since Rachel Saint's arrival. Over the last thirty years, it seemed, almost everyone—the state ministry of education, the provincial departments of education, the state oil company, the foreign oil companies, CONFENIAE, the Catholics, other Protestants—had tried their hands at teaching the Huaorani the ABCs, the multiplication tables, the capitals of France, China, the United States. But no one bothered to seriously assess the impact of those efforts until a Frenchwoman named Laura Rival made it the subject of her doctoral dissertation for the London School of Economics. Her study is widely regarded as the only work of substance on formal education in the territory. From 1988 to 1990 Rival spent eighteen months doing fieldwork among the Huaorani. For part of that time she taught at the school in Dayuno; later she moved to Quehueire Ono. (She is the only nonmissionary *cowode* woman to have lived among the Huaorani for any significant length of time.) The conclusions she reached are interesting, even compelling, for any number of reasons, not the least of which is that they are those of an academic—for whom, presumably, the whole notion of Western education has self-evident merit.

Overall, the portrait Rival draws of the educational system imposed on the Huaorani is one of immense destruction, of ethnocide, emotional and physical trauma, deracination. But she poses a riddle, as well: Why do so many Huaorani continue to clamor for schools, even while blaming them for the destruction of their culture?

It is no secret that the contracted goal of the Summer Institute of Linguistics was to replace the traditional Huaorani life with a life based on school and church. To the American Christians, tradition meant Satan-inspired savagery. As for the state, life in the forest failed to contribute to the national good, because the Huaorani produced nothing for external consumption. The schools became a way to convert them to farming, to participation in the market economy. They were required to live near the schools, in large villages. As the hunting diminished they had to plant bigger gardens and grow a wider variety of crops, which meant they had to stay in one place. They were made to contribute food, labor, and, on occasion, cash to support the schools.

By 1990 there were seven schools in the territory, and though the state was nominally involved in some of them, it was the American missionaries who selected the teachers and gave them airplane flights into the villages, and who provided the schools with books, meals, pencils, schoolbags, and uniforms. By contract the *evangelistas* were also permitted to teach the Bible in the schools and to officially inspect them three times a year. To receive their uniforms the students had to recite Bible stories, in Spanish, and acknowledge the glory of God. Meanwhile, the schoolteachers, most of whom were Quichua, became village potentates, with powers that extended far beyond the classroom. Some of them opened stores, for example, and the Huaorani went into debt.

For the first time in Huaorani culture—in which, traditionally, personal autonomy is paramount, and, as Rival notes, "no orders are given, and requests are few, and no one is allowed to be in distress"—children were forced against their will to complete assigned tasks, and, often, to perform extracurricular work for the personal benefit of the teachers. Sexual abuse, if not frequent, was common enough. The children were regularly beaten—an outrage in a society that so values family harmony that raising a hand against a child, or a wife, was unimaginable.

Above all, however, the Huaorani were taught that "to go into the forest was uncivilized," and that becoming civilized was their only hope for survival. No element of Huaorani culture was allowed to enter the curriculum. The Huaorani learned about European plants but not about the plants that grew around them in the forest. They learned the nutritional value of an urban diet—rice, ham, salt—but not the value of their typical foods (which were, if anything, superior). They learned to sing in Spanish—to the president and to God—but were forbidden to learn the chants that told the stories of all that made them what they were. (Once, outraged that his children were not being allowed to help him hunt, Dabo nailed the Dayuno school shut with the teacher and students inside.)

After interviewing adult Huaorani who had gone through the first wave of evangelical education, in Toñampare and Tihueno in the 1960s and early '70s, Rival concluded that their "education" was a form of religious literacy only: The missionaries had stressed reading, not writing, because "reading was conceived to be the individual reception of God's sacred word in one's own language." Instruction in writing, on the other hand, was reserved for a handful of fervent believers; in any case, twenty years later they no longer wrote. The quality of formal Huaorani education improved somewhat through the 1970s and '80s, but not much. For most male students, and for all females, school ended at the sixth grade, a level they did not generally attain, if at all, until they were sixteen or seventeen. By then, estranged from the forest, they had little choice but to take whatever place they could find on the lowest rung of a catastrophically poor society—to become, in other words, slaves.

The Huaorani are nothing if not keen observers, and they readily identified the schools as the main reason they were losing their nomadic way of life and becoming alienated from the forest and dependent on the *cowode*. Sometimes the Huaorani would leave the school villages to start new settlements, or they would drive the teachers away. Yet it would be wrong to say that the Huaorani were being "educated" against their will. Many not only wanted the schools but were proud to have them. Laura Rival believes they saw in them a "means of domesticating outside reality on their own terms." That is, the schools were valued not for their academic content but because they offered the Huaorani a model by which they could become "civilized." The Huaorani were eager to learn how to walk, talk, dress, and eat like the *cowode*, because being "civilized" meant easier access to *cowode* abundance: tools, food, radios, boots, airplanes.

One very effective way to get those things, the Huaorani cannily observed, was to learn how to write for them. Delivered in person to the Company or the government, a written demand—an *oficio*—readily produced a host of *cowode* goods, particularly when it included language that invoked threats of violence and when the authors appeared in person brandishing spears. Letter writing, in other words, raised the Huaorani practice of hunting and gathering—or, as their *cowode* victims tended to see it, raiding and looting—to an entirely new level, a "civilized" level. As Moi had said when I told him what I did for a living, "Writing is a very good way to get things without doing work."

Quehueire Ono was founded not by retrograde Huaorani shutting the door on modernity (though there were certainly elements of that) but by the most literate part of the culture. Most of the residents were from Dayuno, where the students had received broader exposure to Western thought and practice than was permitted the residents of Toñampare, Tihueno, or any other school village. One of Moi's older brothers had spent two years in Quito attending a literacy course at the Catholic University. Moi, too, had spent considerable time in Quito, and five years on oil crews, and six years in elementary school. He had a working grasp of Spanish, and he wrote letters all the time—not only *oficios* but stories, plans, dreams. And while it was true that he and Nanto and Amo often asked *cowode* to help them draft ONHAE *oficios*, to give the letters a certain style that they were incapable of producing themselves, one measure of their comprehension is that sometimes they would recopy the *oficios* in their own hand and insert deliberate mistakes to make them appear more "authentic."

This is not to overstate the Huaorani command of Western literacy. As Rival notes, the Huaorani read newspapers all the time—out loud, slowly, to one another—but seldom understood them in any meaningful way. Nor should their manipulation of the *cowode* be interpreted as cynical. Rather, it was one more very practical way to assure *abundancia*, and the real value of *abundancia*—indeed, the inspiration for virtually everything the Huaorani do—is not material gain but to keep the family together in peace and harmony.

In 1988, under pressure mainly from the country's large Andean Indian population, Ecuador's then-president, Rodrigo Borja Cevallos, initiated a project to make genuine bilingual, bicultural education an option within the national curriculum. Texts were to be prepared and classes taught in the language of the local people, with Spanish employed as a secondary language, and strong emphasis was to be placed on the preservation of cultural identity. As with so many well-intentioned initiatives in Ecuador, however, resources for the program were woefully limited, and in this case they were earmarked almost entirely for the Quichua-speaking population. In the Huaorani territory, the evangelical missionaries branded the program "Communist" and succeeded in blocking it by warning that if it were implemented the mission would end its support of the schools.

In 1990, however, the Huaorani of Quehueire Ono opened their own school—without the missionaries. Instead, it was run under the auspices of Napo province, which was committed to the new bilingual, bicultural education program. Napo was poor, however, and the school had few of the amenities of the other Huaorani schools. It was little more than a dirt-floor shack, and pencils and notebooks were hard to come by. But for the Huaorani it was an approach to formal education that they saw as honoring their culture and incorporating its knowledge of the forest into the curriculum. It would take a long time for the program to prove itself—the teacher, in fact, was a Quichua and could speak only minimal Huaorani—but it struck me as an honest attempt to join the best of both worlds. To Moi, it was "education for five thousand years."

IN THE MORNING Ali stayed at Moi's house to tend the nursery he was starting for Quehueire Ono, but I waded across the river with Moi's sister and mother and we set off down the trail to the communal hall. At home they had worn only shorts, but for the asamblea they put on clean white blouses and skirts dyed the traditional Huaorani red. Canoes bearing families were drifting down the river, and on the trail people were stacked up like commuters, carrying pots of chicha, babies, machetes. By the time we reached the center of the village, at least three hundred Huaorani were gathered there, or roughly 20 percent of the entire population. They had traveled for days and weeks, from Dayuno and Tzapino, from Garzacocha, from Toñampare, from most of the seventeen Huaorani communities then known to exist. Those who couldn't make it, like Penti from Cononaco, had sent messages. Any notion that ONHAE was not representative of the Huaorani as a whole—the charge was raised whenever ONHAE spoke out against the Company—was disspelled by such broad participation in the congresos and asambleas. (At asambleas, which were held every few months, the Huaorani discussed issues among themselves; a congreso was called for elections, and to formally address the world outside.) The Huaorani would meet for three days, from dawn to dusk—until everyone who wished to had spoken, and until consensus had been reached. From dusk to dawn, they would dance.

Nanto and Moi and Amo had already been at the hall for hours, drawing up the final agenda for the meeting. I talked to them briefly.

They were upset. Enqueri had not come, and he had not spread the word of the *asamblea* to all the villages, as he had said he would do. Fortunately, word had filtered out on its own—there are no secrets in Huaorani territory. But Moi and Nanto and Amo weren't mad at Enqueri; they were mad at Samuel Caento Padilla. Word from Toñampare had it that Samuel had stopped Enqueri from doing his job, because tourism in the Huaorani territory was one of the issues the *asamblea* was to address and Samuel did not want his business threatened. And by then they understood what had happened at their meeting in Quito with William Hutton, the Maxus *gerente*. Naturally, they were upset, though they seemed more disappointed than angry. "We asked Samuel to translate what we said," Nanto told me. "We did not ask him to speak for us." Meanwhile, a recent copy of a Quito newspaper featured a photograph of Samuel, taken at the airport. The caption said that he was on his way to a meeting in New York to discuss "the defense of the human rights of the Huaorani." Nanto and Moi were worried that Maxus was behind Samuel's trip.

Moi asked for my sunglasses, and then he and Nanto ducked into the hall and called the *asamblea* to order.

I watched from outside, standing at the entrance to the hall. Dozens of log benches had been set up inside, and they were now filled with men, women, children, a couple of spider monkeys on long leashes, a macaw. At the front of the hall stood two school desks. Amo sat in one, earnestly taking notes, and Nanto and Moi took turns in the other. As vice president, Moi had the job of moving the agenda along, and of recognizing speakers, but Nanto was the orator. "The Huaorani live well and will continue to live well," he said to open the meeting, "because we are the bravest people in the Amazon and we will defend our land!" A roar of approval erupted, but Nanto appeared to pay it no mind. In Coca and in Quito he had often seemed confused, or preoccupied, or somehow thrown off kilter. But up there in front of his fellow Huaorani, he was a different man. He looked handsome, in command, sure of himself.

Nanto spoke for more than an hour, in a strong, clear voice, though at one point he nearly passed out on his feet. He wandered outside then and told me that his head hurt and that he was feeling pains in his back. "Maybe I drank some contaminated water when I visited Quemperi," he said. More likely he'd suffered a concussion when he fell out of the canoe and hit his head on a rock. But he sipped some Yupi, and thus fortified went back into the *asamblea* and persevered.

T H E *asamblea* was serious business, but it also fit rather nicely into the Huaorani tradition of feasting—of "seeing all the Huaorani whose faces are known." People milled in and out of the hall. In front of the hall, next to the river, big pots of rice and manoic were cooking, and old, long-eared warriors were hanging about. Sometimes they sat in on the meeting, but mostly they left the politics to the younger Huaorani and held their counsel for later, around the fire. One old man in particular stood out: Mengatohue, the last of the true Huaorani shamans.

Moi had said Mengatohue was his grandfather. There was no direct line of descent, but for the Huaorani, a "grandfather" is a teacher, a man who brings the young into the forest and passes on the knowledge of the ages. Almost everyone in Quehueire Ono called Mengatohue grandfather. He was sixty or more; no one really knew. He was Quemperi's brother and looked like his twin. He was completely toothless, but his hair was thick and black, his body one tight knot of muscle. He walked around with a live ten-pound woolly monkey sitting right on top of his head, held there by a cord woven of chambira. Mengatohue seldom wore more than a pair of grubby shorts, and often not even that. He also wore a necklace made of a jaguar tooth and a dental mirror, and, always, an expression of complete absorption, of intense concentration: The Huaorani zone in its highest form. Wherever he went his eyes traveled slowly across the scene, as if taking in every detail and examining it until he understood its essence and had extracted from it that which he could use and which would have been found, too, by his father and his father's father.

I spent a lot of time with Mengatohue. Walking in the forest with him was like visiting an immense library with a master librarian. No matter how seemingly wild, every patch of ground had a history: Here he had planted chonta palm that in the time of Moi's children would provide wood for spears. Here balsa had reclaimed an old manoic garden and would be harvested for earplugs and rafts. Here a man had been spear-killed; here a jaguar appeared now and then. Here were plants for treating snakebite, diarrhea, skin rash. Here was a patch of the hallucinogen ayahuasca that would soon be ready to brew into tea. I began to see the forest not as wild and unknown but as managed and inventoried, shaped and maintained by man as much as it shaped and maintained him.

The Huaorani attributed to Mengatohue gifts beyond the realm of common human knowledge: He could enter an ayahuasca trance and become a jaguar. He could repair a broken leg or arm by grafting onto it the bone of a monkey. He could diagnose illness by touch. When Moi introduced me, Mengatohue took my hand and looked into my eyes, gripped my elbows and shook my arms, felt the back of my neck. He grunted to Moi.

"What did he say, Moi?"

"He said you work too hard."

For many years Mengatohue had lived as an exile. He was born in the Yasuní region, but sometime in the early 1970s the missionaries herded him into their protectorate. However, it wasn't long before they branded him a witch doctor, an agent of the Devil, and forced him out. By then the Yasuní Huaorani considered him "dead," because he had left the clan; to return there to live would have meant war. So he and his family wandered in the forest until Quehueire Ono was established. At first he had been uneasily accepted. Influenced by the missionaries and the *civilizado* schoolteachers, the young Huaorani had grown up ridiculing men like Mengatohue, who wore their hair long and sometimes walked naked into the schoolhouses to show the uniformed children how the Huaorani had once lived. But as Moi began to mine the cultural past for whatever would help the Huaorani survive the future, he had come to revere Mengatohue, and the shaman had regained something of his rightful place. Following Moi's example, the Huaorani officers cut their hair as the elders did, long in back and straight across the front. They often quoted from Mengatohue in their *oficios*. Moi called Mengatohue "The Captain."

Thus far, however, only Moi had attempted to follow Mengatohue into the deeper world of the forest. Only Moi had partaken of ayahuasca; only Moi was interested in learning the skills of the shaman. Only Moi believed that in all that the Huaorani had been taught to discard from the past they would find the knowledge and skills that would help them navigate the present. That conviction set him apart from Nanto and Enqueri and Amo, who were among the first Huaorani to have grown up in a world of constant contact with the *cowode*, and who were oriented out, away, toward a future that, no matter how inevitable and incomprehensible, they understood to be a *cowode* future that could be survived only by learning a *cowode* way of life.

There was heroism, and something essentially Huaorani, in the fact that, through ONHAE, such disparate and conflicting visions—visions that clearly held the seeds of doom—had merged into something unique and strong. In the late 1980s, as the Ecuadorian government moved toward granting them land title, the Huaorani had come under great pressure to form a national organization. CONFENIAE was involved, and the national ministry of colonization, the missionaries, and the military. ("*Mucha confusión,*" Moi said of those times. "Everyone was telling the Huaorani what to do.") At first Moi and the people of Quehueire Ono had wanted to form their own organization, apart from the Huaorani influenced by the missionaries. But the Huaorani way is to include rather than exclude, and there were *asambleas* and *congresos* in Quehueire Ono and in Toñampare to discuss the problem. In the end, in March of 1990, the Huaorani came together as one. The first election was held in Toñampare, which had the largest population. Many of the residents were related to Nanto and, rightfully, Nanto had been elected president. (He defeated a candidate supported by Rachel Saint.) By then Quehueire Ono's population was the third-largest in the territory, and Moi was elected vice president. Amo was from a smaller village, Tzapino; as secretary, he represented the inclusion of interests that fell outside the main villages.

Ali Sharif had been around to observe ONHAE since its earliest days. "I find it incredible the way they've organized themselves," he told me one afternoon. "It's only been two years, but ONHAE is up and alive and a real thing. It is *such* hard work. It pulls them away from their home life, and from that serenity of running through the forest and hunting and being with the community family. I mean, look at Amo— he's just had a kid, for godsakes. They *love* their kids. There's never a stern word, just love. They'll tear an animal to pieces, but when they see a kid, it doesn't matter whose kid it is, they'll let him crawl all over them. So you can see how grueling the ONHAE work is. It takes them a week to mail a letter, and then they find themselves stuck in Coca with no money, no food, no gas for the canoe. They do it all on nothing. But they're prepared to go all the way with it, you know?"

IN SOME WAYS ONHAE may have been hardest of all on Moi. Unlike Nanto and Amo, he was not married, and as much as anything, marriage is the cornerstone of Huaorani culture. Everything flows from it: alliances, work, play, feasts, hunting rights. The act most critical to a successful marriage is, simply enough, staying around, sharing the partnership completely. But Moi just didn't stay home enough to make a good husband. He traveled, constantly and widely. He had been to see the ocean ("Chong, the water rose up before it bit the land!"). He was in and out of Coca, and he knew Quito pretty well. He'd spent time in jail: From what I could tell, he had been in Tena, a town near Coca, when the national Indian confederation called a strike and shut down highways all over the country. The Tena police had rounded up every Indian in sight. There was a flood that day, and Moi passed the night standing in water to his knees.

Moi had even been to a place called Los Angeles. Ali Sharif had taken him there once to try to get help for the Huaorani. It was a short trip, and it passed like a dream. He remembered little about it except that Los Angeles was a city somewhere on the other side of Quito, that he had been in an airplane for some time, and that the people he met were barbarians: They ate no meat, only leaves. He did not want to go back there again, ever.

At twenty-six it was, for Moi, high time to get married. But the complex marriage laws of the Huaorani severely limited the number of eligible women, and Moi said that he was thinking about marrying a *cowode*—a Quichua, perhaps. (Huaorani men think Quichua women make especially good wives, because they are quiet, hardworking, and beautiful.) The fact was, however, that women left Moi paralyzed with shyness. They were the only force I'd seen, in forest or city, that inspired in him anything that might be called fear. Of course, in every place I have ever traveled with Moi, women have tended to appear out of nowhere and attach themselves to him, but he always seems oblivious to their attentions. But I happened to be around the day he got snakebit by a leggy twenty-one-year-old Swiss heiress named Marie, and it's fair to say that nothing he had learned in the forest or his travels had quite prepared him for that sort of *cowode* invasion.

Marie had the summer off from school and was bumming around Ecuador when she met Moi in Coca. In that she was not unusual. What was unusual is that she found her way to Quehueire Ono, which is like saying Cortés found his way to Mexico. Quehueire Ono had never seen the likes of her. She was built with the precision of a Swiss watch, and proud of it. Stripping down to her shorts to swim, she would stretch and bend languorously, the sun flashing off her long, white limbs, and would so fluster the Huaorani men that they couldn't eat, which is power of a high order. She was wealthy by any standard, and had the loud and aggressively flirtatious manner of the insecure young rich, and the attention span of a gnat. It didn't take her two days to tire of Quehueire Ono. She didn't like the food and she didn't like the bugs and she didn't like what happened to her skin, and after a while she didn't like all those people who wanted to see just what a white girl's body looked like. ("Skinny," Moi's mother said. "I hope she gets well.") But this didn't stop her from jumping all over Moi—touching him, grabbing him by an arm to lead him here or there, running her fingers through his hair, hugging him while she demanded that I take photos with her camera. The Huaorani were astonished. All of them except Moi, that is, who seemed to regard Marie with the same indifference he did any of the *cowode* women he so often attracted.

Late one night, however, I heard their voices near me on the sleeping platform. Marie was stretched out on her mat, and Moi was kneeling over her.

"I invite you to be my wife," Moi said.

"You invite me to do *what?*"

"I invite you to stay and live with me here in the forest, where we are safe from all the dangers of the world. I will protect you with the heart of a jaguar and we will have many children."

"You are such a dear man."

"I have made this crown for you."

"It is truly beautiful. Thank you."

"Then you will be my wife."

"Oh, Moi. I am so sorry."

There was silence then. In the morning old Dabo brought the canoe around, and he and Marie set course for the Shiripuno bridge. She was wearing the crown. It was much like Moi's, an elegant mosaic of eagle, toucan, owl, and turkey feathers. Moi didn't see her off. He disappeared instead into the forest behind his home, where he spent the day alone, disconsolate and confused, clearing a field. All day I could hear the steady whack, whack, whack of his machete, driving out his disappointment.

I didn't see him until late that night, when I awoke to find him lingering over the fire. He was feeling old, he said. His work for ONHAE had kept him away from Quehueire Ono for too long. He said there was a Huaorani woman that he cared for, and she cared for him, but now she was married to another man. They had children. Maybe he could find a wife in Quito, he said. "What do you think, Chong?" he asked. "Would a *cowode* woman come here to live with me?"

"I think it would be difficult for her," I said. "She might like it for a time, but it would be hard for her to stay for a long while."

He thought this over. "Yes," he said. Then he laughed, hugely, and held up his right foot and wriggled the toes. "And she would not come to live with a man who does not wear shoes, would she?"

OVER THE three days of the *asamblea*, the Huaorani passed several resolutions, by majority vote. They addressed education (they wanted schools, but they wanted them to be run under the government's bilingual education program and to be independent of missionary influence); tourism (they were against it until and unless a program could be devised that allowed them to participate and to retain control); and health care (they would ask the government to fund a program to train their own people as health workers). The dominant topics, however, were colonization and the Company. "We are opposed to oil development, but we know it cannot be stopped," Moi told me one night, after the day's talk had ended and the night's dancing had begun. "What we want is a moratorium."

"What is a moratorium?"

"We believe that the Company should stop for ten years. That seems reasonable. Right now, everything is happening too quickly.

There is no control. The Company is killing the forest, and no one is watching out for the Huaorani. We want the Company to stop, to count the damage that has been done so far, and to come up with a serious plan to limit damage in the future. We think that is fair."

Clearly, some of what Moi was saying had been picked up from *cowode* of various sorts. (For example, the idea of a moratorium came from the Quichua.) But I had little doubt that he understood full well what these things meant, and the resolutions that had emerged from the *asamblea* seemed well thought out.

"Well, of course," Ali Sharif said later. "They are excellent observers. Their lives depend on seeing *everything*. When they are given time to make decisions, to act at a pace they're accustomed to, they don't make many mistakes. It's not the sort of life that has traditionally been very forgiving of mistakes, you know? But now they are being asked — forced, really — to make decisions at our speed. Too often, they have to act before consensus is reached. *That's* when they make mistakes. Given the proper amount of time and space, they tend to act in the best possible way. But the oil business doesn't leave a lot of time."

On the last day of the *asamblea*, I asked Nanto and Moi and Amo about the petition the Sierra Club Legal Defense Fund had filed with the Inter-American Commission on Human Rights — the petition that charged that oil development in the Huaorani territory would lead to ethnocide and called for an investigation. The names of the organizations meant nothing to them, and they knew nothing of the petition. That wasn't surprising. The petition had been prepared and submitted under the auspices of CONFENIAE, and, three years later, a representative from SCLDF had yet to visit the Huaorani territory. Still, Nanto, Moi, and Amo were intrigued, and pleased, to hear of the effort being waged on their behalf. ("Let the whole world come and see," Moi said. "Tell them to bring your president.") They had no trouble understanding *ethnocide* — "It means the Company is going to kill us," Amo said — and they were ready to move forward: "If they are our lawyers, we must invite them to come and meet us."

Did Amo know what a lawyer was? "Yes," he said. "It is someone who speaks for you when you cannot speak for yourself."

Nanto and Moi decided that Amo would return with Ali and me to Coca, borrow a typewriter from the Capuchin mission, carry it into the territory on his back, and type up an invitation to the Sierra Club Legal Defense Fund, which would be signed by the other officers. With luck Amo would have time to squeeze in a visit to his village, to see his wife and his two-month-old baby girl. He would then travel to Quito. Ali would be out of the country by then, and in any case, given his precarious political position, he could not involve himself in such activity. "Chong," Moi said, "Amo will come to your house, and you will send the letter to the United States of North America."

IT WOULD BE many months, possibly a year, before Ali would be able to return to Quehueire Ono, and on the last night of the *asamblea* there was a *despedida*, or going-away ceremony. With all three hundred of the Huaorani gathered around Ali, two old men sang a blessing, sending the jaguar to protect him on his journey and to bring him quickly and safely back to the land of the People. Moi gave him a feathered crown, old Pego a spear he had carved during the *jornada*. "When you come back, Ali," Moi said, "we will find you a wife."

The next day Amo led us out of Quehueire Ono on foot. We traveled for twelve hours, eating nothing until we bedded down that night in a clearing near the Shiripuno bridge, when Amo produced a mound of rice wrapped in a banana leaf. He refused to take any for himself. In the morning we flagged an oil truck, and in Coca we shared a coconut. I drew Amo a rough map of Quito, marking my apartment, and gave him fare for the thirteen-hour bus ride. Then Ali and I bid him luck and good-bye.

"I just hope Amo's letter makes it to someone who can do something," Ali said later. "There's a billion of us, but there's only thirteen hundred of them. When they're gone, they're *gone*."

12

A MO NEVER made it to Quito. This much is clear: He got on the jitney that picks up Indians and colonists along the Vía Auca. Nanto and another Huao, a man called Pancho, were inside the vehicle, and Amo was riding on the roof, as he often did. One way or another, he fell off. Nanto and Pancho saw Amo drop from the roof and shouted for the driver to stop. The driver slowed, Nanto and Pancho hit the ground on the fly, and the driver sped away. For two hours Amo lay by the road unconscious but alive. Suddenly, he sat up, vomited blood, said, "My head hurts," and died.

Four hours later a pickup truck from the Capuchin mission arrived and took the body to Coca. There was no investigation, by either the military or the police. A doctor who later examined Amo's body—but refused to do an autopsy, for fear the Huaorani would blame him for the death and exact revenge—told one of the Capuchin priests that Amo had landed on his head with such force that a small stone was driven through his skull and lodged in his throat.

A few weeks later, when I was able to speak to the Huaorani about Amo's death, I found no one who believed it had been an accident. I went first to the Vía Auca. Amo had died near the office of the Shuar colonist association, not far from where Babae and his clan lived. Several of the clan members had seen his body. "He had a round hole in the back of his head, and the hair around it was burned," Babae's wife said. "It was a small hole, like the hole a bullet makes in a pig, and you could see the place in his throat where something was trying to push through. How would a stone get all the way down there?"

From the Auca I made my way to Toñampare, where I spoke first with Nanto. Though he said there was some possibility that Amo had been hexed by a witch, he endorsed the more widely held belief that Amo had been shot in the head by a Shuar colonist who was on the roof with him. "I heard the dead man screaming," Nanto said. "Then I heard a sound like a gunshot. When I looked out the window, he was flying off the roof. He wasn't falling, trying to grab things as he went—he was *flying*."

Amo's body had been flown home for burial. (Arranging and paying for this flight was the last thing Ali Sharif did before leaving for the United States.) Nanto said that Enqueri would assume Amo's duties as secretary, and that he too believed that Amo had been assassinated. "The Shuar want our land," Nanto said. "They think they can get it by killing us." Enqueri, he said, was scared and angry. Meanwhile, Amo's grandfather was said to be beside himself with grief and rage: Quemperi, word had it, was looking for revenge.

I HAPPENED to arrive in Toñampare the day before a village *asamblea* was to be held to discuss the Company. I ran into Salomón, in whose hut I had slept during my first visit. He led me across Toñampare and down the trail to the clearing where Enqueri's family had made their home. We found the Condorito in his hammock, staring at the sky. He jumped out and gave me a hug. "José!" he said. "You have come back to live with the Huaorani!"

It had been six months since I'd last seen Enqueri, and, once again, I almost failed to recognize him. He had adopted the short-in-front, long-in-back hairstyle worn by Nanto and Moi, and he had pulled his hair into a ponytail. His eyeglasses now sported elegant wire rims. In the right circumstances he might have passed for a hip young Latino, at least until you saw his shoes—a pair of ersatz sandals that he had fashioned from cheap rubber boots by cutting out the tops and the tips. They were at least two sizes too small for him, and his toes lapped over the edges.

"How is your wife, Enqueri?" I asked, and Salomón howled with laughter.

"I did not get married," Enqueri said.

"Why not?"

"She moved to another country."

"What country?"

"Ecuador!"

"Tell José about the thing!" Salomón said.

"The thing!" Enqueri said. He glanced at Salomón, and both of them choked with laughter. "The thing," as it turned out, was a penis ring. Enqueri had seen one on an Australian who had come into the territory and done the usual—gone native, or what he imagined to be native, and run around naked for a couple of weeks, until bug bites and skin fungus drove him mad. Enqueri made a ring for himself. One day while he was walking the territory, he stopped at the village of Damuintaro, an evangelical community, and went down to the water to bathe. He was bathing naked, which the missionaries prohibit, "so I was hiding behind a rock, and I put my thing on the rock, and then some people came down to the river. When I got out of the water, my thing was gone! So now I have a place for a thing, but no thing!"

"Enqueri has no thing for his thing!" Salomón said. "Watch out for your thing, Condor! They will steal that next!"

When I asked about Amo, however, the Condor turned somber. In many ways Amo's death affected him more directly than it did anyone else, because now he was the secretary of ONHAE. "I believe that the Shuar had an arrangement with the bus driver," he said. "It was an assassination. The Shuar had told the dead man that they were going to kill him if he didn't give them land. The last time I walked out of the territory the Shuar stopped me and said, 'We are going to do to you what we did to the dead man.' I told them they will have to kill all the Huaorani before they will get our land. I was alone, or I would have fought them right there." The idea of Enqueri fighting anyone seemed preposterous, yet I had no doubt that he was serious.

THE *asamblea* began that afternoon. It was of a somewhat different order than the one I'd seen in Quehueire Ono, in that it was attended mainly by the inhabitants of Toñampare. But it was a significant gathering nonetheless, because almost a fifth of the Huaorani population lived in Toñampare. More significant, perhaps, was that Moi was not there. There were problems, Enqueri said, but he was reluctant to discuss them. All he would say was that Maxus had offered the Huaorani a contract, and they were going to talk about it.

The *asamblea* was held inside the Toñampare school. Maybe eighty Huaorani were there. The schoolhouse was far grander than anything in Quehueire Ono—it had blackboards and a wood floor and chain-link fencing on the windows and a corrugated tin roof—but the *asamblea* itself was a much more subdued affair. Nanto ran the show. His mother had painted jaguar whiskers on his face with black dye, and he and Enqueri wore crowns. They sat in front of the room, squeezing themselves down behind a tiny table meant for children. The effect was oddly comic—they looked like overgrown kids.

Nanto seemed both tired and frenetic, on edge. He appeared to speak with little of the confidence or authority I had seen so powerfully displayed in Quehueire Ono. He stopped and started and looked at the ceiling or at the floor. This was, I suppose, no surprise. Amo's death had been shock enough, and there were rumors that the Shuar had issued a death threat against Nanto. More daunting, however, was the presence of Rachel Saint, who took up a seat at the rear of the meeting and furiously scribbled notes and interrupted the proceedings again and again to shout to Nanto or Enqueri or the crowd itself. I had no way of knowing what she was saying, because the meeting was entirely in Huaorani, but it wasn't hard to read the nervous glances Enqueri shot her way whenever she spoke—it was the same sheepish manner he'd displayed when I'd seen him telling Bible stories in her chapel the year before.

Rachel, it turned out, was the reason Moi was not in Toñampare. He would not tolerate her presence at such a meeting. But Moi, of course, was fundamentally different from Nanto and Enqueri. He had long since escaped Rachel's influence. He had made a new home with his people, in a place where animals still ran wild in the forests, and the people sang and went naked, and the shaman spoke in the jaguar tongue. But Nanto and Enqueri had grown up wearing Rachel Saint's uniforms and eating Rachel Saint's food and flying in Rachel Saint's airplanes and studying in Rachel Saint's school. They had learned that the way their parents hunted and the way they ate and the way they dressed and the way they made love were evil. If to some degree they had also learned, in time, to reject Rachel's teachings, there was clearly a part of them that could never escape her entirely.

After the meeting Enqueri told me that for the moment the People were not willing to sign with Maxus. But he was worried. He himself did not want to make any such deal, he said, but "the Company is sitting on Nanto's head."

Later I went to visit Rachel Saint. She told me that Texaco and Petroecuador and the rest of the Oil had been bad news, but Maxus was a different story. Like her, William Hutton was a devout evangelical Christian, and he had already provided funding for a secondary school in Toñampare. Rachel was coordinating its construction and staffing with the Christian mission in Quito. "Bill Hutton's a good Christian man," she said. "And he says he's an environmentalist, too. I don't think the Aucas could ask for much better than that."

I said that I had spoken with Moi, and that he seemed adamantly opposed to Maxus.

"Moi?" she said, as if trying to recall who he was. "Isn't he the one from that rebel village? With the Communist school? My guess is he probably drinks a lot."

"I've never seen him drunk."

"Yeah, well. He's a little crazy."

That night Nanto told me that Maxus had paid to fly a group of Huaorani from the Christian compound in Shell to Toñampare, for the *asamblea*, and had bought the Huaorani two hundred pounds of rice — enough to feed everyone at the *asamblea*.

"Does that mean you are working with the Company?" I asked.

"No!" he said, quite forcefully. "It was the only way everyone could eat."

On the surface, or at least to a *cowode* way of thinking, Nanto's acceptance of the rice and his denial of collaboration with the Company seemed hugely contradictory. But I was beginning to understand that, from the Huaorani perspective, this was not necessarily so. Basically, the Huaorani consider it their right to collect whatever they can from whatever *cowode* they happen to cross paths with, and to feel no obligation in return. It is thus among themselves: To accept a gift leaves one with no obligation to respond in kind. The act, not the gift, is the real point of any such transaction, for it demonstrates that the giver is so capable of securing *abundancia* that he or she can share without fear of further need. Of course, the Huaorani see securing goods from the Company as something more substantial than the mere receiving of gifts. For them it has become as intrinsic and necessary a skill for surviving in the forest as hunting monkeys or gathering ungarawa nuts. What carries over, however, is the belief that they incur no debt or obligation. That, and the absolute conviction that they are the rulers of their land and have in no way forfeited their right to evict the Company—or any other *cowode*—whenever they want to.

WHILE I WAS in Toñampare a valve in an oil well near the Napo broke, or was left open, and for two days and a night raw crude streamed into the river—at least 21,000 gallons and perhaps as many as 80,000, creating a slick that stretched from bank to bank for forty miles. Ecuador's downstream neighbors, Peru and Brazil, declared states of emergency, but Petroecuador shrugged off the problem. "It looks much worse than it is," an official said. "The water underneath is perfectly fine." Three weeks later the pipeline itself burst, in the Andean foothills that rise beyond the west bank of the Napo, and spilled another 32,000 gallons into the watershed.

WHEN I GOT back to Quito, I called the Maxus offices and tried to arrange an interview with William Hutton. I'd tried before and been politely but firmly rebuffed. Señor Hutton was out of town; Señor Hutton was in a meeting. This time, however, I was offered the opportunity to speak with an executive involved with working out an agreement with the Huaorani. I got a cab and headed for the *petrolero* district.

The Maxus offices weren't hard to find—they were the same offices Conoco had used. Signs that read MAXUS had replaced signs that read CONOCO, but other than that little had changed. The same armed guards shook me down in the foyer; the same secretaries greeted me upstairs on the tenth floor; the office into which I was led offered the same million-dollar view of the snowcapped volcanoes that surround

Quito; and the spokesman I sat down with was the same well-manicured Ecuadorian, Jorge Jiménez, who had held a similar position with Conoco. The bottom line hadn't changed, either. "The oil is going to come out of the ground," Jiménez said. "We don't have to negotiate with the Huaorani; we don't need their approval. But we'd like to be good neighbors. We'd like to be fair."

He gave me a copy of the Maxus management plan for Block Sixteen. It was, for all intents and purposes, identical to the old Conoco plan. There had been no independent review of the plan and no more than token public participation in its development. The Huaorani didn't see it until three years after it was finished. (Later, when I showed my Spanish copy to Enqueri, he was incredulous. He read aloud from a page that stated oil development would pose "no threats to the health, safety, or long-term welfare" of the Huaorani. "Have these people ever seen the Oriente?" he asked.)

I asked how the company could claim that its project would not threaten the Huaorani. Jiménez, who has a degree in petroleum engineering from the University of Texas, spoke in fluent English. "Well," he said after a moment, "you're right. No one knows what the impacts will be. There are so many things to consider: the road, the rivers, how the seasons affect the work." He sighed. "Yes, I have to say there will be an impact."

According to a study that had been commissioned by Conoco, the most devastating potential impact of developing Block Sixteen would be colonization of the Maxus road. Ecuador had the greatest population density in South America and its highest rate of population growth, and the pressure to colonize every inch of land was enormous. The report had warned Conoco that for the Huaorani "to lose any more land or resources will result in deculturation and genocide." But nowhere in the entire Amazon, let alone Ecuador, had anyone ever been able to prevent colonization of a road—except by not building one. Maxus could have developed Block Sixteen with helicopters, but that would have cut into profits. Instead, Maxus proposed a system of guards and gates. In the end, Jiménez said, "I really believe that when the colonists understand the road is on Indian land, when they understand that land belongs to other people, they will respect that."

Although the project would hit the Huaorani hardest, the road would start in Quichua territory near the Napo River, and Jiménez made no bones about the Maxus strategy regarding the contract it had worked out with the Quichua: Divide and conquer. The company had ignored CONFENIAE, gone directly to the Quichua communities through which the road would pass, and gotten them to sign. Valerio Grefa had howled at this invasion of what he considered his own domain; Jiménez was unmoved. "I could call Valerio Grefa right now and make a deal," he said. "We could set up a foundation and make him president and he would sign on right away. I don't say that in a negative way. He's a very good businessman; he would work out a very good deal. But there would be no way we could guarantee that whatever it was we were giving him would make it to the communities that will be receiving the impact of our work.

"Let me tell you something," he continued. "I have been working on this for almost three years. I have gone into the Quichua communities and I have gone into the Huaorani communities. I know more about what goes on in there than Valerio Grefa does, and I know more than the environmentalists do, because I have put myself on the line. Do you understand what I am saying? Let me tell you what happened last year, when there was a big meeting in Pompeya, the Quichua community where the road will start. There was supposed to be an eclipse that day. I knew I would have to speak, and I am not a very good orator, and I was worried. What will happen if it goes dark all of a sudden? What will they think of me? What might they do to me? But I got up in front of the Quichua and I said, I come here now to speak for myself. I know you have no reason to trust me, or the people I work for, so I ask you to judge us by what we do. Try us out and see if we keep our word.

"And then I finished and sat down and the eclipse happened. It didn't get too dark, and things seemed all right. The next day they said, okay, we'll sign the contract. Sure, they signed with Maxus, but they also signed with *me*. Do you understand that?

"Three weeks ago, I went into Toñampare to talk about a contract, and the Huaorani said, We want a high school. I said, Yes, we will build one. We have already made a deal with a contractor. And we will give air passage for a teacher, and money for books and desks. No strings attached."

But I'd been to Toñampare, and I'd heard about the new school from Rachel Saint. The evangelical missionaries were coordinating it, and they were on record as opposing the bilingual education system the Huaorani had expressly stated they wanted. When I pointed this out to Jiménez, he appeared to be shocked. "I'm a firm believer in bilingual education," he said. "When you lose the language, you lose the culture." Proudly, he showed me two bilingual coloring books Maxus had produced for the Quichua. "My own daughter enjoys these," he said.

William Hutton, of course, had his own ideas about educating the Huaorani. Still, what the high school illustrated was not overt malice by the Company but the covert malice of a system that conspired at every turn to keep the Huaorani politically powerless. All too often anyone outside the Company or the government who tried to help the Huaorani was threatened with deportation, jail, or worse. The Huaorani were forced to negotiate contracts and other agreements without the counsel of lawyers or advisers, and they remained almost completely ignorant of their rights under Ecuadorian law.

When I voiced these thoughts to Jiménez, he looked genuinely surprised. "The Huaorani don't need advisers," he said. "Why should they? We are going to make a fair contract with them. It will be a simple contract. It will be so simple, in fact, that they will not need help reading it."

I WENT to the Quito office of Dr. David Neill, an associate curator of the Missouri Botanical Garden. Maxus had hired Neill to catalog and replant the forest that would be destroyed as the Block Sixteen Road was built, and, with great fanfare, pointed to Neill's project as proof that it could extract oil from the forest without doing permanent damage. Neill started to describe his reforestation program for me, then stopped, let out a long sigh, and said, "Technically, our program might work—we can grow trees—but so what, if somebody comes in and cuts them down? I'm not optimistic. People need to survive. The colonists are going to go in there, because they have no alternative."

· · ·

ONE OF the rights nominally guaranteed to Indians in Ecuador is to be shielded from contact with private petroleum interests. Manuel Navarro, the Petroecuador executive charged with overseeing the relationship between the Indians and the Company, told me that under Ecuadorian law foreign oil companies were prohibited from negotiating directly with the Indian groups, because such contact jeopardizes the Indians. (It was just this law, in fact, behind which such companies as ARCO and Texaco hid when they were accused of ignoring the Indians on whose land they were drilling for oil.) I spoke with Navarro in his Quito office. That very day, he said, he had written a letter to Maxus, because he'd heard that Maxus had been dividing the Huaorani by creating "hateful differences" between various groups.

Then why, I asked, did he permit Maxus to deal directly with the Huaorani?

Navarro smiled, then narrowed his eyes and squinted, as if delivering a lecture on the fundamentals of petroleum jurisprudence: Maxus didn't like that law, so it didn't apply to them. "They don't have much confidence in us," he explained.

So, as part of the deal that allowed the company to develop oil in the Huaorani territory, the Ecuadorian government had essentially put Maxus in charge of Huaorani health and education—much as it once had the Summer Institute of Linguistics. The government's bureaucrats had a dozen different ways to justify this, but the heart of the matter was that they were only too happy not to have to bother with the Huaorani.

To Moi, at least, it all boiled down to a rather basic equation: "We were sold like meat."

PART THREE

Among the Cannibals

13

I GOT a lot of weird telephone calls in Quito. The lines crackled
and popped without logic. A call from the United States might
come in clear as a bell, and a call from down the street would
sound like a hurricane. Or the phone would ring once and stop,
and five minutes later I would pick it up and find someone on the line.
Or three or four people. One day the phone rang, I answered and said
hello, and behind a wall of static I heard a small, distant voice. "José,"
it said. "*Change.*" And then nothing.

"Hello?" I said again.

"José. *Change.*"

"Hello, this is José," I shouted. "Who is speaking?"

"José. *Change.*"

I hung up, but a few minutes later the phone rang again, and we ran
through the same routine. This time, however, the voice was louder,
and I thought I detected a slightly nasal inflection. "Moi?" I asked.
Nothing. "Nanto?" Nothing. "*Enqueri?*"

"Yes! *Change.*"

Later, I would learn that the Huaorani spoke on the telephone as if
they were speaking face to face. I was supposed to know who was on the
line without being told. As for *cambio*, the Spanish word for "change,"
in this case it was the equivalent of the English word "over." Enqueri
may have grown up without a telephone, but he had long since mastered the lingo of the radio transceiver.

"Enqueri, where are you?"

"I am here. *Change.*"

"Where?"

"Speaking to you. *Change*."

"Yes, but *where*? What *place*?"

"I am in Quito! I am coming to your house! *Change*." He had found his way to the office of the Rainforest Information Centre, but Ali Sharif had gone to the United States of North America and Enqueri didn't know any of the other cannibals. He said that he had the map I had drawn for Amo, and that he could get to my apartment without my help. There was no talking him out of it, though I took some comfort from the fact that the RIC office was only six blocks away.

"Enqueri, are you alone?"

"Yes! *Change*."

"Be careful. Come directly here."

"I will be there right now. José, I need some shoes! *Change*."

I hurried down to the street to wait. I waited there for three hours. Finally, I spotted Enqueri loping up the block, looking solemn and purposeful. He had said he was alone, and I suppose by Huaorani standards he was. Behind him came a line of six other Huaorani, ambling slowly and silently up the sidewalk single file: Nanto; his wife, Alicia, and on her back their two-year-old daughter, Rocia; Salomón; and Yacata and Tigue, from Garzacocha. Each of them had a small string bag slung over a shoulder, and Enqueri and Nanto were carrying spears. Alicia wore a red cotton dress, the men T-shirts and blue jeans. Their clothing was clean but thin, and their shoulders were hunched against the chilly Andean air. When they reached me they simply stopped walking and stood on the sidewalk and looked at the ground or at the sky, as if waiting for a signal.

I stuck out my hand. Each man gave it a pat.

"Good life," I said. "Are you still alive?"

"We are still alive," Enqueri said.

"We are hungry," Nanto said.

"We are cold," Enqueri said.

"We came in a taxi from the bus station," Nanto said.

"The taximan took all our money," Enqueri said.

"Come," I said.

They rode the elevator in silence. They looked scared, and after we entered my apartment Enqueri pushed the door to make sure it was shut tight and then he bolted all three locks. "Now we are safe," he said. "Where do you keep your clothes?"

Before I could answer him the Huaorani had distributed themselves throughout the apartment, and they emerged from the various rooms wearing jackets, sweaters, sweatpants, hats, sunglasses, and, in Salomón's case, my one tie, wrapped around his head like a crown. Nanto turned on the radio, found some *rocnrol*, and pumped up the volume. The others reclined on the floor and on the couch and within moments appeared to have entered a state of grace that from all outward signs was nearly as complete as if they'd been in their hammocks in the forest.

I went into the kitchen to fry up a couple of chickens. Alicia followed me every step of the way and imitated everything I did. She looked in the refrigerator, she turned on the water faucet. When I stepped toward the stove, she stepped toward the stove; when I stepped back, she stepped back.

"What are you doing?" I asked.

She laughed, shyly. "So I can know your world," she said.

I showed her how to cook the chicken, and then we put it out on the table with some bananas and avocados and bread, a pineapple, and three cans of tuna fish. When we had finished eating, each of the Huaorani said thank you, and then they carried the plates into the kitchen and washed all the dishes. They came into the living room and Enqueri opened his string bag and pulled out a hammock. It was a spectacular piece of work, woven of hand-spun palm cord and dyed the traditional Huaorani red, from achiote seed.

"This is for you," Enqueri said. "My mother made it."

"It's beautiful," I said. "She must have worked very hard."

"Three weeks," Enqueri said. "Sometimes she rested, because her hands swelled up as she worked."

I offered to pay him for the hammock, but he would not hear of it.

"Where will we sleep?" he asked.

We hauled out three mattresses and arranged them side by side on the living-room floor. Enqueri chose to sleep alone in my office, but the others yanked sheets out of their string bags and handed them to me. Nanto explained that they always carried sheets because they never knew where they might be sleeping. A few nights ago, he said, they had camped near the Shiripuno bridge. "Last night we slept in a bus station," he said. "We were cold like ice cream."

"Do you have any ice cream?" Alicia asked.

"No," I said. "We will find some tomorrow."

"And pizza," Nanto said.

"The sheets!" Salomón said. They arranged themselves carefully on the mattresses, one next to another, and told me to put the sheets on top of them. I tucked each of them in. They cackled with glee.

"Blankets!" Salomón commanded, and I went into the bedrooms and brought out four heavy wool blankets and piled them on one by one.

"More blankets!" Nanto yelled.

"More!" Alicia squealed, and little Rocia waved her tiny hands. I pulled out three more blankets.

"More!" Yacata said. "The Huaorani need ten blankets in Quito!"

By the time I had finished I had buried them under every blanket in the house, a pile six inches thick. I was exhausted then, and went to bed. A little after 3:00 a.m. I awoke to the smell of smoke. I pulled on my pants and raced into the living room. Smoke was billowing out of the kitchen. Squinting, I saw Enqueri and Nanto and Salomón huddled over the stove.

"José, are you hungry?" Enqueri yelled.

At first I couldn't tell what they were cooking, except that as I looked at it it seemed to be looking back at me. Then I saw the feet. When you buy a chicken in Ecuador, the claws and head come stuffed inside the body, and when I had prepared dinner I had discarded them. Salomón had fished the scraps out of the garbage, and then he and Nanto and Enqueri burned them to a crisp.

They ate everything, including the bones.

I went back to bed. Two hours later Enqueri jostled me awake. "What is for breakfast?" he asked.

THE HUAORANI could not have come at a better time for me. It had been two weeks since I had put my wife and daughter on a plane for the United States. In the months they had been in Quito, we had settled into a routine so comfortable that I had all but forgotten it would have to end. But end it did, my wife's maternity leave stretched to the breaking point. I'll be home soon, I'd promised. What was left unsaid was that there was no way to predict when that would be. I knew only that there was much about what had brought me to Ecuador that I did not yet understand.

Into the gloom of my isolation the Huaorani spilled like a traveling circus. My apartment filled anew with talk and laughter and the cries of a small child. That next morning, while we ate breakfast—oatmeal, rice, boiled eggs, a kind of sweet tamale called *humitas*, pineapple, peanut butter, lollipops—Enqueri read the newspaper aloud, loudly, as if reciting its contents for a class. "José," he yelled at one point, "who is Clinton William?" And, "What is the difference between *national* and *international?*" And, "In the United States of North America, do airplanes have ovens and karate movies?"

A story on the front page said that the national Indian organization, the Confederation of the Indigenous Nations of Ecuador (CONAIE, under which both Andean and Amazonian Indian federations, including CONFENIAE, were incorporated), had called for "civil disobedience" to protest the latest round of economic austerity measures. Ecuador had recently elected a new, conservative president, Sixto Durán Ballén. Immediately after the election, Sixto flew to the United States to meet with George Bush and try to borrow some more money; shortly after he took office the price of staples once again tripled overnight (and the Bush administration nominated the president of a Texas oil company to be its ambassador to Ecuador). The CONAIE uprising was a bold move, an almost frontal attack on the new government by the largest Indian confederation in the country. There had been scattered bombings, and the government had fully mobilized the armed forces; there were tanks in the streets. And yet, though the Huaorani federation was, ostensibly, one of the groups CONAIE represented, the newspaper report held about as much interest for the Huaorani as if it had been about the war between Iran and Iraq.

"Engineer Enqueri," Nanto said, "read me some more things."

"Doctor Nanto, educate yourself!" Enqueri said, and tossed the paper at him.

"Professor Salomón," Nanto said, "what does this newspaper say about life among the cannibals?"

"Doctor Nanto," Salomón said, "this newspaper says that the can-nibals wear things on their things!"

Ingeniero, doctor, profesor—these were the titles by which petro-leum officials most often referred to themselves, and the Huaorani invoked them with the exact tone of inflated self-importance. It was a hilarious performance; I'd forgotten what excellent mimics they were.

There was another story in the day's paper that was lost on the Huaorani but was perhaps of far greater import to them: The new government had announced that it was withdrawing from the Organi-zation of Petroleum Exporting Countries. By doing so it would be free to increase oil production in the Oriente, which it proposed to double within five years.

THE HUAORANI HAD come to Quito to do business. Nanto said that the Company had promised to build a school in Garzacocha, but it had given the money to the Quichua federation in Coca and put the Quichuas in charge of the construction project and there was no school. "The Company says it does not trust us with the money," Nanto said. "But if the school is for the Huaorani, then the money should go to the Huaorani." He intended to talk to the Company about it.

Meanwhile, he and Moi had sent another letter to Maxus that said the Huaorani did not want Maxus in their territory. Nanto said that Maxus had invited him to come to Quito to discuss the letter, and that morning he and Yacata, Salomón, and Tigue were going to go there. They knew the way. "Enqueri will wait here," he said, and so would Alicia and Rocia.

After they had gone, I asked Enqueri why he was staying behind. He shrugged. "Nanto is my chief, and that is what he has told me to do, and so that is what I must do." His tone was one of unquestioning obei-sance, and it represented a new and distinctly modern attitude that had crept into Huaorani culture with the arrival of the evangelical mission-aries and the strict authoritarianism of their schools and teachings. Until then the Huaorani had been highly egalitarian—no orders were given, few requests were made. While ONHAE appeared to have in-corporated this traditional sharing of power—the *asamblea* in Que-hueire Ono, for example, had been a wide open, if not chaotic, affair—at times it also displayed the fanatical devotion to central authority that has, in one way or another, been the legacy of the Summer Institute of Linguistics throughout Latin America. I asked Enqueri if he still considered himself an *evangelista*.

"Only at one time of the year," he said.

"When?"

"Christmas."

Meanwhile, Enqueri appeared to be taking his new position as secretary quite seriously. He showed me a pamphlet he had picked up somewhere in his travels: *How to Manage People*. "I want to be the best officer in ONHAE," he said. He had been appointed to his current positions, but he aspired to elected office. "Now is my chance to prove myself," he said. "I could have been elected vice president instead of Moi, but at that time I thought it would be better if I advised Nanto and helped him to do his job. But now I am ready to serve my people." He said that he had given Nanto a copy of the pamphlet, but Nanto had ignored it. "I am worried about him," he said. "He has something strange going on with the Company. That is why he did not bring me to this meeting today. The others, they will do anything. But Nanto knows that I will know, and so he keeps me away. Did you notice that he is getting fat?"

I had noticed: Nanto was growing a potbelly. Compared with the tautly muscled bodies of the other young Huaorani men, it stood out like a watermelon on a putting green.

Nanto and Salomón returned a couple of hours later. Nanto had a wild look in his eye, as if the city had wound him up to the bursting point.

"How did it go?" I asked.

"More or less," he said, and wiggled his right hand in the way the Huaorani sometimes do, as if to say, "There is more going on here than I know how to explain in your language." Yacata and Tigue were gone, he said; they had set out for Garzacocha.

"How will they get there?"

He shrugged. "There are ways," he said.

Salomón simply laughed and displayed a small clay pot somebody had given him. To my eye there was nothing exceptional about it, but I knew Salomón well enough to know that he would carry it for weeks, then give it away. In fact, he would manage to range far and wide—from Quito to Shell, perhaps, and then maybe to Tena, and then, eventually, down the Vía Auca or through the forest and back to To-ñampare—carrying nothing but the pot and the clothes on his back and his stories about sex with rocks and trees and horses. Light as a bird and free to fly, the nomad's nomad.

THAT AFTERNOON I had errands to run and an appointment to interview Judith Kimerling. Nanto and Enqueri and Salomón insisted on coming with me: Perhaps there would be food. Alicia would wait in my apartment, because Rocia was terribly sick. She had a severe respiratory ailment of some sort, quite possibly an early stage of tuberculosis. She had hacked all through the previous night, from deep in her lungs, loudly and painfully. But she had not cried—she was a brave child, Huaorani through and through. Nanto said that she had been sick for weeks, and that he hoped to get medicine at a hospital in Quito. He did not know how he would pay for it.

We went down to the street and set off on foot in a light rain. As ever the Huaorani walked in single file, heads down, checking the pavement for snakes. At corners I had to grab them before they plunged into traffic. At one corner I turned around and they were gone.

I ran back the way we had come, and off to my right, down a side street, I saw what looked like a small huddle of people and hurried toward it. It was the Huaorani, their arms wrapped around one another. Lost in the midst of cannibals, they'd circled their wagons, such as they were. The problem? As we had crossed one street, a *cowode* wearing a bright blue nylon jacket like mine had passed in front of them, and Enqueri, glancing up, had turned and followed him. "But then you stopped and turned around and you were not you!" Enqueri said. Then he and Nanto and Salomón laughed—in its way it was simply another canoe disaster. But they had been seriously frightened. I understood their panic: They felt exactly as I had in the forest, when after a few wrong steps into the bush a green wall had closed around me and I had felt cut off from any return to the world I knew.

We walked.

"Engineer Nanto," I yelled over my shoulder, "what shall we eat today?"

"Professor José, we shall eat chicken and rice!"

We went to a supermarket—the Supermaxi—and I planted them in front of a bin of frozen chicken, dozens of plump carcasses skinned, plucked, wrapped in plastic, and displayed for the choosing. "Pick some good ones and put them in the shopping cart," I said, and went to buy bread and fruit. I came back ten minutes later to find the cart still empty and the Huaorani standing almost exactly as I had left them. Briefly, I watched them from a distance: Nanto would whisper something to Enqueri, and Enqueri would whisper to Salomón, and one of them would start to pick up a chicken, then recoil. The forest seldom presented such an array of choices all at once: If the chickens had been wild turkeys, the Huaorani would have killed what they could and the rest would have fled. But a supermarket—that was *abundancia* of a whole new order.

I grabbed three big birds and threw them into the cart. The Huaorani followed me single file through the store, and when we hit the street they hoisted the bags on top of their heads and marched through the cement jungle with an air of great purpose, if not destiny.

JUDITH KIMERLING'S apartment was stacked with books and papers and files. The Huaorani sat themselves on a couch and took coffee when it was offered and studied the room in silence. I had no doubt that by the time we left they would have memorized nearly its entire contents.

Kimerling asked them about Amo's death. Nanto explained the burn holes and his suspicions of how Amo had died.

"Did you ask the police to examine the body?" Kimerling asked.

"We had no money to buy a doctor," Nanto said.

"You do not have to pay for something like that," Kimerling said. "In Ecuador, the police are obligated to make a full investigation of such a death. It is your right to have the body examined if you want that done."

"The police have to do that?" Nanto asked.

"Yes. If you want, they can do it without cutting open the body— they can put it on a machine that sees right through the skin."

The Huaorani looked at one another in amazement.

"This is just one of many rights you are guaranteed," Kimerling continued. "You are also guaranteed the right to live in a clean and safe environment. Do you know what that means?"

"It means the Company cannot poison us," Enqueri said, urgently. "And it means that the Shuar cannot take our land and that we can fight them if we need to."

"If the Indians are busy fighting one another, the Company can do as it pleases," Kimerling said. "The Huaorani and the Shuar and the Quichua must try to work together. All of you have certain rights that the whole world has agreed to. You have the right to live in a healthy place. You have the right to survive in the way you judge to be best. You have the right to stop the Company from destroying your way of life." She said that these rights and many other things would be discussed at the meeting in Coca.

"What meeting?" Nanto asked.

Kimerling looked surprised. There would be a meeting in Coca the following week, she said. All the Indian nations had been invited, and all the environmental groups in Quito, and all the colonists who had been poisoned by the Company, and many other people from around the world. "No one can fight the Company alone," she said. "But if we work together, the Company will have to listen to us."

"Why were we not invited?" Enqueri asked.

"CONFENIAE told me they had invited you," Kimerling said.

In the silence that followed you could have heard a toucan feather drop.

"Well, you must be there," Kimerling said. "If you are not, everyone else will speak for the Huaorani."

"That is what always happens," Enqueri said. "CONFENIAE will speak for us, and they will arrange it so they can steal things for themselves."

"If you feel that way, then you must be there," Kimerling said.

"We will be there," Enqueri said.

WHEN WE GOT back to my apartment it took us a good ten minutes to talk our way in. Alicia had locked every lock and dead bolt and couldn't figure out how to undo them. Imagine my surprise, then, to finally get inside and find Moi and his cousin Raúl kneeling on the living-room floor, bent over a set of maps.

"Good life, Chong," Moi said, without looking up. Raúl said nothing at all.

"Good life, Moi," I said. "How did you get here?"

"Everything and everyone is entering from all sides," he said. He was studying a map of the oil concessions. "More contamination, more colonization. This must stop. If it does not stop we will have to kill people." He said this so matter-of-factly that I believed him entirely. Finally, he looked up. "We are hungry," he said.

I went into the kitchen and unloaded the bags. Raúl followed me in. I put a stalk of bananas on the table, and while I unpacked the groceries he ate the bananas one by one, until he had eaten all thirteen of them. He piled the skins neatly on the counter, and he didn't say a word. I hadn't met him before. He was a powerfully built man, even for a Huao. He smelled as if he'd been living in the same pants and shirt and cheap tennis shoes for a week, and I assumed he was a backcountry rookie brought out of the territory to catch a glimpse of life among the cannibals. As it turned out, he was the president of Quehueire Ono. He had helped organize the split from the missionaries, and he had been instrumental in opening the school. Now he figured it was time to talk to the new president of Ecuador. "We have told the Company to get out," he said. "Somebody does not seem to understand."

Then he went into my bedroom and took off his clothes and found some clothes of mine and brought his laundry out and asked me to wash it. When I said I would, everyone else gave me their clothes and sheets and followed me into the tiny laundry room and watched while I loaded the *máquina*. "Use lots of soap," Raúl said. Other than that, no one said a word. Later, when the machine had finished, they followed me back into the laundry and lined up along the walls and watched me hang things up to dry. I felt like I was being stalked.

That evening, squeaky clean, we walked to a nice restaurant not far from my apartment. When the Huaorani entered, they were met by chilly stares from diners and staff alike. I'd forgotten how it was. The restaurant was across the street from the Oro Verde, the best hotel in the city. A standard single room cost more for a night than a Huaorani laborer could earn in a three-month shift for the Company. It was where the U.S. Agency for International Development put up its employees while they were looking for housing; one AID couple I knew had spent six months in a suite that cost $200 a day, a fact that lent perspective to the $15 millon budget AID was overseeing for the development of "ecotourism" and "sustainable resource extraction" in Ecuador. On more than one occasion I'd run across U.S. Army troops garrisoned in the Oro Verde while on their way to the Oriente.

We sat down and the waiter distributed menus and left. I explained the various choices: soup, bread, "leaves" (salad); fish, beef, chicken; rice, beans, plantains.

The waiter returned.

"Ice cream," Nanto said.

"Ice cream," Enqueri said.

"Ice cream," Moi said.

"Ice cream," Alicia said.

"Ice cream," Salomón said.

"Ice cream," Raúl said.

I ordered dinners for all of them, great platters of everything on the menu. They dove into it. Halfway through the meal I felt the table rocking and I glanced up to find Enqueri convulsed in silent laughter.

"What?" I asked.

"Enqueri looked at his hands and look how he found himself eating!" he said. He held up his hands, a fork in each.

"Two forks!" Nanto said, and erupted in laughter.

"Like this!" Enqueri said, and made a carving motion, as if one fork were a knife.

"Two!" Moi said, and threw his head back and roared.

"Two!" Raúl said. He laughed so hard his forehead hit his beans.

"Two!" Salomón said. "Maybe the Condor has two things!"

After a while they went back to work. Raúl was sitting next to me. He asked, "Where does the president live?"

"In his palace."

"Where is that?"

"Not too far from here."

He thought about that. Then he said, "I think we should go there and kill him." He said this as much to himself as to me, and then he was silent.

We cleaned every plate on the table. We ordered ice cream. We ordered more.

Raúl spoke up again. "I know how we could do it," he said.

"Do what?"

"Kill the president."

"How?"

"We will put fishhooks in his rice." He nodded to himself, satisfied that this would work. Then he bent himself to the task at hand, as if concentrating on his plate with every bone in his body.

BACK AT THE apartment building the night watchman was on duty, and as we entered he took me aside. "Sir," he whispered. "These people are savages." He gave the Huaorani a nervous glance.

"Absolutely," I said.

"There is no telling what they might do."

"No telling at all."

"They have spears . . ."

"They will pierce a man like butter."

"Nice shoes," Moi called out, and then he ducked into the elevator.

Enqueri worked the elevator without a hitch. Once inside my apartment he started to bolt all the locks.

"Enqueri," I said, "it is safe here. You don't have to worry so much."

"Can the police get in?"

"Of course."

"I thought so," he said, and continued until nothing short of a battering ram could threaten us.

Sometime during the night the Huaorani made their plan: Enqueri would travel down the Vía Auca and from there go to as many Huaorani communities as he could in a week's time and bring them to Coca for the meeting. Raúl would return to Quehueire Ono to fetch Mengato-hue. Moi and Salomón would take a bus directly to the Napo River, to alert some of the Quichua villages to the meeting. "Let everyone come and talk," Moi said. To pay for bus fare they would sell the spears they had brought to Quito. Once in the forest, they would travel entirely by foot.

When he had finished explaining this plan to me, Moi said, "Chong."

"Yes?"

"After the meeting you will come with us into the forest and you will stay with the People again. You will come to the center of the world, where you will be safe."

Nanto and his family left town the next morning, bound for Toñampare. Nanto would miss the meeting; Rocia had to be at home. They would stop at a medical clinic in Quito—someone at the Rainforest Information Centre had arranged a visit—and then they would travel by bus to Shell. From there they would try to latch onto an Alas de Socorro flight. I gave Nanto and Alicia some baby clothes my wife had left behind and let them pick through my own clothes for things that would keep them warm on their long journey. (They asked the same question of each item: "Is this waterproof?") They chose baseball hats, a pair of old tennis shoes, a couple of pairs of khakis, and a beat-up day pack. "Gift me your sunglasses," Nanto said, and after he had settled them in place he and his family walked out the door, looking as if they were bound for Disneyland.

Late that afternoon I found Moi in my office, fingering my backpack, a state-of-the-art model I'd brought from home.

"This *mochila* is very beautiful," he said.

"Of course," I said.

"In the forest one could walk many days with this *mochila*."

This was followed by a moment of silence, but I knew I'd been had.

"It is yours," I said.

He grinned then, and hoisted the pack on his shoulders. "*Puro cowode*," he said.

I asked him about the Maxus situation. Building of the road had begun; it would reach the Huaorani territory in a matter of months, and if all went as planned, the first production well would open within a year. Moi seemed concerned but not upset. "We will kill the Company if we have to," he said. He thought for a moment. "The Huaorani protect the forest for the whole world," he said. "If the whole world will come and see what the Company is doing, the whole world will make the Company stop."

"Do you really think the Company can be stopped?"

"I know it," he said, and pointed out that in Huaorani, his name means "dream," as in a vision.

"Chong," he said.

Along the pipeline

Ruptured oil-waste pit

On the Cononaco River

Enqueri (right)

Quemperi   Moi (left)

Mengatohue showing Huaorani schoolchildren how the Huaorani dressed before the arrival of the evangelical missionaries

ONHAE leaders at the Toñampare *asamblea*, from left: Tementa, Pancho, Salomón, Nanto

Enqueri (right) and Nanto conferring with Rachel Saint during the *asamblea* at Toñampare

Enqueri (with microphone) and Moi addressing Coca meeting

Dinner being prepared in
Huaorani home,
Cononaco

Author, Moi, Mengatohue
(in background) at
Moi's home

Moi (right) on the
Shiripuno River

Mengatohue gathering
ayahuasca

Mengatohue (left), author

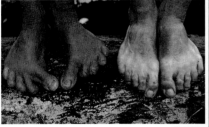

Mengatohue

Amo in Coca

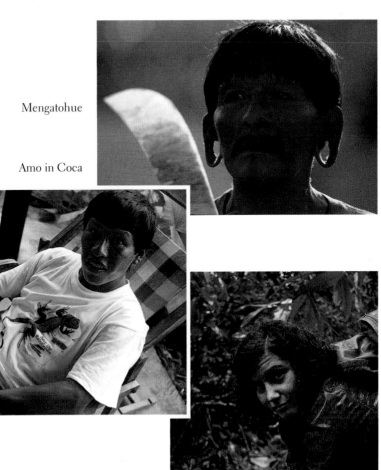

Judith Kimerling at former
Texaco well site

Nanto and family

Inside Huaorani home, Cononaco

Home of Moi's family, in Quehueire Ono

"Yes?"

"If we do not stop the Company the Huaorani will disappear forever."

MOI AND Raúl and Salomón left my apartment that afternoon. Later, I rented a car, a sturdy four-wheel-drive Trooper, and the next morning Enqueri and I picked up a couple of my friends who needed a lift and we set off for Coca. I had some research to do there, and Enqueri was bound for the Vía Auca. However, in the wake of Amo's death and the subsequent threats by the Shuar, Enqueri was afraid to travel alone, and he asked if I'd drive him to the Shiripuno bridge.

"What about the checkpoint?" I asked.

"Enqueri will arrange it," he said. "Enqueri has friends everywhere."

We drove into the frigid dawn, climbed to the continental divide, and for the next ten hours followed the twisty, desolate dirt track that runs down through the eastern slope of the Andes into the Amazon. Somewhere short of Coca the road straightened out for a couple of miles, and we were humming along at forty miles an hour when without warning the road bent tightly into an S curve and spilled onto a log bridge one side of which had been washed out. We slid through the curve snapping right and left like a caiman tail and came screeching to a halt at the extreme left side of the bridge, rocking like a teeter-totter on the right-front and left-rear wheels. The left-front wheel gripped nothing but air and bobbed up and down over a thirty-foot drop directly into a river. I set the hand brake and kept my foot on the brake pedal while Enqueri and the others inched out the right-rear passenger window and stood on the right-rear wheel and then I limboed after them and we stood there on the wheel and listened to our hearts race and tried to hold the truck in place. We waited for what seemed like two hours before a bus approached from the other direction and eighteen men, some barefoot and some in rags and some drunk, climbed out and slung ropes and cables around the truck and heaved and hauled it back to safety. "You were lucky," the driver said. "Last week a bus drove right off the bridge."

It was still two hours into Coca. Enqueri's thin shoulders shook all the way there. He didn't say a word until we hit town and went to the Huaorani Hotel and found some Huaorani hanging out. Enqueri told them the story of our near-fatality three times, and by the final telling he had worked through his fear. "Once I almost killed José and now José almost killed me!" he said. Then he laughed as if he'd never heard anything funnier in his life.

IN THE MORNING we went shopping for shoes. We visited three of the plank-and-tin stalls that line Coca's market block before Enqueri found precisely what he was looking for, a pair of plastic-coated Colombian-made loafers with bright gold-painted buckles.

"Thank you," he said, gravely.

He was wearing his new shoes and a serious expression the next morning when we drove out the Vía Auca. At the checkpoint he convinced the soldier on duty that I was some kind of petroleum worker. Three hours later we passed the office of the Shuar colonist association. Enqueri didn't say a word, and he remained silent at the spot where Amo had died. But he brightened when I left him near Babae's settlement. I told him I'd see him in Coca in two weeks.

"I will bring you a spear," he said. "And a string bag for your wife. You will tell her, 'Enqueri cannot be with us, but he is here in this *shigra*.'"

"She would like that," I said. "Be careful."

"Yes," he said. Then he was gone, his bright golden buckles flashing through the mud.

NANTO AND his family arrived back in Toñampare three days later. The news that Nanto received then was not good: The Company had begun seismic testing within a mile of the village. The work was being performed by Seiscom Delta, an American subcontractor that had a reputation for arrogance extreme even by the standards of the Oriente. Indian communities—especially the Cofan, the Secoya, and the Quichua, whose lands had been the most heavily explored—charged that the company regularly entered without informing them and without doing so much as the minimal paperwork required by the government, and cut seismic lines and blasted dynamite without regard for homes, villages, hunting trails, or water supplies. It had been only a few months since a Quichua federation along the Napo had waged a strike against the company, blocking all access roads. At about the same time, the Cofan had kidnapped an entire crew that they caught working illegally in their territory.

In Nanto's absence the Huaorani of Toñampare had handled things in their own way: They raided the camp. The workers fled, and the Huaorani took whatever they could carry. The military escorted the workers back; the Huaorani raided the camp again. Shortly after Nanto's return, Petroecuador officials flew into Toñampare to try to smooth things over. They spoke with Nanto. "What do you want?" one of the men asked, and his co-workers reached into the Company helicopter and hauled out a plastic bag filled with aluminum pots, cigarettes, knives and forks, rice, bath soap, candy bars, and chocolate-chip cookies. The man showed Nanto an envelope full of cash. Torn between the political position of ONHAE (absolutely opposed to the Company) and the old loyalties of clan and family (what do you have to eat?), Nanto opted for the latter, accepting the gifts and distributing them in Toñampare. The money he kept for himself.

Nanto's decision meant that the Company would be back. They would bring more things; they would look for their oil. If they found it, one day the rivers in Rachel Saint's protectorate—where 80 percent of the Huaorani lived, where the resources they depended on were already stretched precariously thin, and where the Huaorani had little choice but to stay, since there was nowhere else for them to go—one day, surely, those rivers would run black with Amazon crude.

14

WHAT DOES the future hold for the Huaorani?" José Miguel Goldáraz, the Capuchin priest, repeated when I asked him. "Go see Lago Agrio." Around Coca the oil business was still relatively small, just getting its legs, but up in Lago the Company had been pumping oil big-time for twenty years.

From Coca I drove north on a wide, oil-soaked dirt track. The forest had long since been cut back from the road, obliterated, but out toward the horizon you could see fragments of canopy swaying in the breeze. Three hours later I was in Lago Agrio. It was maybe five times the size of Coca. Five times as loud, five times as filthy, five times as desperate. It wasn't supposed to be that way. When the Company carved the town out of swamp and forest, it promised prosperity such as the Oriente had never known. Today, 90 percent of the oil produced in the Oriente flows through Lago Agrio, but Lago itself is a violent, disease-ridden slum. A gallon of gasoline, or, for that matter, access to any device that might require it, is a luxury beyond the means of all but a few, and only then if there is gas for sale. The day I showed up, every pump in town was dry. At midnight electricity was cut off in those parts of town that had it, and Lago Agrio went black. Everywhere, that is, but at the military compound near the edge of town, where bright fluorescent floodlights shone all night long on a giant Petroecuador billboard. The billboard featured an oil well poised over a company slogan: "Returning the earth's riches to the people."

I had arrived in Lago late in the day, and I left as early as I could the next morning and drove east along the Aguarico River, passing through the hamlet of Dureno. It was near here, in the Cofan settlement also known as Dureno, that Texaco perforated its first commercial oil well, in 1972. The Cofan Indians had a small but thriving nation then; today Cofans still inhabit the area, but they are a listless and defeated bunch. The few who have survived the oil boom with their dignity and spirit intact have fled far down the Aguarico, beyond the oil roads. Dureno proper is a handful of colonist shacks. So is Pacayacu, the next hamlet along the road, but the oil well there is newer. It was installed after the town had sprung up, and to placate the outraged locals the Company built a church right in front of the well. The church is blue and white, the Petroecuador colors, and the Petroecuador logo is painted on the floor of the vestibule.

The Cuyabeno Wildlife Reserve begins not far beyond Dureno. Cuyabeno is an area of extraordinary biological wealth, famous the world over for its spectacular lakes and *varzeas*, or flooded forests. It is so rich, in fact, that it was the first wildlife reserve created in Ecuador, and in 1991 its territory was increased by half, to some 1.6 million acres. It enjoys the highest level of environmental protection afforded under Ecuadorian law. Yet Petroecuador, City Investing (which is based in Texas), and Clyde Petroleum, a British company, are producing or have produced oil in the reserve. Occidental has begun exploration, and many of the Texaco wells are nearby. The oil roads opened more than a third of Cuyabeno to colonization, though this is expressly forbidden by law, and more than four thousand families have settled there. The government has made no attempt to remove them. Illegal logging is so widespread that the military was called in to stop it, but couldn't. So much of the original reserve has been destroyed by oil development that in many areas there is no wildlife left to protect.

Between 1984 and 1990 there were at least six major oil spills in Cuyabeno. Five of these were ignored, but when news of the sixth reached Quito, Petroecuador was forced to stage a cleanup. It hired colonists to remove some 44,000 gallons of petroleum from the polluted waters by scooping the waste up bare-handed and dumping it into plastic bags. The bags, some of them already leaking from tears and machete holes, were then buried near the lakes.

Crude oil is extremely toxic, and in Quito I had asked Manuel

Navarro, the Petroecuador executive, to confirm the reports about the cleanups. Navarro didn't dispute the facts, but he said that times had changed. "We learned all we knew from Texaco," he said. "Now we have assumed control of the Texaco operations. For a foreign oil company to treat Ecuadorians in such a manner is one thing, but for us to treat our countrymen that way would be unconscionable. We have hired the very best consultants to help us design and implement the most modern techniques of contaminant treatment. Any suggestion that we would ask men to clean up oil with their bare hands is a gross distortion of the facts."

But as I crested a small hill deep inside Cuyabeno, what I saw before me was no mirage. A hundred men were distributed around a lagoon of oil the size of three football fields. Some of the men were pushing wheelbarrows toward a dump truck parked at the roadside, but most of them were standing in the lagoon, scooping mud and oil into wheelbarrows, or cutting up oil-soaked logs with chain saws and axes. Some of them were ankle deep in the lagoon, and some were in it up to their knees.

It was two o'clock in the afternoon there on the equator, and the air fairly sizzled. The men were more than happy to take a break. A skinny, one-armed black man buttonholed me with his good wing, and a short, stout Latino asked me what I was doing.

"I am looking for contamination," I said.

"Here it is!" the black man said, and laughed. The spill had happened twelve years ago, he said. Though we were well inside the reserve, this lagoon was part of a coffee field—*his* coffee field. He had asked the Company to clean it up, but for twelve years it had ignored him. Now word was getting out about Cuyabeno—getting out of Ecuador, that is—and the Company was hustling to hide what it had done.

"They will be here to throw you out in about five minutes," the Latino man said. His name was Miguel. All of the men were colonists, he said, but their land was so polluted that they could grow hardly anything at all. The only way to survive was to work cleanup for the Company. They were paid about a dollar a day. They worked six days a week, sunup to sundown. The Company gave them boots and a liter of diesel fuel to wash up with. "We asked for gloves," Miguel said, "but the Company refused."

By then a crowd had gathered. To a man they were covered with crude from their feet to their waists, and from their hands to their shoulders. When I asked about their health, several men thrust out their arms, and beneath the dark film of crude I could see raw, infected skin. "These things you can live with," Miguel said. "But there are more serious problems. Malaria, and intestinal problems, and hard breathing and pains in the chest." That was not surprising. Baking in the equatorial sun, the spilled crude gave off the same sort of heavy fumes that I'd inhaled when patching my house with roofing tar. Here, though, they were far more intense. Though I'd been out in the open air less than fifteen minutes, my throat was completely parched, I felt dizzy, and my head had begun to ache.

"If you get sick and don't show up for work, you don't get paid," Miguel said. "A man who is sick will keep on working until he passes out on the job."

Did this happen often?

"One or two men a week."

Did they tell this to the Company?

"Yes, but they say we are lying."

Did they have access to medical care?

"No."

"The price of coffee is down," the one-armed man said, "and the price of everything else is up." They were glad to have any work at all.

Suddenly a gleaming yellow pickup truck barreled over the rise and skidded to a halt, and two men in Petroecuador uniforms and mirrored sunglasses jumped out and inserted themselves between me and the workers. As they hustled me away, a man yelled from the crowd. "They say it is the colonists who cause the contamination," he said. "But it is not us—it is the Company! Be sure you tell people that!"

THE TWO MEN led me to the white-brick Petroecuador headquarters, which fairly sparkled in the afternoon sun. I followed the truck in through an electronic steel gate, past a chain-link fence topped with barbed wire. The air smelled of jasmine. The *jefe* was gone, and so was the *subjefe*, but the *subsubjefe*, Hugo Vargas, showed me into a cool, dark office. An air conditioner hummed in the background. Vargas reached into a refrigerator, pulled out a bottle, and poured a glass of mineral water. He had long, black whiskers, and his thick, black hair was piled high on his head in a greased pompadour. His Company-blue shirt and pants were starched, pressed, and spotless. He handed me the glass and smiled. The glass was ice cold.

"What are you doing here?" he asked, and continued to smile.

"I have heard there were problems."

"Problems? Perhaps you misunderstood."

"I was told there were oil spills here, things like that."

"There are no problems. As you can see, we are engaged in a vigorous cleanup program. But sometimes people get the wrong idea. They exaggerate the . . . conditions. Yes, some oil has been spilled here. But do you know what? It is only on the top."

"I beg your pardon?"

"That's right. It is only on top of the water. The water beneath the oil is perfectly fine. People never hear that side of the story."

"What about the crew? Surely that work makes them sick."

"As far as I know, those men do not have any problems with their health," Vargas said. "None at all. At least, none that have been caused by the work."

"Have they been examined by a doctor?"

"That is not our responsibility," he said. "We hire a subcontractor in Lago Agrio, and he hires the crews." He exhaled forcefully, as if with impatience. "We run a clean operation. But people often say terrible things without knowing the real facts. Someone sneaks in at night, some terrorist turns a valve, the oil spills, and we get blamed for it. Is that fair?"

"There are terrorists around here?"

He nodded gravely. "Communists," he said. "Guerrillas."

"Where?"

"Everywhere."

No guerrillas had ever been caught, let alone identified. But Vargas seemed satisfied that I was not a terrorist, and to my immense surprise, he said I could go back into the oil field if I wanted to. He was in charge only for the day; perhaps he didn't know any better. Perhaps he honestly thought the Company ran a "clean operation." Perhaps he didn't care one way or the other.

• • •

BY THE TIME I returned to the cleanup site, the crew was quitting for the day. A couple of the men got into my car, and a couple of others jumped up on the rear bumper. As we rolled down the road passing their friends, they grinned and hooted like lords of the realm. At the far end of the lagoon a drainpipe extended through a dike, dispensing into a creek a stream of water that fairly glowed with the blue-gold sheen of raw petroleum. "Perfectly fine," Hugo Vargas had said. The creek itself drained into a small river, which in turn drained into one of the lakes that have made Cuyabeno famous. At the current rate of contamination, by some reliable estimates, many of the lakes would be dead within a decade.

Each of the men carried a bar of soap and a one-liter plastic soft-drink bottle filled with diesel fuel. About a mile farther on we stopped at another creek, and the men stripped down to their shorts and plunged in. Standing waist deep in the creek, they wiped their boots with fuel, then rubbed themselves with it, working their arms and legs over slowly, trying to break down the gummy residue of the day's work. Other men joined them, until a dozen were standing in the creek. Their skin beneath the oil was black: They were from the Pacific coast, near the oil refinery at Esmeraldas.

"No work there anymore," one of them said.

"Are you worried about the petroleum?" I asked. "Does it make you sick?"

"Oh, it is killing me little by little, of that I am sure," a man said. He looked about fifty. His hair had gone white, and he had spindly legs and an enormous belly. He broke out his bar of soap and took his time lathering up, until his dark black skin was covered in white. "But the managers have to drink the same water as we do, do you understand me?"

"No, they do not," another man said. He was younger, lean, his muscles sinewy.

"They don't?" the first man asked.

"They have special water."

"They use that in their soup, too?"

"Yes."

"Really?"

The men had a camp across the road, a three-room, dirt-floored plank shack built by the subcontractor who had hired them. In one room a man sweating through a malarial fever tossed about on a dog-eared foam mattress; in another, two men were asleep in hammocks. In all, twenty-two people shared the three rooms, including a couple of wives, at least six children, and a cook. Of the dollar a day each man earned, half went for room and board. They were charged for Sundays, too, though that was their day off and they weren't paid. The Company gave them a pair of boots and a daily ration of kerosene to wash with, but the men bought everything else themselves—medicine, bedding, clothing. Many of the men had families near Lago Agrio, and for a while they had ridden a bus there on Sundays, to visit and, not incidentally, to save on room and board. But recently a new austerity program imposed by the government had doubled the price of the trip, and now it was cheaper to stay in the camp. All told, if a man didn't drink, didn't gamble, didn't dally with the prostitutes that followed the camps, didn't go home to see his family, didn't get sick, didn't destroy more than one shirt and one pair of pants, he might, after the six weeks or so that such jobs typically last, find himself with a dollar or two in his pocket.

On the way out I caught up with the dump truck, making its last run of the day. Half a dozen men were hanging off the back. They signaled me to follow them. We rumbled up the hill, and as we cruised past the Petroecuador office a security guard raced out of the gate and frantically waved me over. I ignored him and followed the truck into what had once been a well site. The truck backed up to the well's waste pit, but the bed wouldn't rise, so the men shoveled and pushed logs and oil and mud down into the pit by hand. To me, it looked an awful lot like the "cleanup" was a matter of pulling oil waste out of one hole and dumping it into another, more hidden one.

Nearby were five more pits, laid out in a row down the hill. In one a bloated animal carcass the size of a large pig floated on its side, the hair burned completely off. Each pit was full to the brim except for the last: Its walls had broken, and a black swath of crude had flowed to the bottom of the hill. Some chickens and a couple of piglets were foraging in the middle of it. The spill ended right at a shack, in front which bright bits of cloth were hanging on a tree to dry. From their size and shape, they appeared to be the shirts and pants of small children.

I DROVE through Cuyabeno for three days and didn't cover half the roads. It seemed as if they were being built as fast as I drove them—I saw crews everywhere, hacking down the forest. I got the impression that the Cuyabeno Wildlife Reserve was one big toxic sponge. There was oil waste in the water, in the air, in the ground. A colonist I will call Wilfrido took me out in front of his house and sliced into the hillside with a machete. Black gunk bled through the soil; it looked as if he'd cut into a piece of chocolate cake. There is a well not six hundred yards from Wilfrido's house, and in 1989 its waste pit ruptured and flooded his patch of land. All the coffee bushes on the hillside were dead, and a thick layer of tar covered the pond at the bottom of the hill, on which he had once depended for fresh water.

"It has been three years, and my wife is still covered with rashes," he said. "I have eight children. All of them have been sick with rashes, flus, their stomachs, swollen throats. We did not have that before the spill. Sometimes a doctor comes to Lago Agrio and I take them there, but the doctor always wants to give them injections. Do you now how expensive they are?"

Despite his troubles, Wilfrido smiled a lot, flashing two gold-capped canines. He said that he had spoken out about the contamination, and that the Company had punished him. "My family was not allowed to ride on their trucks anymore, and that is our only transportation. We were trapped here. Then after many months we were allowed back on the trucks, but we had to pay twice the regular price."

Wherever I went in the Cuyabeno I heard some version of Wilfrido's story. José Cruz and his wife, Loja, had been in Cuyabeno for ten years. They had two young children, and because there was no school for the colonists, Loja taught her kids and those of other colonists in her home—a blackboard was set up on the porch. José cut a coconut from a tree by the porch, sliced it open, and gave it to me to drink. Then he took me up the hill behind his house, to a creek that bisected his land. The creek was black with crude oil. Oil had splashed up onto the underbrush, and it had washed down the creek for several hundred

yards. In the swampy areas next to the creek it was underfoot everywhere. It was up the hillside, too, all the way to the well that stood above
José and Loja's land. The path ended at a waste pit that had been
bulldozed over. A few yards above the pit the Company had dug a new
pit, two years ago, and already it was overflowing.

José said he had taken his case to Ecuador's Tribunal of Constitutional Guarantees. "The Court ruled that the Company was guilty of a
gross abuse," José said. "But the Court has no power to enforce the law.
So . . ." He shrugged, and then we headed back down the hill, slipping
and sliding on a film of oil.

THERE ARE hundreds of oil-waste pits in the Oriente, perhaps more
than a thousand. Many of them are situated right on the streams that
provide drinking, fishing, and bathing water for local communities. A
typical pit is about the size of an Olympic swimming pool and is
nothing more than a hole dug out of the forest floor. Raw crude oil,
toxic drilling wastes, formation water (water that is pumped up from the
ground along with petroleum and carries such heavy metals as arsenic,
cadmium, cyanide, lead, and mercury), maintenance wastes (including industrial solvents and acids), and the related effluvia of the oil-
extraction process are regularly dumped into such pits, and the pits
regularly wash out in the Oriente's heavy rains. In 1993 a team of
Harvard scientists, doctors, and lawyers visited the Oriente and tested
water from thirty-three sites. In particular, they tested for polycyclic
aromatic hydrocarbons, or PAHs, an element of crude oil so toxic that
the U.S. Environmental Protection Agency considers any amount at all
to pose an exceptionally high risk of cancer. In drinking supplies the
Harvard team found levels of PAHs up to a hundred times those legally
permitted in the United States.

Texaco's contract to produce oil in the Oriente expired in 1992.
During the twenty-year life of the contract, Texaco opened 339 wells,
cut 18,000 miles of seismic trail and nearly 300 miles of road, and built
more than 600 toxic-waste pits. In a lengthy document presented to a
juried hearing of the International Water Tribunal in Amsterdam in
1992, D. York LeCorgne, who had been president of Texaco's Ecuadorian operations, defended the company's record in the Oriente. He

claimed, among other things, that while waste pits "may not be aes-
thetically pleasing, they are not an inherent cause of pollution." Furthermore, he said, the Texaco pits were leak proof, and were designed
to prevent accidental overflow or runoff. As for pipeline spills, the vast
majority were caused by unpreventable acts of nature, and while it was
true that there had been deforestation in the oil fields, that was the work
of colonists, not Texaco. The company, he wrote, had complied not
only with Ecuadorian law "but also with oil industry standards of best
practice and our own Guiding Principles and Objectives, which affirm
our commitment to the environment."

The jury concluded otherwise. It ruled that Texaco had discharged
"large quantities" of hazardous waste into the soil and water of the
Oriente; that it had taken "at most superficial measures" to minimize
spills and contamination; that there was "no evidence that the defen-
dants adopted a precautionary approach in undertaking their activities";
and that Texaco was obligated to compensate its victims. Finally, the
jury expressed doubt that "the economic benefits accruing from the
defendant's oil exploitation were adequately balanced against the negative effects on . . . the local population."

But the tribunal is an international body, and, as LeCorgne pointed
out in his letter, it has no legal jurisdiction in the Oriente.

IN SOME WAYS Randy Borman was as typical a thirty-eight-year-old
American male as you were likely to come across. He had shaggy,
sun-bleached blond hair and a neatly trimmed mustache, clear blue
eyes and a perpetual tan. The day I met him, he was raking weeds out
of his backyard. A solar-powered compact-disc player was blasting the
Beach Boys. His wife and father-in-law were working nearby, and his
three-year-old son was playing in the mud. There was a constant stream
of banter. As soon as Borman could repair the outboard, they were all
going fishing.

I must also say that Borman was wearing a dress. Actually, it was a
cushma, as the traditional garment of the Cofans is called, and the
language he was speaking with his family was Cofan, because they are
Cofan Indians, and he was ripping out the grass around his house
because it tended to breed snakes. It is true that the sound system was

playing "Little Deuce Coupe," but it is also true that Borman was hunting woolly monkeys with a blowgun years before he saw his first car. As for his home, it is made of bark and thatch, and it is hidden in a corner of the Oriente so far from anywhere at all—on the far eastern side of the Cuyabeno Wildlife Reserve, almost at the Colombian border—that even by military air transport and powerboat it takes longer to get there from Quito than it takes to get from Quito to New York City.

Randy Borman is the de facto leader of what is left of the Cofan nation. He is a humble, soft-spoken man, but you don't get this far along the Aguarico unless, in one way or another, you have his permission. In October of 1991, twenty-three employees of Seiscom Delta, the American seismic-exploration company, showed up near Borman's community thinking they'd look for oil. Borman and seven Cofan men surrounded the crew in the forest and demanded to see the authorization papers that, by law, the crew was required to have. The crew had no authorization, of course, but such is the power of law in Ecuador that the crew chief threatened to call in the military. Fine, Borman said. In the meantime you are coming with us. Now.

So began an extraordinary turning point for the Cofans, who had long been known as the most pacifist of the Oriente nations. They held the crew for a day; Borman traveled to Quito and spoke to newspapers and appeared on Ecuador's top-rated television show; an embarrassed minister of agriculture deputized the Cofans as guards of Cuyabeno (in which, technically, they reside). In the following months, the Cofans detained other Company personnel, burned a Company heliport, videotaped the Company in the act of breaking the law—in short, they put the Company on notice that business as usual was over. The Cofans were the group hit first and hardest by oil exploitation, and for decades they had either run from the Company or died in its path. Finally, they had said no.

"What were we supposed to do?" Borman asked me. "We have been pushed all the way to the Colombian border. We have nowhere left to go. You are talking about a completely hopeless and defeated nation that has finally said, That's it, we draw the line right here." In doing so, they underscored an essential truth of the Oriente: "We are finally learning what the Huaorani have always known—in the Oriente, you don't get respect until you get violent."

Randy Borman has spent most of his life in the Oriente. He was born there, in Shell, in 1955. His parents—his father is from Illinois, his mother from California—were Summer Institute of Linguistics missionaries assigned to the Cofans. Borman was the first gringo baby the Cofans had ever seen, and they raised him as one of their own. He remembers the time of his youth as a golden age for the Cofans, when the hunting was good and they had the entire Aguarico River to themselves. The trader who came down the river once a year to buy hammocks and skins was one of the few Spanish speakers he saw before 1964, when seismic crews arrived in the Cofan territory. Texaco drilled its first exploratory wells three years later. One was right at Dureno, where Borman lived. He and his Cofan uncle and cousins hiked into it. "We thought it was a lot of fun," he said. "All this clanking machinery and the helicopters flying in and out. The workers gave us some rice, and some spoons to eat it with. They let us keep the spoons. Four spoons! God, we thought we were wealthy."

The Company told the Cofans that a road would come soon, and that it would make steel and beads and knives and kettles cheaper and enable them to fetch higher prices for their hammocks and skins. Among the few Cofans who had an inkling of what was really coming were the chief and his brother, a powerful shaman who had had a premonition of a time when the forest would be gone and smoke would fill the air. One day the chief announced that he was leaving on a long hunting trip. He said a special farewell to Borman's father, using a word for "good-bye" that the Cofans use only when they are going on an extended journey, and asked the missionary to take care of his people. That night the chief drank as much of the white man's liquor as his stomach could hold, and by morning he was dead.

The traditional Cofan response to the chief's death would have been to scatter, but with the missionary station in place, they made the unusual decision to stay where they were. It was a tragic mistake. Randy Borman is not a missionary, and though he defends the SIL—he says that at times its linguistic work was all that kept the Cofan culture alive—he also acknowledges that it made serious errors. "The missionaries were the only outsiders the Cofans knew, and one of the things the missionary community did was to create among the Cofans a false sense of security about the outside world," he said. "But by and large, the missionaries didn't understand how to handle the world of politics and development."

In 1972, having studied at a private high school in Quito, Borman moved to the United States to attend college. He quit after two years ("It was the first time I realized—how should I put this?—that all English speakers were not intellectually capable people") and decided that home was the Oriente. By then colonists were flooding over the mountains on the new road the Company had blazed from Quito, and Lago Agrio, once a prime hunting area, had become a city. "It felt like this huge machine was coming in on top of us," he said. "We didn't understand it, and we didn't know what to do. If we opposed the oil company, they brought in soldiers."

The missionaries prevailed on the government to recognize at least some of the legitimate Cofan land rights, and they were granted title to nine thousand acres. Borman directed the demarcation. Texaco plowed a road right through the demarcated territory. For most of the Cofans, it was the final blow. About six hundred still survive, but most of them continue to live around Dureno, in what can be described only as abject poverty. "They are completely defeated," Borman said. "If you want an example of ethnocide, that's it."

Had he ever spoken to Texaco about these problems?

"I tried," he said. "But who could you talk to? I was as ignorant of the way that world worked as the next Cofan. You went to the Texaco compound and they wouldn't let you past the guard post. The most we ever heard from them was when we saw one of their propaganda movies that had pictures of some Cofans walking along the pipeline. The attitude was, 'Well, nothing's changed much.'"

Borman married a Cofan woman, and they fled with their clan far down the Aguarico. About fifty Cofans now live there, in a traditional way, give or take the odd solar collector. And they have devised a strategy for survival that is, Borman rightly claims, "ten years ahead of the conservation movement."

At about the time Texaco began its work, the Ecuadorian government created the Cuyabeno Wildlife Reserve. Part of the reserve was on Cofan hunting territory, and the Cofans were banned from it. In 1991, when the government expanded Cuyabeno, the new "protected area" once again encompassed Cofan land. This time, however, the Cofans demonstrated that they were ready to resort to force to defend their land rights, and they won a compromise from the government—one that is unique in the Oriente: To secure rights to eighty thousand acres within the new reserve boundary, the Cofans designed a tiered system of usage based on the principle that the people who live in the forest have the most stake in protecting it. They divided their land into three zones: Section One, for gardens and housing, is located along the river flood-plain, where the best soil is; because the river's meander keeps this zone in constant flux, whatever damage does occur is unlikely to be perma-nent. Section Two is "intensively used" forest—land set aside for tra-ditional native uses, including hunting, fishing, and the gathering of seed and materials for crafts, canoes, and blowguns, with the proviso that it will always remain forest. Section Three is maintained as "wild" land, to act as a reservoir for regeneration of species in Section Two, and for limited fishing and tourism. As deputized guards of the reserve, the Cofans are legally empowered to enforce the laws that protect it, up to and including throwing the Company out.

Meanwhile, to provide themselves with an economic alternative to working for the Company, the Cofans have devised a program that is, in my experience, a first not only in the Oriente but in the Amazon as a whole: "ecotourism" that can truly be said to be run by the local people. The Cofans cut sixty miles of trekking trail in Section Three of their territory and built huts on the trail and a trekking "village" across the river, so that their own village would not be disrupted by tourists. The first trekkers arrived in 1993—an Ecuadorian tour company brought them to a certain point on the Aguarico, and the Cofans took over from there. Trained by Borman, who had once worked as a guide for an American travel company, the young Cofan men carried all the gear, the women prepared all the food, and the older men were guides and lecturers. Participation was voluntary, and proceeds were split equally among all participants.

Tourism is Ecuador's fourth-largest source of foreign exchange, and since 1987 the number of visitors to the Amazon has grown by an average of 12 percent a year, making it one of the few bright spots in the Ecuadorian economy. But the hard truth is that the Cofans could not have achieved what they have without the savvy of a man like Borman, who can operate in two worlds—a man whose white skin gives him a distinct advantage when dealing with the media, government officials, the Company, travel companies in Quito and the United States. In any case, in the face of the Company it is a vision as fragile as a thatch hut in a hurricane. Tourists do not want to see wells and helicopters and oil spills.

"We don't have complete control over the land," Borman conceded, "but, theoretically, anyone who is coming in here has to go through us, including the oil companies. That is why we pushed the Seiscom Delta situation. Either the government makes the Company obey the law, or we are ready to take things into our own hands. Then their only choice is to send in the military." If that happens, Borman said, "They've got a guerrilla war, and that is another story."

Was he concerned about his own safety?

"Let me put it this way," he said. "Ecuador doesn't have a history of bumping off enemies, but it would be easy to do, and I'm sure the oil companies have discussed it." He laughed then, but not much.

15

COCA WAS packed to the gills when I returned. Along the roads Indians and colonists were filtering in on foot and bicycle, carrying babies and baskets of food. Down on the Napo the bank was clotted with canoes, and late that evening two busloads of environmentalists and human-rights activists—Ecuadorian, American, European—rolled in from Quito. They hobbled off the buses stiff-kneed and gibbering from the jangly fifteen-hour ride, slogged through the ankle-deep mud, and made straight for the best bar in town.

That's where I found Judith Kimerling, her eyes glistening with excitement. "It's really going to happen!" she said. She meant the meeting, but she meant something else, too. It had been more than a year since the Conoco-NRDC debacle, and she hoped this gathering would kick-start the rebuilding of the fragile alliance that had once existed among *ecologistas* and Indians and colonists. "There will always be differences," she said. "But if you can define the work, it will get you past them—the work becomes the point of common purpose."

The main goal of the meeting was to organize a campaign to force Texaco to clean up the mess it had made in the Oriente. But Kimerling didn't intend to stop there. She and the Quito-based *ecologistas* who had organized the meeting had prepared detailed profiles of each of the oil companies working in the Oriente, and they wanted to bring together all of the people who would be affected by that work and help them begin to devise strategies for protecting themselves.

The first target on their list was Maxus, because Block Sixteen was the next oil field scheduled to come on line. The Huaorani presence at the meeting would be crucial. But the Huaorani weren't the only indigenous group Valerio Grefa had neglected to invite to Coca. He hadn't invited any of them. Kimerling had done that herself, traveling to the far corners of the Oriente in the preceding weeks to get the word out. And they had come: the Siona, the Secoya, local Quichua federations so far removed from the larger world that they hardly knew who Valerio Grefa and CONFENIAE were. Colonists had come too, and so had people who had once worked for the Company, maids and cooks and field hands who wanted to know why their skin was constantly swollen and itchy, why their children always had diarrhea, what those lumps were on their chests.

In the morning I went to the Capuchin mission to look for the Huaorani. School was out for vacation, and the Capuchins had volunteered their grounds and dormitories for the meeting. Children were running through the gardens, and women knelt in the grass and carefully unfurled banana leaves filled with manioc and rice. I found José Miguel Goldáraz out behind the men's dorm, wearing a beret and a bemused smile. Whatever else the meeting might accomplish, he said, one thing was already clear: For most of the people who had come, this would be their first opportunity to see that they were not alone.

Even in such a crowd it wasn't hard to pick out the Huaorani. They'd taken over a corner of the men's dorm, cordoning it off with a wall of crossed spears (which, when found on a trail in the forest, mean death to anyone who passes them). On the floor were two big aluminum pots of *chicha* and, leaning against a wall, a haunch of smoked peccary. Salomón was asleep on one of the cots, with an arm around Raúl, who was leafing through a comic book. Moi and Enqueri sat on another cot, bent over a notebook. They were wearing bird-feather crowns. Plastic briefcases lay at their feet. Moi was shirtless, with palm-thong armlets wrapped around both biceps, accentuating each mass of muscle. Enqueri was wearing his Colombian shoes. He'd been walking in the forest almost every day of the last two weeks, and the buckles had begun to tarnish.

"Good life," I said.

"Chong," Moi said. He handed me a cup of *chicha* and motioned for me to sit next to him. "There are many cannibals here," he said. "The whole world wants to speak for the Huaorani."

"Only the Huaorani can speak for the Huaorani," Enqueri said.

"Many of them want to help the Huaorani," I said.

"Many of them want to steal from the Huaorani," Enqueri said.

They had prepared a speech. Moi read it to me from his notebook. "The Huaorani are the bravest people in the whole world," he began. "The rivers and the trees are our life. We protect our life for the whole world. We are the protectors of the forest. We are not afraid to die. We are not afraid to kill. Now the Company is invading our land. Our land is where my grandfather was born and my father was born and I was born. We will fight the Company. We will fight like Huaorani fight. The Huaorani are the bravest people and we need no one. But the Huaorani will be friends with the whole world that does not try to destroy us. We invite the whole world to come and see how the Huaorani protect the forest. We come to this meeting to sit and talk with those who want to be our friends."

"That is powerful," I said.

"Yes, it is," Moi said. "But it needs more cannibal words—words they will understand. Like . . ." He paused. "*Environment*—that is a word that pleases them, no?"

"Your own words are fine," I said.

"There is more," Enqueri said. The second part was an attack on Valerio Grefa, who "says he is a friend of the Huaorani but he will sell us like meat if he can."

The meeting began that afternoon, in the school's main hall. Perhaps seventy participants gathered in the center of the room, sitting around a horseshoe of rickety tables and school desks. A hundred or more observers crowded in back and along the walls, and others stood outside, peering in through the windows. A microphone appeared. One by one the participants identified themselves. It was an uneventful drone until Moi and Enqueri rose and stood before the crowd.

They had dressed in *cowode* clothes, though Moi also wore his crown. As he began to speak I saw in him an uncharacteristic hesitation, and a slight averting of the eyes, and at first his words limped out in an indecipherable mumble. It was no easy task for him to address such a gathering of cannibals. Nor for Enqueri, who stood at Moi's side and now and then whispered something in his ear. But then Moi's voice began to gather force, and Enqueri began to take turns at the microphone, and before long they were roaring like jaguars in a mishmash of

Huaorani and Spanish delivered at a frenetic tempo. Their initial awkwardness gave way to an aura of undeniable power, and it quickly settled over the entire room. There were many present who could legitimately call themselves people of the forest, but none more so than the Huaorani. They lived in the forest's deepest reaches; they alone were truly warriors. Cameras clicked and whirred and people sat up in their seats. After ten minutes or so Moi and Enqueri paused to rest; the room burst into applause.

When Moi and Enqueri turned their attention to a far corner of the room, where Valerio Grefa had hidden himself away, and said that, above all, the whole world must know that CONFENIAE did not speak for the Huaorani, that only the Huaorani spoke for the Huaorani, it was, in its way, a shattering and defining moment. Delivered before such a large and public assembly—and, especially, before so many *ecologistas*, few of whom had spent any time in the Huaorani territory—their condemnation of Grefa challenged, if not destroyed, whatever was left of the long-standing myth that the Indians of the Oriente speak as one, a myth as convenient as it was false.

If there was any remaining doubt about how the Huaorani viewed Valerio Grefa (it was hard to see how there could be, so direct was their attack), Raúl quickly relieved it. He jumped out of the audience and grabbed the microphone and launched a fifteen-minute assault that was the verbal equivalent of the guanta slaughter I'd witnessed on the Shiripuno River. He stopped just short of walking over to Grefa and beating on him until the blood burst out his ears.

When Raúl finished, the room was hushed in shock.

Cornered, exposed, Grefa had no choice but to respond. For a moment he let the silence hang. No one had ever gone after him in quite so public a way. A *"vaca sagrada"* was how José Miguel Goldáraz described CONFENIAE—a sacred cow that none dared criticize for fear of being labeled a racist, or an agent of the Company, or worse. The letter the Huaorani had written denouncing Grefa was well known inside activist circles in the United States, but it had been quite deliberately buried, lest it destroy the illusion of "indigenous solidarity," as the phrase so often had it. "Grefa's a monster," an American who worked with him once told me, "but he's *our* monster."

When Grefa finally chose to respond, he did so without rising from his chair, and with uncharacteristic brevity. "We admire this statement of independence from the Huaorani," he said, "and we respect their right to make this choice. But it is not a choice they have made on their own. Clearly, they are being manipulated by outsiders. These are not the Huaorani speaking." He said no more, leaving the identity of the "outsiders" unaddressed.

Grefa saved his most powerful words for later in the day, after the meeting had adjourned. If the Huaorani were officially withdrawing from CONFENIAE, he told the meeting's organizers, then CONFENIAE would withdraw from the alliance. Grefa, in other words, was prepared to kill the alliance in its infancy.

DESPITE SUCH high drama, that night the meeting took on the air of a fiesta. People were fed from great vats of beans and rice, and as they ate they mingled freely, Indians and Latinos and Anglos. While the meeting hall was being converted to a dance floor I found myself sitting on the grass with Angel Zamarenda, the Shuar who was vice president of CONFENIAE. As we spoke Zamarenda's two toddling daughters climbed all over him.

Zamarenda is stocky, running to fat, but shrewd and intelligent. His Spanish is excellent and his energy intense. If he was no longer really a man of the forest, neither was he all that far removed from it. A century ago the Shuar were warriors and headhunters, as feared as the Huaorani, and while today they are mainly farmers and ranchers and colonists and traders—they have adapted to the market economy more swiftly, and with greater success, than any other nation in the Oriente—they are no less zealous.

From where we sat we could see a British photographer taking pictures of Moi, perhaps twenty yards away. Moi had outfitted himself in full Huaorani regalia. A European boycott of Texaco was being planned; Moi would appear on the poster.

Zamarenda was in a sputtering rage.

"Huaorani this, Huaorani that!" he said. "Why do all you people applaud them, these Huaorani? You did not see me applaud when that Moi spoke. Indians carving themselves to pieces in front of the ecologists! It was a *disgrace*."

I said that I had recently traveled throughout the Oriente, and that the smaller Indian nations, as well as many of the Quichua communities, agreed with what Moi had said: CONFENIAE was no longer looking out for their best interests; CONFENIAE had not invited them to this meeting because it did not want to share its power.

"That is absolutely not true," Zamarenda replied. He gently pulled one of his daughters off his head, but his eyes said he was ready to explode. "Look around—they are all here. The Huaorani, the Secoya, the Siona—everybody."

"That is because Judith Kimerling invited them."

He didn't say anything to that. Instead, he paused to wipe the runny nose of his other daughter. Then he said, "These smaller groups, we invite them to this meeting and that meeting and we give them money for traveling expenses and they never show up. What is the point? Then they go out and make their own deals with the oil companies at the same time they tell us they don't want oil development on their land. How do you propose we handle such hypocrisy?"

"Did Valerio sell his land to the Company? Is that hypocrisy?"

"It is not as simple as that," Zamarenda said, as if lecturing a child. "That was private land, not communal Indian land. He has the same right as you, or me, or anybody else to sell that sort of land."

"What happened to the money that came to CONFENIAE for the Huaorani to cut their border?"

"Who knows?" he said. "It's like the travel money—it just disappears. When the Shuar cut their boundary, we didn't get help from anyone, no outsiders, no money, nothing. But the Huaorani—they *sell* themselves. They are *pawns*. They are *pathetic*."

Later I spoke with Valerio Grefa. He did not appear upset by the day's events. He was smiling—gloating, really, full of himself. "They will say I killed this alliance," he said. "And they will be right!"

By then we could hear the fevered beat of a Colombian *cumbia* blasting from the hall. Inside, I found the dance floor filled, but the Huaorani were standing along one wall, as if not quite sure how to behave. All of them, that is, but Moi, who was out in the middle of the floor, dancing with a woman I didn't recognize. The Quichua and the Quiteños moved with certainty and flair, but Moi's steps were careful and controlled and not necessarily in accord with the dense and sinuous rhythms of the music.

Then Valerio Grefa jumped into the middle of the floor, reeling and pumping with such wild abandon that everyone else pulled back to give him room. He was all elbows and knees, but he had the moves, and he spun himself and his partner across the room and back, laughing and shouting and waving like a king.

I left then. As I slipped out the door I noticed Moi still at it, off to the side of the floor but dancing all the same, with a look both solemn and serene, as if the whole world and everything he needed from it were right there beneath his two feet.

I WALKED through the mud back toward the Hotel Auca. It was past midnight, but the sky was clear and the moon full. A breeze whinnied up and carried from the forest a balsam so rich it overrode the odor of petroleum rising from the street. I found myself thinking about Moi and Enqueri. It had taken real courage for them to stand up and denounce Valerio Grefa. But there was no denying the truth of what Grefa had told me back in Quito: The Huaorani were alone.

Then again, the Huaorani had always been alone, cut off not only from the world outside their borders but, often enough, from one another. And what was "alone"? Moi, for one, seemed to move between cultures without losing any sense of himself. He was a natural student, and naturally charming, with a poet's talent for interpreting life in ways that applied universally. Enqueri, too, crossed cultures with facility, though differently. Moi acted; Enqueri reacted. He was not as fluid as Moi—his charm was that of the clown, of one who calculated and curried favor—but he had more tools. He had a better command of Spanish, for instance, and he dealt more cunningly with *cowode* authority figures. (Certainly, his intense exposure to the evangelical missionaries had subjected him to a kind of behavior modification that Moi had mostly escaped.) Perhaps, I thought, the combination of Moi and Enqueri was just right—one that could work all sides, and in doing so could lead the bravest people in the Amazon safely into the future.

I was lost in these thoughts when I felt someone tug at my sleeve. It was Salomón, wearing a goofy grin. He handed me a dog-eared piece of paper, which my flashlight revealed to be a photocopy of a computer printout that read, in Spanish, and in its entirety:

Today, the ninth of September 1992, in the offices of Maxus, there was a meeting between representatives of the Huaoranis—Nanto Huamoni, Yacata Yategue, Salomón Oname [*sic*], and Tigue Oname—in which they expressed the following points, which were decided in a meeting of the Huaorani Congress:

1. They decided that Maxus may begin to construct a road in the territory; the road shall be five to six meters wide.
2. They need Maxus's support in providing equipment for the primary and secondary school.
3. Colonization controls, which will be worked by the Huaoranis.
4. Generator for the night school.
5. Payment for a machinist to cut wood.
6. Transportation: Gasoline and two outboard motors.
7. Provision of medicine and health care programs.
8. They declare that they wish to make only one contract between the Maxus Company and ONAHE [*sic*].

Today, September 9, we sign this act of the meeting, in agreement, with all the points mentioned.

The contract had been signed by the four Huaorani it named—signed, according to the date, while they had been staying at my apartment, on the day that Nanto had ordered Enqueri to remain behind while he went to meet with the Company. Yacata and Tigue had told me they were adamantly opposed to the Maxus road, but they were, I was fairly certain, illiterate. Standing there in the Coca mud, meanwhile, Salomón said he hadn't been at the Maxus meeting. "Nanto came to me with this piece of paper," he said. "It was folded like this." He folded the agreement in fourths so that only his name was showing. "He told me I had to sign my name, so I did. When he went to sleep I stole it out of his pants. What does it mean?"

As for the "congress" the contract referred to, it was true that there had been a Huaorani congress, at the Shiripuno Center, nine months before the date of the Maxus document. And it was true that oil issues had been discussed. But the resolution that had come out of that *congreso*, and that had been written down and signed by all the ONHAE officers and the representatives of the various villages, hardly approved what was, essentially, the sale of the Huaorani birthright for what amounted to beads and trinkets. Rather, the resolution stated, among other things: "We do not want the presence of the petroleum companies, because the crude oil contaminates the rivers, the land, and the environment, and destroys the health of the People. The Huaorani want no more advancement of oil development, because the roads are the first step in the invasion of colonists. We do not want the contamination, the noise, or the disruption of the oil companies. . . . We will apply our law, the pain of death, and we are ready with arms to defend our territory against all invaders, because we are the bravest people in the Amazon."

I asked Salomón if he had shown the contract to Enqueri and Moi.

"No," he said. "No one has seen it."

They saw it the next morning, however, and Enqueri quickly grew agitated. "This is what I was telling you about!" he said. "Nanto is making a deal with the Company, but he does not want us to know. The Company is sitting on his head—they get him alone, and he does not know what to think."

Moi received the news with more equanimity, though no less concern. He said that unless such an agreement was signed by all the officers of ONHAE, and approved by all the Huaorani, and stamped with the ONHAE seal, it had no meaning. "This is not how the Huaorani do things," he said. "If we make an agreement and the agreement is good and we all talk about it, there is no reason to hide it."

He and Enqueri discussed the contract with Judith Kimerling. "The Huaorani might not consider this a real document," she told them, "and it might not be a real document according to the laws of Ecuador. But now Maxus has a piece of paper that it can take to America or Europe or anywhere and say, The Huaorani have made an agreement with us. That makes it easier for them to work in the Huaorani land."

But even this explanation did not appear to inspire in Moi anything like anger. He remained calm and pragmatic, and Enqueri followed his lead. When they returned to the territory, Moi said, he and Enqueri would find Nanto and they would speak with him. Then he and Enqueri would go to all of the Huaorani, walking and canoeing the territory for as many weeks as necessary, and they would have an *asamblea*, and they would address this issue once again. Then they would go to Quito and, once again, they would find the Company.

MEANWHILE, the meeting had stirred up other strange currents.

The night before, Enqueri had stayed at the dance for about an hour after I left, but Moi had danced all night. In the morning he told me about the women he had met: the *ecochicas*, he called them.

It is one of the ironies—or, perhaps, inevitabilities—of Ecuador that for all the macho posturing of the dominant Latin culture, an inordinate amount of the hardest work in environmental and human-rights activism is done by women. In fact, if there is any one person who can be considered the heart of "green" Ecuador, it is Esperanza Martínez, the fiery and charismatic Quiteña who had been the first coordinator of the Campaña por la Vida. She and Judith Kimerling had organized the Coca meeting, assisted by the dozen or so women who were most active in the various groups joined under the Campaña umbrella. The *ecochicas* were young and articulate and well educated; most of them had children; several were divorced—still a rarity in heavily Catholic Ecuador. A few lived together communally, sharing child care and rent. They worked hard and they played hard. They put in twelve- and fourteen-hour days; they set up picket lines; they occupied offices; they confronted businessmen; they made noise; they danced all night. This was old stuff in the United States, but it was bold and a little dangerous in staid and patriarchal Ecuador. The *ecochicas* were out there, on the edge, making up the rules as they went along.

Now they'd found Moi.

"We are going to have a strike," he told me, in the same tone of dead certainty with which, from time to time, he would announce that he had friends in the United States who were going to send bombers to attack the Company, or that on a good day he could walk ten kilometers in ten minutes. "The Huaorani and the *ecochicas*. A hundred Huaorani will come to Quito and we will go to the Company and we will make a camp and we will not leave until we tell the Company to get out."

Later I spoke with some of the *ecochicas*, and they confirmed this plan, with one additional bit of information: There would be a day set aside for *paseo*, for the Huaorani to spend hanging out and enjoying themselves in the big city. Moi, one of them told me with an air of utter befuddlement, had said something about karate movies. Did I have any idea what he meant?

From every conceivable angle, the strike was a bizarre proposal. The Huaorani raided oil camps and stole things and killed people; they didn't go into the city and carry picket signs and occupy offices. As for the *ecochicas*, I knew them just well enough to believe they didn't understand what they were getting into. It was one thing to take a gang of urbanites to the Maxus office and make a ruckus and get your picture in the newspaper, but to bring a hundred Huaorani out of the forest and all the way to Quito was something else altogether. Moi had said a hundred Huaorani, for example; that could mean ten or a thousand. They would have to be fed and transported and clothed and treated for the inevitable colds and flus they would contract. They'd march around Quito in bras and underpants. And what if the old warriors decided to go to work with their spears?

THROUGHOUT THE WEEKEND a nattily dressed little man scurried around the meeting hall videotaping everyone who spoke. There were several video crews at the meeting, and no one paid the man much mind until late the second afternoon, at the meeting's final session, when one of the former oil workers remembered where he had seen the man before: He was an Ecuadorian soldier.

The oil worker leaped to his feet. "Spy!" he yelled, and when the suspect's credentials proved fraudulent he was hauled to the front of the room. He didn't deny the charge; he didn't say anything at all, and he didn't look particularly worried. His tapes were confiscated. Then, one by one, each person at the meeting was asked for identification, and two more spies were found. They were paraded in front of the crowd and denounced and insulted by various people and then an officer from the base appeared and without apology or explanation took custody of the three men and demanded that the meeting's organizers hand over the tapes. Angel Zamarenda had been the last person seen with them, but he claimed not to know where they were. Voices rose, accusations flew, and the meeting threatened to devolve into spectacle.

I was sitting with Enqueri and Esperanza Martínez. "We should just give them what they want and get them out of here," Enqueri said. "This is a waste of time. Nothing is going to happen to the spies. At least we should act in a way the military respects, and preserve our dignity."

Martínez endorsed Enqueri's idea. "This is a public meeting," she said. "We are not keeping secrets, and we are not breaking the law." But the officer's request was refused, and after half an hour of angry haggling he stomped out of the hall with the spies in his wake.

That evening word came down that Judith Kimerling would be arrested the next morning, at the airport, when she was scheduled to leave Coca. Until then she had been elated by the success of the meeting. Despite Valerio Grefa's threats to withdraw, the alliance she envisioned appeared to be coming together, and Grefa, recognizing that it would go forward with or without him, had backed down. People from all sides had sat together and talked and worked. A commission of Indians and ecologists had been formed to organize the campaign against Texaco, and another to plot strategy against Maxus. Lines of communication had been worked out—no small step, given that many of the meeting's far-flung participants had little access to telephones, mail, or reliable transportation. There had been workshops to explain such things as which companies had rights to which blocks, where the blocks were, what the steps of oil production are, how to identify contaminated water and soil.

But as Kimerling sat that night eating dinner with José Miguel Goldáraz and Esperanza Martínez, she looked drawn and agitated. The exhilaration evident throughout the weekend had drained from her face, replaced by fear and frustration. "Have you ever been arrested in Coca?" she asked of no one in particular. "Believe me, you don't want to be. The jail, it's a dirty little cement box with a teeny little hole for light. You have to wait a couple of minutes for your eyes to adjust just so you can see who else is in there. Last time it was six men."

Last time, José Miguel had helped to negotiate her release. This time, he wasn't sure what might happen. "The stakes are higher every day," he said. Kimerling had broken no laws and, legally, could not be held more than a day without charges. But as everyone well knew, charges weren't the point, and the law didn't count for much. "They want me out of here," Kimerling said, "and they want me to think real hard about coming back."

At midnight the power went off and Coca went black. I walked Kimerling to her room at the Auca. By moonlight I could make out three men standing in the street in front of the hotel. As we approached they melted into the darkness and slipped away, but I easily recognized them as the three spies.

In the morning two dozen people escorted Kimerling to the airport, and she boarded the plane without incident. But no one doubted that the threat of arrest had been real, or that it would shade every subsequent trip she made into the Oriente.

As for me, I climbed onto the bed of a pickup truck piled high with gas and food and Huaorani and slipped out Coca's back door—over the Napo, through the checkpoint, and on down the Vía Auca.

16

I DID NOT know, then, that I was taking my final trip into the territory. As the truck hit the last rise in the Auca and we dipped down into the endless canopy of the Shiripuno valley, into miles upon miles of green, I thought quite the opposite. The day was clear and cool and filled with the simple joy of movement. Huaorani hung off the sides of the truck and crowded wall to wall in the bed and I had a foot in my face and a head in my lap and once again my nostrils were filled with the fragrances of sweat and smoke, wild game and river musk. Once these had seemed alien and threatening, but now they signaled a return to something familiar and cherished. We had food, we had time, and I felt among friends, with no purpose but to return to the center of the whole world.

At the Shiripuno bridge the truck erupted in cheers: The river was up and the snags safely hidden, as if the forest had rolled out a welcoming watery carpet. Battered and patched like an old warrior, the canoe rested right where Moi had left it, and we quickly put in and within minutes rounded the first bend and glided into a different world. Though we stopped to hunt and to swim, we made the Shiripuno Center before dark and feasted on piranha and manioc and the fiery hot peppers now coming to fruit on bushes planted by Ali Sharif. Since my last visit the center had changed in only one way: A board was nailed across the small cabin that Amo had used as his office. Two dried flowers were tucked behind the board, and painted across it, in bright Huaorani red, was the word MUERTO: Spanish for "dead."

• • •

IN QUEHUEIRE ONO I helped Moi around his home, carving blowguns and spears, repairing the sleeping platform, hauling manioc and water. He always had a gaggle of kids trailing after him. He taught them to write, to tie shoes, to swim—Moi's being the first generation of Huaorani to have mastered these skills. (The Huaorani did not learn to swim until they moved down off the ridgetops and settled along the rivers.) We hunted and fished, and at night we sat around the fire and drank *chicha* and ate ungarawa nuts, monkey, the catch of the day. Sometimes Moi's uncle, Dabo, would sing me to sleep.

One evening I came back from washing in the river to find Moi, Salomón, and Mengatohue sitting around the fire, stirring a small pot filled with what looked like mud and bark. "*Huando*," Moi called it. He said that he had taken *huando* six times; four more and he would pass a milestone toward shamanhood. "The last time I drank *huando*," he said, "I could see right into the earth. I saw whole cities there beneath the ground. Cities filled with people who had died, and many women. I ran through the forest all night long with no moon. I did not fall once."

What could I say? What I did say, in Huaorani—and I am translating roughly here—was, "Spare a hit?"

Mengatohue spoke to Moi: "It would be better if we tied this cannibal to a tree."

"Yes," Moi said, in a serious way. "Like a monkey."

I responded with a Huaorani epithet that means, literally, "Piss on yourself." Salomón and Mengatohue and Moi howled with laughter. Salomón passed me a tin cup of *huando*. It tasted like, well, mud and bark. I gagged a little as it went down. Then I sat back and waited . . .

. . . for nothing, as near as I could tell. Two hours later the sum effect of the *huando* was that my mouth was so dry I couldn't spit. Moi and Salomón were sitting at the edge of the sleeping platform, pointing at the night sky and chattering like machine guns.

"I have had about all the fun I can stand," I announced. "I am taking myself to my sleeping place now."

I awoke sometime later with a powerful need to urinate. Moi and

Salomón were asleep, or what passed for asleep. I stepped to the edge of the platform and balanced on the log frame and took aim into the forest. Nothing happened. I edged down off the platform to stand on level ground. Again I aimed; again I failed. I stood there for maybe twenty minutes.

Nothing.

At three o'clock in the morning, of course, all nightmares are true, and I began to suspect—no, I *knew*—that I was harboring the dread candiru, a tiny, parasitic catfish that survives by swimming up the gill streams of much larger fish and implanting itself with a set of external spines. However, a candiru can't always distinguish between fish gill and human urethra, and once it is lodged inside the urinary tract there is no way to remove it but to cut it out. The closest thing we had to a surgical tool was my Swiss Army knife—that or a machete. And the Huaorani, for all their familiarity with the forest, have no knowledge of anesthesia.

"Moi!" I screamed. "Salomón!"

I heard Moi mumble from the platform: "Piss on yourself!"

"I can't!"

"It's only something we *say*. You don't have to do it!"

"I can't piss at all! There's a fish in my pipe!"

Mengatohue wandered in out of the dark. "We should have tied him to a tree," he said.

I tried to go back to sleep. I might as well have tried to fly to the moon. But I had a vision, of sorts: I knew that if I survived this episode, it was time to go home to the United States. I didn't know exactly why, but I knew it for a fact.

At first light I was on my feet. I steadied myself; I took aim. A few minutes later, a couple of drips trickled out, then a flood. It burned like a freight train. No words can describe my joy.

I danced a little jig and turned to the sleeping platform to find Moi and Salomón and Mengatohue and Moi's family and assorted neighbors studying me with something akin to amazement. I fumbled through my Huaorani vocabulary. "Now making good water!" I said.

"That is quite a talent," Mengatohue said.

◆ ◆ ◆

THE NEXT few days passed in a sublimely peaceful haze. Maybe it was the *huando*; maybe it was the place. One day as I was lolling in a swimming hole, I heard a voice calling from somewhere up in the trees along the far bank. At first it sounded like it was saying, in English, "Come here, Joe," and I thought maybe it was the *huando* talking. But then it came a second time, more clearly, and that was exactly what it was saying. A third time, and I recognized the voice as Enqueri's.

I found him high on the ridge, resting in a hammock in Mengatohue's barren hut, a pile of banana skins on the dirt beneath him, before him a million-dollar view of the Shiripuno valley. I'd lost track of Enqueri after we reached Quehueire Ono, and as it turned out, he'd been staying with Mengatohue, working over some things that were weighing heavily on his mind.

In Coca, he told me, he had run into his brother Pedro. Many months ago Pedro had left his wife and run off with a Quichua woman, an oil-camp whore. Now Pedro was afraid to return to the territory, because he believed his wife's brother would kill him. Enqueri was at a loss. He said, "I told him, 'Pedro, you must go home and be with your wife. This is how the world is. I will sit down and talk with the family and make it right.' Pedro wanted money to take a bus to Puyo, and I said, 'No, I will buy you a Coca-Cola, but that is all.' But he said he would go anyway, because he knows a Communist in Puyo who sells drugs and will give him money and he would not have to work very hard for it. I said, 'Pedro, the police will catch you and put you in jail and never let you out. Come back to the People and we will keep you safe.' "

But Pedro had elected to leave the People, and Enqueri was vexed beyond consolation. The Huaorani had always been on the move, but they had never left the forest. However dangerous that life might have been—to walk through any part of the forest was to hear stories of Huaorani who had suffered or died there—it had been whole. But that was changing. Now the Huaorani could go away and never come back; now they could go to a place where there was no forest at all and they were no longer Huaorani.

"Pedro will suffer," Enqueri said. "But I cannot help him. He said, 'Enqueri, you have many cannibal friends, tell them to help me,' but I said, 'Pedro, they are my friends but they cannot help you. That is the way the world is.' "

"And how is the world, Enqueri?" I asked. "Moi tells me you have a woman here in Quehueire Ono, and another in Toñampare who is going to have your child."

"What!" Enqueri said. "That Moi! He is always saying things about me! He is such a liar!" The Condor laughed then—ha-ha-ha-ha-ha—and leaned back in his hammock, but he did not seem at peace.

THAT NIGHT Enqueri came to Moi's home, and they sat around the fire and talked for a long time. They made plans for an *asamblea* to discuss Nanto's contract with the Company. "Now we must talk about the strike we will have in Quito," Moi said when they had finished. "Come here and help us, Chong."

I didn't know quite what to say. My experience with *huando* had only brought to a head a tangle of emotions I'd been struggling with for some time. I found it thrilling to travel with the Huaorani and know their life and have them visit me and know mine. I considered Moi and Enqueri my friends. But it was one thing to witness what was happening to them, and to record it, and quite another to participate directly in their political work. This struck me as a line I should not cross. I could argue that it was a matter of physical danger—I could get thrown out of the country, or worse—but what it really came down to, in the end, was the sad knowledge that the only proper way to be further involved with the Huaorani was to commit myself without limit. To be with them for a few months more, even a year or two, would do little but make them dependent on me for advice, clothing, shelter, any number of things. True, I had a wife and child, and sooner or later I had to return to them, but this was more an excuse than a reason. Had I been alone, I was not sure I could have found it in myself to step out of the world I knew and completely into this one. I could not, in other words, commit myself in the way that, say, Rachel Saint had; whatever else one might think of her, you had to admire her courage.

I believed that if Moi and Enqueri were truly serious about their strike, they would have to forge their relationship with the *ecochicas* on their own. It would be difficult for them, if not impossible, but if they succeeded, they would be far stronger—if for no other reason than that they would have expanded their range of *cowode* friends. But I could

find no good way to explain this to them. They did not compartmen-
talize their lives in such a manner. What had to be done had to be done,
and you did it.

In any case, it seemed, Moi already had his plan.

"We will come to your house in Quito in twenty-two days," he said.
"We will make our camp there, and then we will find the *ecochicas*. We
will tell them to send a bus to Coca or two buses. Enqueri and I will
bring one hundred Huaorani from all villages so the Company cannot
say it is only this village or that village that is speaking. We will make
one hundred spears and one hundred pots of *chicha*."

I agreed to this plan; it seemed the least I could do. I would leave
for Quito the next day, and Enqueri and Moi would begin their long
trek across the territory to rally the People.

We huddled around the fire and ate and talked into the night. At
times the rain beat down on the thatch roof so violently that it drowned
our voices, but we were warm and dry. Sometime before dawn the rain
lifted and I gave Enqueri the backpack I had brought as a gift for Amo's
family and the three of us went down to the river, where Dabo was
already waiting with the canoe that would carry me back to the Vía
Auca. "Be careful," I said to Moi and Enqueri, and handed each of
them some money to use when they reached the city—much, I realized
with a small shudder, as I had Amo when I had seen him for the last
time.

"We will eat pizza!" Enqueri said, grinning, and he and Moi turned
to climb the path to Moi's home. Then Dabo stood up in the stern
and stuck a long pole into the river bottom and with a slight grunt
pushed off. We picked up the current, and soon we were gliding swiftly
and silently back toward the land of the cannibals.

17

TWENTY-TWO DAYS after I left Quehueire Ono, I walked out the front door of my apartment building in Quito and found Moi and Enqueri sitting on the lawn.

"Chong," Moi said.

In my apartment Enqueri bolted all the locks and Moi rummaged a pair of dress shoes from my closet. "Now I am ready for the *ecochicas*," he said.

"Tell me how life is," I said.

Enqueri told me that they had come directly from the *asamblea*, by canoe, foot, truck, and bus, and that they had not eaten in four days. Seventeen communities had sent representatives to discuss the *acta* Nanto had signed with the Company, and all but Toñampare had rejected it outright. Toñampare itself was divided. Those Huaorani who were related to Nanto supported the deal, which only made sense, because they would receive most of the benefits.

"What does Nanto say now?" I asked.

"Nanto does not say anything," Moi said.

Despite their long journey, Moi and Enqueri were fired up by the prospect of the strike, and they asked that I take them directly to the office of the *ecochicas* so they could make their plans. It was a small building in a sunny, run-down neighborhood, with a lock and chain on the door. I shouted up to an open window on the second floor and a face appeared and then a key came flying down through the sharp sun.

Maybe a dozen people were in the office, including many of the *ecochicas*: Esperanza, Paulina, Yvonne, Elizabeth, Cecilia. They hugged Moi and shook hands with Enqueri and sat down in a circle in the center of the room. Moi sat, too, but Enqueri and I stood against a wall. At first Moi didn't seem to know quite where he was, and he launched into a speech about tourism. But then Esperanza asked about the strike, and he shifted course without a hitch. He said they would bring one hundred Huaorani to the Shiripuno bridge on the twenty-fourth of the month, and from there they would depend on the *ecochicas* to get them to Quito. Each village would send at least three representatives. They would strike for three days. The elders were making crowns and spears.

The *ecochicas*, for their part, had already met with Luis Macas, the president of the national indigenous confederation, CONAIE, and he had agreed to provide food, blankets, tents, and clothing for the strike, and to demand a meeting with President Sixto Durán Ballén. (Under Ecuador's complex indigenous political system, Valerio Grefa's organization, CONFENIAE, was incorporated within CONAIE, and Grefa was subordinate to Macas. Macas was intelligent and honest, and though he is an Andean Quichua, he had taken a central role in speaking out against the Company, for which, the following year, he would win—deservedly—the prestigious Goldman Environmental Prize, awarded annually to one grass-roots activist on each continent.)

"Two days for the strike," Yvonne said, "and one day for *paseo!*"

"Yes!" Moi agreed. "Then the whole world will come to Quehueire Ono for a fiesta!"

It was Moi's show. The Condorito hovered in the background. He was not exactly ignored, but neither did he fit in. He was as awkward as Moi was graceful, as odd looking as Moi was handsome. After a while he touched my arm, and we slipped out the door and hailed a cab and left Moi to his fate.

"Enqueri, what do you think?" I asked on the ride back to my apartment.

"Moi has many friends among the cannibals," he said.

"And the strike?"

"We must try," he said.

"Do you understand that I cannot be a part of this?"

"It is time for you to go to the United States of North America and be with your family," he said.

"Yes. Will you be safe here?"

"José, do not worry yourself. The Huaorani will always find what they need."

It was the sort of thing Enqueri seemed to say without thinking, and if it was difficult for me to decipher just how deeply meant it was, I had come to understand that for all the battles they fought, the Huaorani had no sense of apocalypse. They believed, absolutely, that they ruled their land and controlled their destiny. The Quichua, the Cofans, the Shuar might depend on the government, missionaries, tourists, anthropologists, even the Company, but the Huaorani depended only on themselves and the forest, which were as one and had never changed and never would.

This had been brought home to me powerfully only the week before, on Columbus Day, when 20,000 Indians from all corners of Ecuador descended on Quito to stage a mass protest. About half of them made it through a cordon of military barriers erected around the city. I stood among them in a driving rain in the central plaza and listened to Valerio Grefa rail against five hundred years of oppression by the Spanish conquerors. He punctuated his speech with thrusts of a Huaorani spear. It was a tourist spear, from a trinket shop, and maybe half the size of a real spear. But the Huaorani didn't mind. They didn't even know. They hadn't come to Quito, and they hadn't joined the protest, for they were unlike every other indigenous group in the country: As they saw it, they had never been conquered and never would be, because they were the bravest people in the Amazon.

MOI RETURNED to my apartment later that afternoon, grinning and telling tales of his *paseo* with the *ecochicas*—he had eaten noodles and ice cream and walked in the park and met with Luis Macas. He was feeling good about the strike. "The whole world will know about the Huaorani!" he said. "The Company will cry when it sees our spears!"

A couple of hours later someone jiggled the knob on the front door, and I opened it to find Nanto and Alicia and Rocia standing in the hall. Nanto entered without a word and Alicia smiled and Rocia hugged my leg. They settled themselves on the couch next to Moi and watched Enqueri fiddle with the radio and exchanged no greeting that I could detect. They sat in silence for a while and then they spoke among themselves in Huaorani, quietly, and by and by Enqueri remarked to me, casually, that Nanto now thought the strike was a good idea and wanted to see if he could help.

Then Nanto spoke to me in Spanish. "We are hungry," he said. "We would like fish."

I took them to dinner at a small place nearby. Alicia was enthralled to find a dish on the menu called "Corvina Alicia" ("How did they know I would come here?") but too shy to order it. In fact, everyone ordered chicken and rice. Poor little Rocia coughed all through the meal. Nanto held her in his arms while he tried to eat, and whenever her coughing abated he patiently spooned chicken soup into her mouth. Later, as we got up to leave, he folded some rice into a napkin, to feed to her during the night.

At the apartment we pulled out mattresses and blankets and executed the usual routine, the Huaorani giggling and yelling instructions at me. They were asleep by eleven o'clock. About midnight there was a knock on the door, and I opened it and saw a woman holding an envelope. She was short and she appeared to have lightened her dark hair and she wore too much makeup. She looked, in other words, like a typical middle-class woman in Quito. She jumped back when I opened the door, as if she were surprised to see me.

"Who are you?" she asked.

"I live here," I said. "Who are *you?*"

"I am a friend of Nanto's. Is he here?"

"Yes, but he is asleep."

"Please let me speak to him."

"It is after midnight."

"What is your name, sir?"

"What is *your* name?"

"Rossana."

"Rossana what?"

She tried to look past me into the apartment, but I blocked the door. She backed off then, and I told her to return in the morning. Without another word she walked to the elevator and hit the button.

Awakened by the commotion, Enqueri snuck a peek through the door as the woman waited for the elevator. "That is Rossana Faieta," he said. Faieta, of course, was the sociologist employed by Maxus to secure a contract with the Huaorani. "This has been going on for many months now," Enqueri said. "The Company is trying to break Nanto. Rossana sits on his head. She will meet with him only when she thinks he is alone—when Moi and I are not there—because when he is alone he is very weak, especially if he comes to Quito. His head gets so full he cannot think. He will agree to anything."

I went downstairs then, to see if I could find Faieta, but the street was empty. On the way back in I asked the doorman if he had seen her.

"Yes," he said. "She had an envelope for one of your friends—one of those savages. He asked me to take it for him. He said it would be full of money. But the woman would not leave it with me."

In the morning I fired up the coffeepot, and as we sat around the kitchen table eating papaya and sipping gringo *chicha*, Enqueri told Nanto and Moi what had happened. Nanto was feeding pieces of bread to Rocia, who again had coughed violently through the night, and he looked sad and tired. If he was indeed taking bribes, it wasn't hard to see why.

At first, though, I wondered why Nanto had given Rossana Faieta my address—surely he hadn't thought he could keep his dealings with her secret. But the more I thought about it, the less surprised I was. There is no absence of guile among the Huaorani, but until the arrival of the Company, when survival without the clan became, if not possible, at least conceivable, guile that benefited only the individual was impractical. It had been a society in which nothing could be hidden. The Huaorani simply hadn't had much opportunity to hone the skills that promote such solitary action; Nanto still wasn't very good at being corrupted.

For his part, Nanto offered neither defense nor explanation of his behavior, and neither Moi nor Enqueri asked for any. Instead, Moi stood up behind Nanto and massaged his shoulders. "Nanto, Nanto," he said after a while. "We must be strong, Nanto. How can we fight the Company if we take money from it?" To my ears, at least, his voice carried no blame. Despite all the recent turmoil, the three of them remained as close as brothers, and, in any case, the idea that Nanto could have deceived Moi and Enqueri in any real way was ridiculous. As far as they were concerned, Nanto was a victim. Moi nodded toward a spear they had brought me as a gift. "If she comes again," he said, "I will kill her." He might have been kidding, but I honestly couldn't tell.

THE NEXT DAY I called the Maxus office and asked for William Hutton. I was told that he was in a meeting. Did I wish to leave a message?

"Tell him I'm an American journalist and I want to know whether a payment that a Maxus employee attempted to give to a Huaorani man was a bribe."

Hutton came on the phone a few seconds later.

"We have a policy of not paying the Huaorani money," he said, "but let me get back to you." He called in about an hour. "Rossana said she wanted to reimburse Nanto for a trip he made to Quito to visit someone in a hospital. Sometimes we will cover their transportation expenses for emergencies."

I suggested that midnight on a Saturday night was an odd time to be doing business.

"Look, I won't say we've never paid the Huaorani any money, but to my knowledge we haven't," he said. "It's not a good thing to do with relatively uneducated people."

I asked him why, if he had agreed to remove Faieta from her position, she was still on the job.

"I didn't say I'd take her off the job," he said.

I read to him from the transcript of the tape that Moi had made of the meeting in Hutton's office, in which it appeared that he had agreed to do just that.

"That's taken out of context," he said.

I read him more of the transcript.

"Let me get back to you," he said. I didn't hear from him again.

ENQUERI AND Nanto and Alicia and Rocia left that afternoon. I walked them downstairs, and in the street I flagged a cab and paid the driver fare to the bus station.

"Thank you, José," Nanto said. "Come soon to see us."

"Bring your baby," Alicia said.

Enqueri got into the cab last. It was hard to see them go, but him especially. It had been a year and a half since we'd first met, but in that time he'd undergone a decade's worth of change. At my apartment Moi had cleaned up Enqueri's haircut, shaving the sideburns high above his ears, and Enqueri had helped himself to the last of my good clothes. The gawky kid who'd once led me through the forest in his underwear now seemed more like a young man heading off for college. I tucked some money into his hand and made him promise they would get something to eat while they were on the road. He gave me a hug and looked me squarely in the eye. "I will be worried for you out here in this world, José," he said. "Please take care of yourself. And hurry back to the forest."

"And you, Enqueri. Move carefully among the cannibals."

"Good life, José."

"Good life."

M O I   S T A Y E D at my apartment two more days. I didn't see that much of him. I was packing to leave, and he was busy with the *ecochicas* and with Luis Macas. He did ask me to sit in on a meeting, but I declined. "It is not the work I do," I said. "If people like me are involved, then the Company and the government will tell the world that the Huaorani are being manipulated by foreigners."

"What is a foreigner?" Moi asked.

"Someone who does not live in your country."

"But only the Huaorani live in Huaorani country," he said. "So everyone is a foreigner."

I did agree, the night before I was to leave, to accompany him to a party at the apartment shared by two of the *ecochicas*, Esperanza and Paulina, and the children from their respective marriages. Music thundered from a tape player, and couples were dancing and sipping wine; Moi seemed a bit overwhelmed. He was tired, for one thing; as far as I could tell, he hadn't slept more than two nights in the preceding week. He found a spot on a couch and didn't leave it for the next six hours, though he was quite willing to talk to any of the women who wanted to talk to him, and pretty much all of them did.

"Moi has an ability to communicate with people that goes beyond the boundaries of language," one of the *ecochicas* told me.

Another said, "There is something about him—you could almost call it a kind of purity."

"I don't know about that," I said.

"I mean he is natural. He speaks directly from his heart."

"I think that is true," I said.

One thing he did speak from the heart about was his desire to have a schoolhouse in Quehueire Ono, a real schoolhouse rather than a hut, with desks and a blackboard and pencils and notebooks for all the students.

"Moi keeps asking us about 'programs,'" Esperanza Martínez told me later that night. "He has so many plans, and he wants us to help. But how do I explain that 'programs' are not what we do? We have demonstrations, we get in front of people in power, we make the public aware of issues. But we don't work out in the field—we don't have that kind of money. We seem to be having some trouble making that clear."

About three in the morning I looked over to the couch to find that Moi had tucked himself into my windbreaker and pulled the hood down over his face and gone to sleep. I rousted him and gave him my heavy jacket to wear under the windbreaker, and out in the street he drew all the cords tight and snapped all the snaps and zipped all the zippers and cinched down the hood.

"You look like an Eskimo," I said. "Do you know what an Eskimo is?"

"Yes," he said. "An *indígena* who lives in the snow in America."

"Yes."

"And their land has a lot of oil, does it not?"

"Yes, it does."

"And they fought the Company, did they not?"

"Yes, some of them did."

"And now they have a lot of money but they are not *indígenas* anymore."

"It is true that many of them do not live as they once lived," I said.

"So they lost."

At my apartment he stretched out on the guest bed with all his clothes on, and I covered him with blankets and put a glass of water beside the bed. Two hours later we awoke and I called a cab and we were out the door quickly, I on the way to the airport, Moi to the bus

station. He was wearing the black leather running shoes I'd given him—
he'd had them polished—and my backpack and bright blue nylon
chumpa and the sunglasses that he thought helped him to see for many
kilometers. He was a little dazed but in a good mood. It was early, the
streets nearly deserted. He said he would walk for a while. As with
Enqueri, I gave him money for his trip home. He told me to write him
letters and send them to the Capuchin mission in Coca, and I said I
would come back as soon as I could.

"Bring your family," he said. "We will build you a house on the
ridge, next to Mengatohue, and we will protect you."

"That would please me very much," I said. "I will come back as
soon as I can. Be careful, Moi."

"Chong, the Huaorani fear nothing. Good life!"

When my cab pulled away Moi watched me as carefully as he
would a monkey in the treetops. Then he waved. It wasn't a particularly
animated wave—his hand more flopped than shook—and he didn't
smile. But as he faded from sight, I realized that I had never before seen
a Huao wave good-bye. About then I was finally able to identify the
source of the vacuumlike feeling, a hollowness in the gut, that I always
felt when I parted from Moi, Enqueri, Nanto: It always seemed more
likely than not that I would never see them again.

18

ONCE AGAIN on the flight to California I had violent dreams and awoke with my forehead dripping sweat. Once again, when I got home, I immersed myself in my garden and took long walks in stormy weather. I was never quite comfortable if my family were out of my sight, and I hugged them a lot. I did not doubt that I was right to have come back, but it was a long time before I understood that I had left the Huaorani so that, in some very fundamental ways, I could live like a Huao. I thought often of Moi, Enqueri, and the others. I missed them.

Fortunately, even from afar it was not hard to track their strike, or, later, to fill in the missing pieces. Half the people I knew in Ecuador had found their way to it. Indeed, as *El Comercio*, Quito's newspaper of record, put it, the Huaorani "captured the attention of the entire nation."

WHEN THE BUSES arranged by the *ecochicas* arrived in the Oriente—one went to the Shiripuno bridge, the other to the town of Puyo, near Shell—they found more than a hundred Huaorani waiting for them. They had come from every part of the territory—from Garzacocha, from Toñampare, from Quehueire Ono, from Cononaco. There were old barefoot warriors brandishing spears and blowguns, grandmothers carrying pails of *chicha*, young men trimmed out in their best T-shirts and boots and go-to-town pants, young women wearing nothing but the faded pastel skirts and armorlike, lovingly preserved white cotton bras sent to the forest decades earlier from small Christian towns in Texas and Oklahoma. The buses drove so high into the Andes that some of the Huaorani got nosebleeds and their ears ached. Then they plunged down through a corridor of volcanoes and into Quito and came to an exhausted stop at the great park, the Carolina, that stands at the heart of the new part of the city. There the Huaorani made their camp, directly across the street from the high-rise that held the Maxus offices.

A crowd of *cowode* ringed the camp throughout the day and into the night. Sometimes there were dozens of gawkers, sometimes hundreds, many of them getting their first glimpse of genuine Amazonian Indians. One thing they saw whirling about the camp was Enqueri, who threw himself into the strike with every bit of the deep reserves of energy I had seen during our epic trek. His experience as chief of a seismic crew now put to new, if ironic, use, the Condorito took it upon himself to run the camp, to be sure that everyone was kept warm and dry and fed and Yupied.

It was Moi who led the assault on Maxus. Assault seems the right word. In the morning, fueled by rice and beans and Yupi and the sheer exhilaration of their quest, the Huaorani—some of whom hadn't laid eyes on an internal combustion vehicle until the day their bus bounced down the Vía Auca—took up their spears and marched across one of the busiest streets in Quito and positioned themselves in front of the Maxus doors and laid siege to the building. Surrounded by television and newspaper crews, Moi told the guard that he wanted to speak with William Hutton. Instead, Rossana Faieta appeared, and the Huaorani women set upon her, slapping her and yanking her hair and driving her into the safety of the building.

Next the Huaorani marched to the offices of Petroecuador. They massed themselves in front of the building and sang songs of war. Hundreds of people gathered to watch them. Nanto and Moi stood up before the crowd. Judging by the photographs that appeared in various newspapers, they cut striking figures, wearing crowns and quivers and armlets, shirtless, their broad shoulders and deep chests radiating strength, at their sides the long Huaorani spears whose purpose few in Quito would need explained. Moi was handed a microphone. He proclaimed the valor of the "bravest people in the Amazon" and demanded that Maxus get out of the territory. "We do not destroy your home," he cried. "So why must you destroy ours?"

Enqueri stood a little off to the side. Had he been dressed like Moi and Nanto—and, indeed, most of the Huaorani—he would have looked thin and awkward rather than powerful, his bony shoulders lost amid crown and quiver and armlet. Instead, Enqueri chose to present himself in glasses, sport shirt, long cotton pants, and Colombian loafers, on his right wrist the watch that hadn't worked since the day he bought it. In a sea of savages he was an island of *civilización*. If you did not know that he was a Huao, you might not have guessed it.

With the Huaorani blocking the doors and hundreds of onlookers in the streets, Petroecuador and Maxus finally had no choice but to meet with Moi and Nanto. The meeting was closed to the press and the public, but the views expressed by the Huaorani were contained in a letter written to Maxus by Nanto and signed by Moi and representatives of the Huaorani communities and stamped with the ONHAE seal. They said that the Huaorani had met and they had voted and they had rejected the *acta* Nanto had signed with Rossana Faieta; that the Huaorani did not want Faieta in their territory, and this was why the women had attacked her; that the Huaorani did not want any gifts from Maxus; that Rachel Saint had tried to prevent the Huaorani from coming to Quito and making their protest known to the world because she was in favor of the Company; and, above all, that they were tired and wanted to live in peace and did not want the *petroleros* on their land. "Now we have shut the door," they wrote. "We do not want to negotiate anymore."

Publicly, the Company refused to acknowledge that it was having any problems with the Huaorani. According to a Maxus spokesman, the Huaorani were in no way opposed to the Maxus project. They had come to Quito, the spokesman said, because "they wanted assurances about our environmental management plan." The Huaorani had given Maxus a document that the company was in the process of "studying." The meeting with the Huaorani reflected a climate of friendship and cordiality. There had been no violence.

A more telling indication of just how serious the Huaorani problem had become for the Company came the following day, when Nanto, Moi, and Luis Macas were granted an audience with Sixto Durán

Ballén, the president of Ecuador. The meeting was held in the National Palace. According to all reports, it was tense. The price of oil was tumbling, the country's debt was rising, and Sixto was hard-pressed to attract all the foreign oil investment he possibly could, because Ecuador did not have the money to develop its oil fields on its own. The American oil companies had Sixto over a barrel, so to speak, and they were working him. That very week, Maxus, ARCO, Occidental, City, and Oryx had formally demanded changes in the country's oil laws; in particular, they demanded an absolute guarantee that oil production would not be hindered by laws protecting nature reserves, national parks, or indigenous rights.

The last thing Sixto needed was any public sign of unrest in the oil fields. What exactly did the Huaorani want?

Nanto and Moi told Sixto that the Huaorani were a small nation, but the forest was their home, and that while the government might not recognize their law, they nevertheless had a right to defend their home. The Huaorani respected others. They didn't go to the president's house and break all his windows. They didn't throw garbage into the president's house. Yet the president allowed the Company to throw garbage into the home of the Huaorani and pollute the rivers and make the Huaorani sick until they died of contamination. Every culture was different; the Huaorani did not want to exchange their way of life for schools and airplanes. If the president thought the Company way of life was good, then he should offer his own home to the Company, not the home of the Huaorani. They asked the president to appoint an independent commission to investigate the Maxus situation.

Sixto was stern. The government had ministries designed to address such problems, he said. You want me to do something about them even though you haven't discussed them with my ministers. Instead, you have gone outside the government, outside the system of justice that has been established in Ecuador. It would be wrong for the government to accommodate such behavior. "Put yourself in my shoes," he said.

But Moi, for one, was satisfied. Now the president had heard. Now the whole world would know. And he found Sixto's last remark absolutely hilarious.

• • •

THE HUAORANI held their camp for a week, and life in the mountains took its toll. Strangers inserted themselves into the camp; the Huaorani woke in the night to find drunks stealing their food. The rains came, bitter Andean rains, and the Huaorani were cold all the time. They fell ill with fevers, coughs, intestinal ailments. The Yupi ran out, and the novelty of their presence in Quito wore off. Quito was big, life was fast, and their friends had many other things to attend to. Once again the Huaorani were alone.

Nanto left Quito first, on his own, but Moi and Enqueri hung on until the end, when the Huaorani climbed onto the buses to begin the long trek back to the forest. Moi was exhausted but content: The Huaorani had spoken; the world had listened; now everyone knew what the Company was trying to do to the Huaorani. In the *ecochicas* and Luis Macas they had made important new friends. They had told the Company to get out, and they had delivered their message to the president. "Put yourself in my shoes," Moi said as he boarded the bus, and laughed.

For reasons that will become clear, I have no way to confirm Enqueri's thoughts as he followed Moi onto the bus. But knowing the Condorito as I did, I believe this is a fair guess: I don't think he was laughing. I think he would have been keenly aware that his own shoes had already begun to disintegrate, the bright golden buckles tarnished by mud and oil, his broad Huaorani feet pushing out the sides, and that it would be years, if ever, before he would have the money to buy a new pair. I'm sure that many times during the strike he looked across to the Maxus building, to the *cowode* hurrying in and out, so elegantly dressed, so civilized, and so apparently unaffected by the Huaorani presence that they could all but ignore it. I believe he would have been more conscious than ever of how the Huaorani saw the world and how the people across the street saw it and whose point of view really counted. His calculating mind would have been hard at this equation: The Huaorani had been in Quito for a week. They had worked, they had suffered. What difference had they really made?

THROUGH THE spring and summer of 1993 reports continued to filter in from Ecuador. The sources were varied: a letter here, a postcard there, often months in transit; a ravenous, amoebic traveler back from the Oriente, willing to sing for lunch; the occasional static-filled phone call, though these were thin fodder indeed, for anyone even remotely connected with the goings-on in the territory assumed his phone was tapped. Still, from this patchwork network the same stories emerged time and again.

In February of 1993, four months after the strike, ONHAE held its second elections. They were held in Toñampare, but judging by the reports I received, they might as well have been held in the Maxus offices in Quito. According to several observers, Maxus paid not only for all the costs of the *congreso* but for the party held afterward, and for airplanes to bring in selected delegates, during which Maxus representatives suggested to the Huaorani how they should vote. At least half the Huaorani did not participate, and many who did walked out in protest against Maxus. They were led by Moi. Enraged by the Company's interference, he quit ONHAE altogether, choosing to concentrate his energies on the defense of Quehueire Ono, which thus far remained beyond the Company's influence. As for Nanto, his spirit had long since been broken, and he, too, chose to leave the organization. So, with Amo dead, the ONHAE mantle came to rest on the thin shoulders of the Condorito, Enqueri—who, as it turned out, had run on a platform that advocated making a deal with Maxus.

For its part, Maxus did not deny that it had participated in the Huaorani elections, but a company spokesman maintained that it had provided only logistical assistance, and that it had acted in a spirit of friendship and good faith. Yes, Enqueri wanted to make a deal with Maxus, and that was why he had been elected. The Huaorani were free to make their own decisions, were they not?

In the months following the election, Enqueri was spotted far more frequently in Quito, almost always in the company of Maxus employees, and usually escorted by Milton Ortega, a company "anthropologist" who took over Rossana Faieta's role after the strike. I heard that Enqueri stayed in expensive hotels and wore fine clothes; that he had a suit, which he wore with shiny new soccer cleats; that he had a new wristwatch, too, one that actually worked and that said, on its face, MAXUS; that Maxus had given ONHAE thousands of dollars, and set it up with an office near Shell, and arranged for Enqueri to receive a salary. But the comment I heard most often was perhaps the most telling: Enqueri was getting fat.

In August of 1993, six months after Enqueri was elected president of ONHAE, Maxus announced that it had signed a formal agreement with the Huaorani. I called William Hutton to get a copy. He refused to release one. It would be "inappropriate," he said. It was an "involved" document and needed explanation. I asked him whether Enqueri had had the benefit of an independent adviser to help him analyze the contract. Yes, he had, Hutton said—"the government." He dismissed my suggestion that the government was compromised. "There's no compromise at all," he said. "It's a very one-sided agreement. The Huaorani are receiving educational and other benefits from Maxus, and the only obligation they have is to let us come onto their land." Maxus, he said, was legally entitled to exploit the Huaorani land with or without Huaorani cooperation, but it would like to be a good neighbor. In fact, it had begun its community programs inside the territory more than a year and a half before it signed the agreement. "It's our intention," Hutton said, "to work with the people, let them live their lives, and try to avoid any substantial disruption of their culture."

Were the "educational and other benefits" of the agreement being disbursed by the evangelical Christian mission?

"We're simply working through the existing infrastructure," he said, and that included "the missionaries that have been there for a long time." He pointed out, too, that "basically all Christians are interested in telling others about the Gospel, so the term 'evangelical Christian' is kind of a redundant phrase." As for any journalists who might try to sneak into the territory to see what Maxus was doing, he said, "if we find them, we will stop them."

Maxus did release a photo taken at the signing ceremony, which was held in the Huaorani community of Quihuaro. On the left, tall and gray and pale and bald and patrician, dressed all in white, beaming from ear to ear, stood the Ecuadorian president, Sixto Durán Ballén. On the right, tall and gray and pale and bald and patrician, dressed all in white, beaming from ear to ear, stood William Hutton. Between them, standing only to their shoulders, his hair thick and black and his skin very brown, wearing a jaguar-tooth necklace and some sort of shorts and no glasses, stood Enqueri. He was the only man looking the camera in the eye, so to speak, and his expression was as enigmatic as the Mona Lisa's. I'd seen it before: when we were in the forest and he told me we were lost and I asked him what that meant and he said, "It means we might die."

I felt fairly certain of at least this: Whatever it was Maxus thought Enqueri had agreed to and whatever it was the Condor thought he'd agreed to were two entirely different things.

BY ALL ACCOUNTS the Maxus development proceeded about as expected. Eleven days after it signed its agreement with Enqueri, Maxus managed to drill into an Occidental pipeline and spill 55,000 gallons of raw crude near the Napo River. Barges hired by Maxus dumped drilling waste into the Napo and the Yasuní. When people got in their way, Maxus subcontractors broke bones and threatened lives. A confidential study made by a consultant, a draft of which was leaked to me, confirmed that the Maxus "education" program was systematically undermining the "traditional social structures and communication networks" of the Huaorani. "Maxus has pretty well taken over," Ali Sharif told me when I called him in Quito. "They've bought ONHAE." He hadn't seen Moi in months. "I'm worried about him," he said. "I hear that Enqueri has issued a death threat." And by the way, did I know that Nanto had taken a job with the Company?

IN THE FALL of 1993 an American with a video camera managed to make his way into Toñampare and capture portions of a rather telling ceremony celebrating what was, on paper, an extraordinary gesture by the Ecuadorian government: the incorporation of the Huaorani into the administration of Yasuní National Park. In an agreement to be signed by ONHAE and the government's Institute of Forests and Natural Areas, the Huaorani—or at least ONHAE—were accorded a role in policing the park boundaries, enforcing hunting and fishing rules within the park, and, most important, overseeing the park's administration and the enforcement of the Yasuní Park Management Plan, which included environmental monitoring of Maxus.

Making the Huaorani park guards, of course, was not without precedent—Randy Borman and the Cofans had won that status only the year before. But that was as far as the similarities went. The Cofans had won their role by aggressively confronting the Company, and by catching it in the act of breaking the law. The Huaorani, on the other hand, were being brought into the Yasuní administration by the very people they were supposed to watchdog. (The "Park Management Plan" they were to enforce had been funded by the Company and zoned half the park for industrial use, and the contract they signed with the forestry institute was coordinated by SUBIR, the "sustainable resource development" program created by the U.S. Agency for International Development.) About three hundred Huaorani—basically, the population of Toñampare—turned up to witness the signing. As Enqueri moved among them, wielding a bullhorn, the Maxus anthropologist Milton Ortega followed two steps behind him, herding him like a sheepdog. William Hutton was there, too, wearing a Maxus hardhat and starched white Maxus overalls, a copy of *The Wall Street Journal* sticking out of his briefcase. He sat beneath a beach umbrella with Rachel Saint. As they waited, a military helicopter landed on the *pista* and disgorged officers from various branches of the service and a slight, dark-haired woman named Alicia Durán Ballén—the president's daughter, and his chief adviser on indigenous affairs. She was accompanied by Mark Wiznitzer, a "political counselor" from the U.S. embassy.

The director of the forestry institute made a short opening statement applauding the idea that the Huaorani would now be put in charge of monitoring oil development on the land that had so long been theirs. Then, one by one, the various dignitaries signed the document. The last to take pen in hand was Dayuma, and when she had finished, Alicia Durán Ballén removed her gold earrings and presented them to Dayuma as a gift. Dayuma, in turn, gave the president's daughter a feather armlet. Then Ballén turned to Wiznitzer and flashed him a warm smile. "Was that a fair exchange?" she asked, in English.

Smiling just as broadly, Wiznitzer replied, "Well, that's how we got Manhattan."

THE VIDEO included an interview with Enqueri. Feather crown, no glasses. "We did not want the oil company on our land, and we successfully resisted them for years," he said. "But then the government made it clear that the oil company would come whether we liked it or not, so we decided it would be best to negotiate an agreement." He said that the agreement he had signed with Maxus recognized the existence of the Huaorani nation, and he was pleased about that, but that in fact the Huaorani had no power to control the oil companies, so they really had no choice but to trust Maxus. However, if Maxus violated that trust by destroying the forest, "our only choice is to use what we know— attack them with spears from all sides."

It was hard not to laugh at Enqueri's threat—this from a man who could barely control a canoe. But on the whole the interview was infinitely saddening, not only, or even mainly, because the Enqueri on tape seemed far more a public relations construct than a genuine leader. No, somewhat the opposite, in fact. His words felt painfully true to the man I had known. I am sure that he did quite well for himself in the Maxus deal. But I'm sure, too, that he had assessed the situation as thoroughly as he could and had seen no other way. I think that on some level he honestly believed that if Maxus broke its word, the Huaorani could drive the Company out.

It was easy enough for me, for any *cowode*, to see what was coming, and to ask the obvious questions: Where would the Huaorani be in twenty years, when Maxus was finished taking its oil, and the Huaorani territory was crisscrossed with roads and laced with toxic waste, and the money and the gifts that the Huaorani had grown accustomed to—that they had come to depend on—suddenly dried up? But to the extent that the Huaorani prepared for the future, they did so by obeying tradition: by cultivating their manioc gardens, by moving from place to place, by singing, down through the generations, the knowledge of their vast territory and where to find every single thing they might need. Twenty years? The future was right now: How do I get something to eat?

Enqueri gave that interview just over a year after I had taken him to see his first production well. He had seen test wells before that, and he had cut seismic trail, but he had never examined an actual working well. This one happened to be in Quichua territory, a mile or so off the Vía Auca. The well pump, a giant metal locust, roared so loudly that even though we parked two hundred yards away we had to shout to hear each other. Below the well were three waste pits that had mostly col-

lapsed into one big pool. It was quieter down by the pool. At its far end
we found a fruit bat mired in tar, trapped face down a couple of feet
short of the bank. Only its head was free, and at our approach it began
to bob maniacally, as if it could peck its way clear of the film of crude
in which it was dying. It soon wore itself out, and lay there panting, the
action of its tiny, frantically beating lungs highlighted by the black
sheen that coated its back.

Enqueri studied the bat for quite some time, then pointed, in a
startled way, to the gray wall of dead, leafless trees that surrounded the
pit, and then to the massive field of dead trees below the pit's lower lip,
which oozed a long trail of waste crude. "Everything is dead," he said,
as much to himself as to me. "This is what the Company is going to do
to the Huaorani land." It was, however, the look on his face, more than
his words or tone of voice, that has remained with me: a look of real
fear, and as rare among the Huaorani as his eyeglasses. But it was not
without precedent. It was, I imagined, a look very similar to the one his
father must have worn almost forty years before, the first time he had
squinted into the sky and seen flying metal. His father had lashed out,
but soon, tempted and terrified by that new and unfathomable power,
he had surrendered—whether he knew it or not.

INITIALLY, the change in administrations in Washington in 1992
had appeared to augur well for the Huaorani, given the concatenation
of American interests in the Oriente and the fact that, as a senator, Al
Gore had made the preservation of tropical rain forests almost a personal crusade. When Gore became vice president, a member of his
senatorial staff, twenty-nine-year-old Kathleen McGinty, was appointed
director of the White House Office on Environmental Policy, and in
August of 1993, shortly before Enqueri signed his agreement with
Maxus, McGinty was headed to Ecuador's Galápagos Islands and decided to take a look at the Huaorani territory. Maxus and the U.S.
embassy were only too happy to oblige. They whisked McGinty into
and out of Toñampare in a matter of hours—just long enough for a
photo op. The photo surfaced in *The New York Times* a few weeks later:
There, sitting side by side, were William Hutton; Jack Mack, the embassy's chargé d'affaires; and McGinty, wearing a Huaorani headdress

and the somewhat startled expression most *cowode* wear most of the time in the territory. End of visit.

Shortly thereafter, Boris P. Abad, the Maxus manager of government affairs, sent a written statement to McGinty, the State Department, and the embassy, apparently to assure them that the Huaorani agreement was the product of free and fair elections, and an accurate reflection of the wishes of the Huaorani people. Among other things, Abad asserted that Enqueri "was never at" the Huaorani strike in Quito.

I got a copy of Abad's statement, too. I keep it in a file with a photograph taken during the strike: It shows Enqueri and Moi standing before a crowd of Huaorani, in front of the Maxus building, Enqueri's right fist raised in protest.

IN OCTOBER of 1993 Enqueri was brought to the United States by a Maxus public relations team and escorted through Washington, D.C., by Blasco Peñaherrera, the Ecuadorian ambassador to the Organization of American States. Standing before the OAS's Inter-American Commission on Human Rights at that very moment, of course, was the petition filed by the Sierra Club Legal Defense Fund on behalf of the Huaorani—the petition charging that the Maxus project would cause the ethnocide of the Huaorani, and asking the commission to investigate.

The Ecuadorian diplomats helped the Maxus team arrange a follow-up meeting with Kathleen McGinty and a presentation for the OAS. There were other meetings as well. One of them was with an environmental group, one of the largest in the United States, which had a project in the Yasuní area. The woman with whom they met agreed to tell me about the meeting only if I did not reveal her name or that of her organization, which had already come under fire for accepting a substantial donation from the Company, and which in the chorus of voices raised over the Huaorani situation had been conspicuous by its absence. It was a controversial area, she said, and they didn't want to inflame their membership. If the president of the organization learned that she had spoken to the press, she would lose her job.

She said that the meeting was conducted in Spanish, and that

Enqueri was sandwiched between Lucia Rivas Saenz, of Maxus, and Blasco Peñaherrera. Saenz and Peñaherrera described the agreement between the company and ONHAE and requested funding for a scientific station in Yasuní that, they said, would be run by the Huaorani.

"It was extremely sad," the woman said. "Every time I asked Enqueri a question, one of the other people would jump in and answer for him. He finally spoke up when I asked him whether Maxus had built a school—he said, 'Yes.' That was all he said during the entire meeting. I just felt really sorry for him. He sat there dressed up in his feather crown and his suit and clearly didn't know what was going on. It was obvious to me that he was being manipulated. He was nothing more than a showpiece."

Later I received a copy of an odd little note Maxus had prepared as an introduction for Enqueri, a sort of biographical sketch. One sentence in particular leaped out: "Enqueri is married to Kauo Baiwa from the Cononaco group." I had to smile at that. The Cononaco group, of course, was Quemperi's clan; it appeared that our nearly disastrous visit there had borne fruit for the Condorito. Not only had he gained the right to live in the rich Cononaco region, if he so chose, but he had married a good woman. As I remembered Kauo, she was strong and energetic, quick to smile, and a beauty—and she had thought Enqueri something of a clown. But Maxus had made Enqueri a rich man. He had become, as they say, a good catch.

19

I N SEPTEMBER of 1993—a matter of months before Maxus was to open its first well, and more than three years after the Sierra Club Legal Defense Fund first filed its petition—the Inter-American Commission on Human Rights announced that it had scheduled a hearing for the SCLDF side of the case. SCLDF was given two weeks to prepare its presentation. As it happened, the hearing was to be held in Washington, D.C., shortly after the Maxus team had made its rounds with Enqueri. This meant the SCLDF petition would have no apparent authority unless a Huao was there to help present it. So Adriana Fabra, a Spanish human-rights lawyer and one of the two SCLDF lawyers handling the petition, had just two weeks to find a Huao willing to come to the United States of North America and testify.

Fabra flew at once to Quito and looked up Judith Kimerling. The two women made their way to Coca, down the Vía Auca, and up the Shiripuno River to the Shiripuno Center—where, by sheer good fortune, they found Moi. Kimerling introduced him to Fabra, and he agreed at once to go to the United States: He said that he had recently learned, through a dream, that he was about to take a long and important journey. Moi and Fabra returned to Quito and immediately applied for a visa at the American embassy. Fabra explained their mission; the embassy denied their request.

That afternoon, angry and frustrated, Moi went to President Sixto's newly created Office of Indigenous Affairs, which advised the president on the country's increasingly militant Indian groups. Moi met with a staff member, who said there was nothing he could do. Perhaps if Moi would meet with the president's daughter?

The next morning, Moi was ushered into the office of Alicia Durán Ballén. Why, Moi demanded to know, had Enqueri been permitted to visit the United States, but he, Moi, was being denied? Moi said that Maxus was manipulating Enqueri. It was time to denounce Maxus before the whole world, or Maxus would rob the Huaorani name.

While he was sitting there, a door opened and a man from the Company walked in and handed Moi some pieces of paper. They contained a list of goods that the Company was prepared to give to Moi's village: gasoline, wood, cement, nails, paint—in fact, all the materials they would need to build a real school. The Company would pay for everything, including a contractor to construct it. The Company would provide desks and uniforms, and pay the schoolteacher's salary. Later it would build a landing strip for airplanes and helicopters and install a radio. The memo had been signed by Maxus, by Enqueri, and by the head of the evangelical mission. A cover note said that it was based on an agreement that had been made between the Company and ONHAE ten months before. Now, suddenly, the goods were ready for delivery—they would arrive at precisely the time Moi was scheduled to testify in Washington.

MEANWHILE, Adriana Fabra was on the phone to the United States, and at some point that day the fact that a witness in a human-rights case was being denied a visa got through to the State Department. Two days later Moi was on his way north.

Much of this I learned shortly before Moi and Fabra got on their plane in Quito, when I received a call from the SCLDF office in San Francisco. Once Moi reached Washington, I was told, Fabra and Karen Parker, the other attorney working on the petition, would be busy preparing their presentation, and Moi would be more or less alone in a strange city in a strange country. Did I have any suggestions on how best to make him feel comfortable?

I flew to Washington. Moi arrived there right behind me, less than twenty-four hours before he was due to testify.

"Chong," he said, and handed me his bag and his spears and walked into the hotel room and made himself at home.

MOI LOOKED no different, and his spirits seemed as good as ever. But he said that the year since I had last seen him had been the hardest of his life. "Chong," he said, "we were sold like meat." He told me about the strike, about his meetings in Quito, about the election and the agreement Enqueri had signed with Maxus—it had been negotiated in secret, without benefit of outside counsel, and the elders, particularly Mengatohue, were enraged. Maxus had hired an "army" of anthropologists to find ways to "manipulate" the Huaorani, and it was buying off the villages one by one, dividing the Huaorani against themselves. It was cutting Quehueire Ono off from the outside, too—Maxus patrolled the Vía Auca, Enqueri in tow, trying to block Moi's friends from getting up the Shiripuno. He said that Maxus had threatened to control the Huaorani with violence if necessary. It had bribed Enqueri with some new teeth. As for Enqueri himself, Moi said that he still considered him a good man, but that he was weak, and that the Company and the missionaries had a hold on him that could not be broken. "We must win," he said, "or the Huaorani will disappear forever."

And so Moi had agreed to come to Washington, and he had written his letter to the president and asked him to explain why it was that the United States of North America was so bent on destroying the Huaorani. We failed on our first attempt to deliver it to the White House, of course, and the following morning Moi insisted that we try again. Again we found the gate closed. Nearby, however, there were two life-size cutouts of Bill and Hillary Clinton. I explained to Moi who they were. He nodded, stepped between them, slipped his palm into Bill's, and turned stone-faced to the photographer. After the Polaroid developed, Moi studied it seriously, in the way the Huaorani often study photos: He held it upside down, sidewise, and at an angle, to be sure he understood its essence. "Yes," he said. "That is me." Satisfied, he tucked it in his bag. Then we strolled past the Washington Monument. Moi assumed that it was an oil well, because down in the Oriente the only places one sees such an expanse of cleared land and such an immense structure are where the Company is at work. It made sense to Moi that an oil well would stand right in the heart of the center of power in the United States of North America.

IN THE AFTERNOON Moi put on his shirt and tie and crown and quivers and went with the SCLDF lawyers to testify before the commission. I went, too, and saw for a fact that he had taken to heart my suggestion to "use your own words": The hearing was in Spanish, and when it came time to testify Moi roared like a jaguar. However, he did so in Huaorani. The commissioners sat back, stunned. By the time Moi reached his warning that the Huaorani were "the bravest people in the Amazon" and would defend themselves "with spears from all sides," he was half out of his seat with the intensity of his oratory. About then Karen Parker leaned over and said, very quietly, "Now say it in Spanish." Moi switched languages without appearing to miss a beat, and finished with a plea: "Please do not abandon us to the Company."

When the hearing ended, a half dozen commission members gathered around Moi to introduce themselves. As it happened, Moi had brought several string bags with him from the forest. The bags had been woven by Huaorani elders, who depend on such handicrafts to earn a little cash for things like shotgun shells and malaria medicine. He hoped to fetch about five dollars for each bag, and a dollar more for "transport." As Moi figured it, there was no better place to start his sales campaign than with the commission. But the Huaorani are warriors, not traders, merciless to their enemies and generous to their friends. Within five minutes he had given away all the bags he'd brought. He gave away a spear, too, to the commission's executive secretary. "When your sky falls," Moi said, "this will hold up the clouds."

APPARENTLY, Moi made quite an impression, because the next day the commission told his lawyers that it was strongly interested in the petition. However, under the bylaws of the OAS, it could not conduct an investigation unless it was invited to do so by the host country. In this case that invitation had to come through the Ecuadorian ambassador to the OAS—Blasco Peñaherrera. You can see the problem, the commission said. Perhaps Moi would speak to the ambassador?

While the two attorneys spent all the next day trying to arrange a meeting at the Ecuadorian embassy, Moi put his time to good use. Speaking Spanish, he quickly developed a rapport with the hotel's service staff. He learned how to run the elevator, he stuffed his bag with free shampoo, and, as often as he wanted, which was often indeed, he was served a humongous dish the kitchen named the Moi Plate—a bottomless gob of chicken, shrimp, rice, potatoes, and "leaves."

Though his Spanish clearly served him well, Moi was determined to learn English. He wanted to meet some American women, and he was convinced that until he could speak to them in their own language he would be ignored. At his insistence, each night in Washington we sat in a bar, he sipping a soft drink and I a beer, and he practiced saying, "Hello, how are you, Miss?" Late that second night he gave me a nudge and nodded toward a young woman sitting nearby. I asked her if my friend could try out his English on her; she said she'd be delighted. I about had to shove Moi out of his seat. Finally, he walked over and looked at her for a long time. She smiled. Very seriously, he pursed his lips and said, "How . . . how . . . *cómo estás?*" Then he started laughing so hard tears came to his eyes. It was all he could do to slink back to our table, where he collapsed in a puddle of giggles. Every once in a while he'd lean back and coo to the ceiling. "How are you?" he'd say, and then he'd fall apart all over again.

MOI NEVER DID get inside the White House, but he came close. I happened to know an *ecochica* in Washington who happened to know how things got done, and one afternoon Moi settled his crown into place, adjusted his jaguar-tooth necklace, and marched through the metal detectors inside the Old Executive Office Building and into the office of Kathleen McGinty.

Moi told McGinty what had happened after she left the Huaorani territory, when Enqueri signed his agreement with the Company. After the ceremony, Moi said, dozens of Huaorani fell sick with disease, and one little girl died. Furthermore, he said, many of the Huaorani were opposed to the agreement, but they hadn't been allowed to attend the ceremony. In the past, he explained, ONHAE would have held an assembly before making any such deal, and representatives from all parts of the territory would have come together and discussed it until consensus was reached. But only Enqueri and a few others had read this agreement. Many Huaorani believed it to be a deal for T-shirts.

McGinty assured Moi that the White House was interested in the Huaorani and would be keeping an eye on the situation. If I, for one, had no doubt of her sincerity, I knew also that she meant no more than exactly what she said. ("Perhaps when Maxus is done, we could blow up the roads," one of her aides suggested on our way out.) I knew who would win the day even if by some long shot the fate of the Huaorani were to come down to a shoot-out between young Kathleen McGinty and, say, a Texas warhorse like Lloyd Bentsen.

These were things Moi could not have picked up on; still, he seemed disturbed as we left. He felt that he had failed, somehow. In the corridor he said, "The Company can speak whenever it wants to, but this is the only chance the Huaorani will have to be heard. If only the government would come to the forest—if only it could *see*." He was lost in thought until we hit the street. Then he said he was thinking of changing his name. *Moi*, he reminded me, is a Huaorani word that means "dream," as in a vision, but now it was too late for visions. He would change his name to Dica, because *dica* means "rock." "A rock can be struck many times," he said, "but it can never be hurt."

OUR LAST STOP on our last day in Washington was the Ecuadorian embassy, where, finally, a meeting had been arranged. Where the Old Executive Office Building had bustled with activity, the embassy seemed a throwback to colonial South America and an authoritarian order that, centuries after the conquest, continues to dominate nearly every aspect of Ecuadorian culture. The building itself is haciendalike and cavernous, and a ghostly emptiness greets the visitor. The only life in evidence on the ground floor was huddled into a corner: a dozen of the forlorn Latin faces one sees throughout Ecuador, faces reflecting resignation to a long and most likely fruitless wait for an audience with whatever power it was that lay hidden somewhere on the second floor. It was an indication of the seriousness of the OAS case that Moi and his attorneys were ushered into the ambassador's office right on time for their meeting.

Strong coffee was served in tiny cups. Blasco Peñaherrera is a small, dapper man with a rhetorical style that is common, in my experience, to virtually every bureaucrat in Ecuador: parry slightly, then thrust with an aggression meant to buckle the knees. As he sipped his coffee he listened to Moi's proposition: Invite the OAS to study the territory and, if problems were found, impose a moratorium on oil development until they could be resolved. When Moi finished, the ambassador smiled and put down his coffee cup. In a voice that grew steadily more intense, he said that the Huaorani were not a sovereign nation; they were Ecuadorian citizens. Ecuador depended on oil for half its revenue, so to impede production was akin to treason. He lashed out at the two lawyers: What right did they have to interfere in the business of Ecuador? How could Moi claim to speak for the Huaorani? Just two weeks before, their elected leader, Enqueri, had sat in the ambassador's office. He had come to the United States with the Company, and he seemed very happy with the agreement they had made. As far as the ambassador could tell, the Company was doing a fine job.

Moi listened impassively and, to all outward appearances, patiently. For the Huaorani, political discourse is a long discussion aimed at achieving consensus; aggression means spears, and putting one's life on the line. When the ambassador had finished, Moi had only one point to make: If the Company was doing a fine job, what harm could there be in an open investigation? Everyone could participate: the Company, the government, the Huaorani, the OAS, the whole world. Let everyone come and see. Let everyone speak.

Blasco Peñaherrera was silent for a moment. Then he said, "Do not think for one second that there will ever be a moratorium on oil development. But I will talk to the commission and tell them about our discussion today. And then we will see."

WHILE WE were waiting to hear from the commission, we took the train to New York, where I had some business to attend to. For the first hour Moi amused himself by adjusting his seat. Then he practiced English: "Hello, how are you, Miss?" and "Good morning" and "Thank you." He leafed through a mail-order catalog—jackets, shoes, watches— and asked the usual question about each item: "Is this waterproof?" He found Chesapeake Bay beautiful and added its name to a list he was keeping of cities and towns. After we entered the industrial corridor north of Delaware, however, his face lost its glow. We passed a field of giant tanks used for storing chemicals; to Moi, they looked exactly like the tanks the Company uses to store oil.

For a long time he didn't say a word. Then he asked, "Chong, are there any Indians here?"

"No."

"Were there Indians here before the Company came?"

"Yes. There were Indians everywhere."

"Were they killed?"

"Yes."

"All of them?"

"Almost all."

From there to Pennsylvania Station, we rode in silence. Once in New York City, however, Moi perked up. Proceeding at his usual slow, steady gait, he slipped easily through the crowds milling in the station. Only one thing seemed to throw him. As we stood in line waiting for a cab, he bumped me with his shoulder and nodded toward the two young women ahead of us.

"You are on your own," I told him.

He went into the Huaorani zone, as if to summon every ounce of courage he had. When he returned, he looked at one of the women, and said, in perfect English, "Hello." She smiled at him; he froze. Then he turned, looked me right in the eye, and said, "How are you, Miss?"

Over the next couple of days we negotiated Manhattan carrying a nine-foot Huaorani spear. ("Cool," someone remarked on Forty-second Street.) We traveled by cab as we had in Quito, with the spear protruding like a jousting lance, scattering pedestrians before it. At the hotel it melted crowds. ("Good Lord," said the doorman.) Moi was impressed, but not overwhelmed, by the immensity of the buildings; perplexed by the terraces that grew forests high above the ground; and flummoxed by the city's pace: "In Ecuador we wait all day for four o'clock. In New York, four o'clock comes with breakfast." Through it all, however, Moi remained utterly himself. One night we ate dinner at a Mexican restaurant, near a drug rehabilitation center. At the table behind us, several men and women were engaged in what might be kindly described as group therapy. They screamed and shook their fists at one another. Moi studied them carefully until a woman pitched forward and passed out on the table. Then he leaned over and spoke to her softly, in a voice filled with compassion. "Good morning," he said. "Thank you."

I INVITED Moi to Oakland, where I live; he agreed to come only after I assured him that he would not have to survive on "leaves." We walked in the redwoods: Moi was astounded by their size but disappointed that they harbored neither jaguars nor monkeys. At my house he turned the bamboo patch into a blowgun factory and stalked squirrels and pigeons, and he engaged me in a running debate about the globe in my living room: Why put a map on a ball? Maps were flat. If the world were round, the water would fall off.

Finally, the day before Moi was to leave, the call came from Washington: Blasco Peñaherrera had spoken to the commission and invited it to Ecuador; the commission had accepted. Though the Ecuadorian government had yet to put the invitation in writing, and thus make it official, the commission believed that this would just be a matter of time.

It was about then that Moi learned how to slap a high five. And then he was ready to depart. "There is not very much to learn in the city," he said. "It is time to walk in the forest again." Then he said, in English, "Hello," and then he was gone.

TWO WEEKS after Moi went home, the Ecuadorian government sent the OAS a letter in which it said that there had been a misunderstanding. It would not extend a formal invitation; essentially, it saw no reason for an investigation. There was no way to get this information to Moi. As far as I knew, he was waiting in Quehueire Ono, ready to roar like a jaguar not only for the commission but for the president of the United States of North America and the whole world.

It would be six months before I stumbled across the documents and made the phone calls that revealed that Blasco Peñaherrera had a son, also called Blasco Peñaherrera, who owned a market research firm in Quito, and that the firm had been hired to promote the Maxus project, and that Peñaherrera the younger had traveled with his father and Enqueri in Washington, D.C. If it was a relationship that suggested a clear conflict of interest in the matter of blocking the commission's investigation, it was also one of which everyone I spoke with who was working on the case, including the lawyer handling it at the OAS, was unaware.

IN JANUARY 1994, three months after Moi's visit, the Ecuadorian government announced that it had withdrawn from development Block Twenty-two, which fell entirely within Yasuní National Park. It was a startling announcement. It had always been assumed, by oil executives and outsiders alike, that Block Sixteen would cover the costs of developing the infrastructure necessary to produce oil from the two blocks, but that the real profit lay in Twenty-two. Officially, no one was saying why Twenty-two had been shut down, because there was no explanation that could do anything but discourage further oil development in the area: There wasn't as much oil in there as had been supposed, or the government had bowed to public pressure to protect the park, or the cost of producing heavy crude had become too high. Most likely it was a combination of factors; in any case, as plenty of people pointed out, the government was free to reverse itself whenever it wanted to—say, when the price of oil rose again, which, sooner or later, it had to do.

But what was most startling about the announcement wasn't that the block had been closed; what was startling—indeed, terrifying—was that at the same time, the government announced that it was putting ten new oil blocks up for bid. All told, the new blocks covered some 5 million acres, or an area about the size of New Jersey, and contained 85 percent of the land in the Oriente inhabited by indigenous groups. Six of the new blocks were to the west and south of the Vía Auca, which meant that virtually every inch of land from the Auca to the Andes was now open to oil development—including almost all the old Huaorani protectorate, where most of the Huaorani lived. Even Moi's village, remote Quehueire Ono, did not escape: On the map released by the government, a concession that would be operated by an American company, Oryx, encompassed the entire Shiripuno River, all the way to its headwaters. The sharp, rectangular black lines of the concession appeared to corral Quehueire Ono, as if capturing the village and all the wild forest for miles on every side of it.

Two weeks later I received a collect phone call from Ecuador. The connection was awful, but I heard "Chong" come swimming though the static, and for a moment I was startled. Then I was worried. Moi spoke as he always did—directly, without introduction or niceties—but his voice had an urgency I'd never heard before. He had made his way to Quito, he said, to the house of a *cowode* friend, who had put the call through for him. The government was after him. They were angry about what he had said in Washington. He'd been threatened. At the least, they would revoke his passport; at worst, he feared for his life.

"When is the commission coming?" Moi asked.

"The lawyers will have to explain," I said, and took down the number.

"Tell them to call right away."

"I will. Be careful, Moi."

"The Huaorani live well!" he said, and hung up.

I heard nothing more from or about Moi until March, when I received two disturbing pieces of mail. One was a copy of a fax sent to the *ecochicas* in Quito after Moi had invited "the whole world" to a meeting in Quehueire Ono. The fax was sent through the Christian mission and signed by Enqueri. It warned the *ecochicas* that if they tried to enter the territory Enqueri would be forced to take "drastic measures" against them.

In the same packet I found a newspaper clipping. It said that Samuel Caento Padilla—the Huaorani half-breed who had offered his services to Maxus—had traveled to Quito to denounce the efforts of the *ecologistas* working with Moi. He claimed to be speaking on behalf of ONHAE. It was, it appeared, a preemptive strike by the Company, because three days later, after yet another epic trek, Moi arrived in Quito with Mengatohue and fifty other Huaorani and marched on the National Palace. They brought with them a letter for President Sixto and his daughter Alicia. Maxus was dividing the Huaorani, it said, and encouraging violence among them. "Why has the government made a gift of the Huaorani people to Maxus so they can destroy us?" Moi wrote, and he asked once again that the government permit an independent study, "by national and international experts," of the impact of oil development in their land.

I called down to Quito as soon as I got the clip. By then, of course, Moi was long gone, but a friend who had managed to stay close to the action inside the territory told me, "The word is that Moi is a dead man." He added that the military had recently picked Moi up for "interrogation." He was released after two days, apparently unharmed. Still, I found myself wondering if I would ever see him again.

In April, Maxus opened a valve, and the first drops of oil gushed from beneath the Huaorani land into the new pipeline and began their journey north.

Meanwhile, the pipeline that runs along the Vía Auca had ruptured where it crosses the Shiripuno—right where, so many times, I had slipped into a canoe with Moi and Nanto and Enqueri, and, turning a bend in the river, the road and the pipeline disappearing behind us and the forest swallowing us up, I had felt that I was leaving one world and entering another—right there, the pipeline had ruptured and spilled so much oil into the Shiripuno that it created a slick more than thirty miles long. The river turned black from the Vía Auca all the way into the Cononaco—all the way down to where old Quemperi and his people lived.

But that was nothing compared with what had happened a few months earlier, in the same place: One of the wells in the Cononaco field burst into flame and burned out of control for nearly a week. It was, by most accounts, the biggest fire ever seen in the Oriente. The oil-fed flames were said to have leaped so high that they dwarfed the great forest itself, and to have spread so fast that no man could outrun them.

Epilogue

I T HAS BEEN a couple of years since I was last in Ecuador, but many of the people I met are still there, and many of the patterns I witnessed endure:

In November 1993 an Ecuadorian lawyer and an American law firm filed a $1 billion class-action suit against Texaco on behalf of some 30,000 Quichua, Cofan, and Secoya Indians. The suit was brought in New York, because Texaco is an American company and because the Indians have no chance of receiving justice in Ecuador. The Ecuadorian embassy tried to block the suit but failed. Judith Kimerling, who continues to work in the Oriente, has agreed to act in an advisory capacity for several of the communities involved in the suit.

Ali Sharif is still in Ecuador, teaching permaculture courses and working with descendants of escaped African slaves in a village on the western slope of the Andes.

Quichua communities living in the ARCO concession, Block Ten, have managed to get the company to the negotiating table. Through public pressure in the United States and Ecuador and the assistance of nonprofit groups (especially Oxfam America) who have an understanding of the Oriente at the grass-roots level, as well as direct confrontations at ARCO's well site that have led to costly delays in bringing the project online, the Quichua appear to have persuaded the company that it would be wiser and cheaper to work with them than to ignore them. While it is too early to tell what real gains the Quichua will make, their success thus far is unprecedented in the Oriente, and their political network has become a model for indigenous people throughout the continent—though no longer, it would seem, for the Huaorani.

A FEW MONTHS after its first well came online Maxus told the Ecuadorian government that its operating expenses for Block Sixteen would be much higher than projected. Maxus says also that the concession holds only two-thirds as much oil as had long been thought. Because its contract with Maxus essentially allows the Company to recover its investment before the government sees a dollar, it looks as if Ecuador will receive far less revenue than it had expected—and that is before factoring in economic values for species loss, deforestation, and pollution.

Ecuador's oil exports increased in 1994. So did its debt. The government imposed new austerity measures, and there were strikes and demonstrations and rumors of a coup.

THE AMERICAN GOVERNMENT pumps a fair sum of money into Ecuador. The most obvious beneficiaries of that largesse are the American oil companies—Maxus foremost—that have taken the lead in developing new concessions in the Oriente. What with embassy support, military support, World Bank and other development loans, intelligence operations, research grants, and USAID funds that assure the cooperation of influential nonprofit groups, the American taxpayer, however unwittingly, has underwritten the Company in a hundred different ways. Without this help it is unlikely that the Oriente's oil fields could have been developed so quickly or widely, if at all.

What do Americans receive for their investment? Tax revenue? Given its losses, Maxus has had to pay few corporate taxes in the United States, while American citizens working in foreign countries are eligible for a tax exemption on up to $70,000 of annual income. Cheap oil? Compared to American consumption, there is so little oil in Block Sixteen that it will have no impact on the price of a gallon of gas. Support for the Company is often justified on the grounds that American operation of foreign oil fields contributes to national security. But in February, with Block Sixteen up and running at last, Maxus announced that it had agreed to be purchased by an Argentine oil company.

The price of Maxus stock rose 46 percent overnight.

AFTER MONTHS of jousting, the Inter-American Commission on Human Rights finally secured an "invitation" from the Ecuadorian government, and in November of 1994 it sent a team to the Oriente. The commission did not enter Huaorani territory. It went no farther than Coca, where it spent only two days. Still, some fifty Huaorani traveled to the Capuchin mission to welcome the commission with dances and songs. Later, Huaorani men and women stood up one by one and spoke about the Company, the colonists, the pollution of their lands. ONHAE does not listen to us, they said. We need help.

The last Huao to speak was Moi. It was Moi, of course, who had brought the Huaorani to Coca, but he was not the same man who had testified in Washington. Thus far he had survived the threats made against him when he returned to Ecuador, but he still believed that the Company or the government would do him serious harm, and he had abandoned his political work and sequestered himself in Quehueire Ono. Tired, frustrated, and increasingly isolated, he had made peace with Enqueri, and the people of Quehueire Ono had let Maxus build a school. Today the children of Quehueire Ono wear uniforms from the evangelical mission, are fed by Maxus, and study from texts that, with only minor variations, are the same the missionaries used when they taught the Huaorani that the way they had always lived was evil. Sometimes the shaman Mengatohue walks into the schoolhouse and tells the children how the Huaorani used to be. They laugh at him.

Moi felt that he could no longer behave as boldly as he once did. In the old days he would have roared like a jaguar, but in Coca he let the other Huaorani do the talking. Only after the people from the commission had said a polite but quick thank you and explained that they were in a hurry did Moi rise to address them. I am sorry to keep you, he said, but there is something I must say: Now you know what is happening to the Huaorani. Please do not forget about us. Tell the world.

Then he led the Huaorani back into the forest, where, as far as I know, he remains to this day.

One other Huao spoke to the commission, but not until it returned to Quito. On the day before the commission was to leave the country Enqueri found his way to the hotel where it was conducting its final hearings. The Condor was due at a meeting in Venezuela and didn't have much time. He said that the Huaorani were having many problems with the Company and that there was much "confusion." The Huaorani wanted only to live in peace; they wanted only to live like Huaorani. Then he excused himself and hustled down to the street, where a Company car and driver were waiting for him.

Oakland, California
April 1995

Postscript

MAY 5: Word comes of an uprising in the Huaorani territory. A few days ago, perhaps a week or more—details are elusive—some one hundred Huaorani overran the Maxus production facility for Block Sixteen. The action was led by Moi, whose passion and fury are said to burn anew, and by a new wave of bold young Huaorani. They were assisted by the same Quichua leaders who helped them gain title to their territory, and who are now battling ARCO. The military was called in and fired a few threatening but harmless rounds; the Huaorani did not back down until the Company agreed to meet with them and, for the first time, conduct genuine negotiations. What they will yield remains to be seen, but at the moment, one can conclude with certainty at least this: The jaguar spirit lives.

Acknowledgments

First thanks go to the Huaorani among and with whom I traveled. Though some of them understand what writing is, I don't believe any of them fully grasped what I was doing—as, I'm sure, I never completely understood what was happening around me when I was in the Huaorani lands. For their friendship and trust they asked only that I "tell the world" about what I saw. I hope I have.

I am grateful beyond measure to my editor, Dan Frank, who is, in his way, much like a Huao: kind, patient, keenly observant, and ever willing to hack away with a machete when the occasion demands. Thanks, too, to Claudine O'Hearn.

It was Joe Spieler who convinced me that this story had to be told and found the means for me to tell it. He is the best agent a writer could have, and an even better friend.

Parts of this book took form as articles for *The New Yorker*. The first piece, the sort of in-depth investigation that would have been possible for no other magazine, was assigned by Robert Gottlieb and published by Tina Brown. The second piece was the inspiration of my editor, John Bennet, who gave so generously of his ideas on reporting, writing, and editing that he could not help but shape this final text as well. Thanks are due also to Bill Vourvoulias, the fact checker, for his skill, tenacity, and good humor under fire, and to Bill Finnegan and Chip McGrath.

I might not have stayed sane, let alone alive, without the help of friends. Zbyszek Bzdak's cool head and warm heart got me through some tough times, as did Joe Karten and his *trompeta*. As he has been for nearly twenty years, Ken Conner was my first reader; in dissecting several drafts of this book he often seemed to know my mind better than I did. If there is one desire common to all writers it is for intelligent readers, and it was my good fortune to have found them in Mike Bryan, Jon Carroll, Fred D'Orazio, Jeff Gillenkirk, Cynthia

Gorney, Tracy Johnston, Mark Plotkin, and Evan Young, all of whom offered insightful comment on the manuscript.

Dozens of people familiar with the Oriente took time to discuss it with me. Most do not appear in the story, but in one way or another every one of them influenced it. In particular, I want to thank Juan Aulestia, Monica Baez, Bruce Cabarle, Gustavo González, Randy Smith, Marijke Torfs, and Leonardo Viteri.

Thanks also to Doug Crichton and American Airlines for logistical support and to Osprey, Inc., for the excellent backpacks donated to the Huaorani.

Everyone I have written about is real, and with the exception of two characters who appear only briefly, so are their names. However, I was aided on my travels by several people whose roles I have not described, either because that was the agreement I made with them beforehand or because doing so would compromise them without adding substantially to the story. My thanks go out to them, along with the hope that I can one day return the favor.

In many ways this story is about family, and in the end it was family that made it possible for me to tell it. My time in Ecuador would not have been nearly as enjoyable or productive without the love, help, and company of Kirsten, Nancy, and Curtis Axell. My greatest thanks go to my wife, Elyse Axell, for her unwavering support despite the obvious hardships she endured: Her love and counsel are the bedrock of everything I do. Finally, it was our daughter, Clare, who showed up right in the middle of things and became my best teacher. This book is for her.

Bibliography

NOTE ON SOURCES

For the most part this book is based on firsthand reporting. However, at times I had to rely on secondary sources for such things as historical background, statistics, and leads, and to help corroborate or interpret events I either did not fully understand or did not witness. The most important of these sources are indicated in the notes for each chapter. For the period 1991–1994 I also found useful information in Quito's newspaper of record, *El Comercio*, and its closest competitor, *Hoy*.

PROLOGUE

Judith Kimerling's *Amazon Crude* is the only comprehensive overview of the environmental and cultural impact of oil development in the Oriente. Its breadth and clarity are remarkable, and its accuracy has never been seriously challenged. *The New York Times* praised it, rightly, as "the *Silent Spring* of the Ecuadorian environmental movement."

The population estimate for the Huaorani is based on a 1992 census compiled by Randy Smith. Smith has probably seen more of the territory than has any other *cowode*—he directed the last stages of the cutting of the Huaorani territorial boundary. His report, *Crisis Under the Canopy*, is an ambitious attempt to catalog the current state of affairs in the Huaorani territory. Particularly illuminating are his analysis of tourism in the territory and his descriptions of threats to the Tagaeri and other "uncontacted" Huaorani.

Books and Reports

Amazon Cooperation Treaty, et al. *Amazonia Without Myths*. Washington, D.C., 1992.

Center for Economic and Social Rights. *Rights Violations in the Ecuadorian Amazon: The Human Consequences of Oil Development*. New York, 1994.

Energy Information Administration. *Annual Energy Review*. Washington, D.C.: U.S. Department of Energy, July 1994.

Hicks, James F., et al. *Ecuador's Amazon Region*. Washington D.C.: The World Bank, 1990.

Kimerling, Judith. *Amazon Crude*. New York: Natural Resources Defense Council, 1991.

——. *Crudo Amazónico*. Quito: Abya-Yala, 1994.

MacKerran, Conrad B., and Douglas C. Logan, eds. *Business in the Rainforest: Corporations, Deforestation, and Sustainability*. Investor Responsibility Research Center, 1993.

Smith, Randy. *Crisis Under the Canopy*. Quito: Abya-Yala, 1993.

Southgate, Douglas, and Morris Whitaker. *Development and the Environment: Ecuador's Policy Crisis*. Quito: Instituto de Estrategias Agropecuarias, June 1992.

United Nations Commission on Human Rights. *Transnational Investments and Operations on the Lands of Indigenous Peoples*. New York, July 17, 1991.

United States Agency for International Development. *Natural Resource Management and Conservation of Biodiversity and Tropical Forests in Ecuador*. 1989.

World Resources Institute. *World Resources 1990–1991*. New York, 1990.

Articles, Letters, Memoranda, Documents

Brooke, James. "New Effort Would Test Possible Coexistence of Oil and Rain Forest." *New York Times*, February 26, 1991.

——. "Oil and Tourism Don't Mix, Inciting Amazon Battle." *New York Times*, September 26, 1993.

——. "Pollution of Rain Forest Is Tied to Oil in Ecuador." *New York Times*, March 22, 1994.

La Campaña Amazonia por la Vida. "Environmental Imperialism in Ecuador?" n.d.

"Environmental Concerns Gaining Importance in Industry Operations." *Oil & Gas Journal*, July 6, 1992.

Ferguson, Douglas G. "Importance of the Ecuadorian Amazon, Indigenous Knowledge, and Activities of the Rainforest Information Centre." Quito: Rainforest Information Centre, 1991.

Gentry, Alwyn. "Northwest South America (Colombia, Ecuador, and Peru)." In *Floristic Inventory of Tropical Countries*. New York: The New York Botanical Garden, 1988.

González, Gustavo. Briefing on the Yasuní Park's Last News. Rainforest Action Network, December 1989.

Hall, Susan E. A. "Conoco's 'Green' Oil Strategy." Boston: Harvard Business School, 1992.

Hamilton, Martha. "Forest's Fate Splits Environmentalists." *Washington Post*, May 15, 1991.

Hayes, Randall. Letter to Edgar S. Woolard. March 18, 1991.

Holstrom, David. "Volatile Mix: Oil and Indians." *Christian Science Monitor*, June 16, 1993.

——. "Ecuador Indians Fight for Forests." *Christian Science Monitor*, June 16, 1993.

"Huaorani to DuPont: Get Out." *World Rainforest Report*, April-May 1991.

International Water Tribunal. Ruling in the case of *CORDAVI vs. Petroecuador, Texaco Petroleum, and City Investing*. Amsterdam, February 20, 1992.

Kimerling, Judith. "Disregarding Environmental Law: Petroleum Development in Protected Natural Areas and Indigenous Homelands in the Ecuadorian Amazon." *The Hastings International and Comparative Law Review* 14, no. 4 (1991).

La Organización de Nacionalidad Huaorani de la Amazonia Ecuatoriana. Letter to DuPont. January 11, 1991.

Parlow, Anita. "Of Oil and Exploitation in Ecuador." *Multinational Monitor*, January/February 1991.

Parrish, Michael, and William R. Long. "Villagers Standing Up to Big Oil." *Los Angeles Times*, November 6, 1994.

Read, Morley. "Arrows and Oil." *BBC Wildlife*, November 1989.

Reyes, Fernando. "Impacto Ambiental Consorcio CEPE-Texaco Comunidad Nativa Cofanes." Quito: Dirección General de Medio Ambiente, 1989.

——. "Petróleo y Medio Ambiente: Aspectos Legales, Institutionales y Operativos." Quito: Dirección General de Medio Ambiente, 1990.

Sierra Club Legal Defense Fund. *Petición presentada a la Comisión Inter-Americana de Derechos Humanos, Organización de Estados Americanos, por la Confederación de Nacionalidades Indígenas de la Amazonia Ecuatoriana (CONFENIAE) a favor de la población Huaorani contra Ecuador*. San Francisco, 1990.

——. *Informe adicional*. San Francisco, 1992.

——. *Informe adicional*. San Francisco, 1993.

Springer, L. D., and A. B. Chapman (Conoco executives). Minutes of Feb. 5, 1991, NRDC Meeting in New York. New York, February 8, 1991.

United States Agency for International Development. "Sustainable Uses for Biological Resources (SUBIR)." Quito, n.d.

Vinueza, Patricia Norona. "Petróleo: Peligro Ecológico." *Vistazo*, July 19, 1992.

CHAPTER ONE

Alejandro Labaca's adventures among the Huaorani are vividly described in *Crónica Huaorani*, a compilation of his journals through 1980; an appendix includes color pictures of the 1987 spearing.

Through Gates of Splendor, written by the wife of one of the five American evangelical missionaries killed by the Huaorani in 1957, describes the events leading up to the massacre; unconsciously, it also evokes the spirit of naiveté and arrogance that drove the missionaries to their death. I found useful analyses of the Summer Institute of Linguistic's role in indigenous affairs in Ecuador in articles by James Yost, an S.I.L. anthropologist and oil-company consultant, and William T. Vickers; both articles are included in *Cultural Transformations and Ethnicity in Modern Ecuador*. For a thorough chronicle of the S.I.L.'s collaboration with the oil industry in the subjugation of indigenous cultures throughout Latin America, see *Thy Will Be Done: The Conquest of the Amazon: Nelson Rockefeller and Evangelism in the Age of Oil*, by Gerard Colby and Charlotte Dennett.

A detailed analysis of the devastating impact tourism has had on the Huaorani can be found in Randy Smith's *Crisis Under the Canopy*. (Anyone interested in visiting the Oriente will want to note that in September 1992 ONHAE formally authorized five guides to enter the territory—Juan Enomenga, Expediciones Jarrín, Sebastian Moya, Samuel Caento Padilla, and Carlos Sevilla—and declared all other guides illegal. A copy of the ONHAE document can be found in Smith's book.)

A note on Huaorani names: Throughout this book I have referred to the Huaorani only by their birth names, as this was the only way I ever heard them refer to themselves. However, to qualify for national identification cards the Huaorani must come up with surnames, and almost every Huao has one. In Dayuno and Quehueire

Ono, for example, many people are named Irumenga, which means "upriver," or Enomenga, which means "downriver." Also, during their lifetimes the Huaorani will often take on additional names, sometimes adding a dozen or more. Thus: Moi Enomenga, Nanto Huamoni, Amo Quemperi, and, for reasons I never fathomed, Ehuenguime Enqueri.

Books

Colby, Gerard, with Charlotte Dennet. *Thy Will Be Done: The Conquest of the Amazon: Nelson Rockefeller and Evangelism in the Age of Oil.* New York: Harper-Collins, 1995.

Elliot, Elisabeth. *Through Gates of Splendor.* Wheaton, Ill.: Living Books, 1988.

Labaca, Alejandro. *Crónica Huaorani.* Quito: Ediciones CICAME, 1988.

Ortiz de Villalba, Juan Santos. *Los Últimos Huaorani,* 3rd ed. Quito: Ediciones CICAME, 1991.

Smith, Randy. *Crisis Under the Canopy.* Quito: Abya-Yala, 1993.

Whitten, Norman, ed. *Cultural Transformations and Ethnicity in Modern Ecuador.* Urbana, Ill.: University of Illinois Press, 1981

Yost, James A. *El Desarrollo Comunitario y la Supervivencia Étnica.* Quito: Summer Institute of Linguistics, 1979.

Articles, Letters

"Ecuador Steps Up Pace of Oil Development Activity." *Oil & Gas Journal,* March 23, 1992.

Enomenga, Moi. Unaddressed letter from "first Huaorani national assembly." March 10, 1990.

La Organización de Nacionalidad Huaorani de la Amazonia Ecuatoriana. Letter to DuPont. January 11, 1991.

Rival, Laura. "Shared, Consumed, Consummated: The Use of Food Consumption and Changing Relations among the Huaorani Indians of Amazonian Ecuador." Manchester, England: University of Manchester, 1991.

Robarchek, Clayton A., and Carole J. Robarchek. "Cultures of War and Peace: A Comparative Study of Waorani and Semai." In *Aggression and Peacefulness in Humans and Other Primates,* edited by James Silverberg and J. Patrick Gray. New York, Oxford: Oxford University Press, 1992.

Springer, L. D., and A. B. Chapman (Conoco executives). Minutes of Feb. 5, 1991, NRDC Meeting in New York. New York, February 8, 1991.

Tassi, Giovanna. "The Emerald Forest." In *Naufragos del Mar Verde.* Quito: Abya-Yala, 1992.

Vickers, William T. "Ideation as Adaptation: Traditional Belief and Modern Intervention in Siona-Secoya Religion." In *Cultural Transformations and Ethnicity in Modern Ecuador,* edited by Norman E. Whitten, Jr. Urbana, Ill.: University of Illinois Press, 1981.

Wirpsa, Leslie. "Oil Companies Invade Ecuador for 'Black Gold,'" *National Catholic Reporter,* May 1, 1992.

Yost, James A. "Twenty Years of Contact: The Mechanisms of Change in Wao ('Auca') Culture." In *Cultural Transformations and Ethnicity in Modern Ecuador,* edited by Norman E. Whitten, Jr. Urbana, Ill.: University of Illinois Press, 1981.

CHAPTER TWO

My description of the creation of the Oriente, and the intensity of its speciation, is based mainly on interviews with Dr. David Neill, a curator of the Missouri Botanical Garden and a founder of the Jatun Sacha Biological Station, which is located near the Napo River.

The story of how Babae came to live on the Vía Auca has been recorded in several places. My account is based on interviews with Babae, Enqueri, Moi, José Miguel Goldáraz, Douglas Ferguson, Joe Karten, and Rachel Saint, and on a paper by Dr. Laura Rival, "Today I Am Going Back to My Father's Land . . . but Now It Is Petro-Canada's."

Books, Articles, Letters

Ferguson, Douglas. "Report on the Huaorani Project." Quito: Rainforest Information Centre, 1993.

Kimerling, Judith. "Dislocation and Contamination: Amazon Crude and the Huaorani People." Revised draft of a presentation made at the Woodrow Wilson International Center for Scholars, Washington, D.C., November 15, 1994.

Neill, David A. "Ecuador Forest Sector Development Project." Missouri Botanical Garden, September 1991.

ONHAE. Open letter. May 23, 1992.

"Puede haber muertos en cualquier momento." *La Prensa*, June 29, 1988.

Rival, Laura. "Today I Am Going Back to My Father's Land . . . but Now It Is Petro-Canada's." Draft article. Quito, 1990.

Smith, Randy. *Crisis Under the Canopy*. Quito: Abya-Yala, 1993.

CHAPTER THREE

For historical background and insight into the health status of the Huaorani living in the Cononaco region I relied on the work of James A. Yost, the Summer Institute of Linguistics anthropologist. My discussion of spear killing and death practices is taken largely from the doctoral dissertation of Dr. Laura Rival, as are the translations of the Huaorani phrases for "happiness," "anxiety," and "kill."

There seem to be a few different versions of how Toña was killed. The version I have recounted here differs in detail, though not in substance, from the version passed on by the evangelical missionaries; it is my understanding of what Quemperi told me, as translated by Enqueri.

A note on *chicha*: At the time I visited the Cononaco, most of what literature was available on the Huaorani said that, unlike the Quichua, they did not let their manioc drink ferment. However, all of the *chicha* I drank on my travels with the Huaorani tasted fermented. *Chicha* is a Quichua word (Quechua, actually, of which Quichua is a dialect) and its common use by the Huaorani, in whose language manioc drink is called *tepe*, may indicate a cultural shift toward a fermented beverage.

Books, Articles, Reports

Brooke, James. "Braspetro's Ecuadorean Oil Search Troubled." *Oil & Gas Journal*, January 7, 1991.

Peeke, M. Catalina. *El Idioma Huao: Gramática Pedagógica*. Quito: Summer Institute of Linguistics, 1979.

Rival, Laura. "Social Transformations and the Impact of Formal Schooling on the

Huaorani of Amazonian Ecuador." Doctoral dissertation for London School of Economics, University of London. January 1992.

Robarchek, Clay, and Carole Robarchek. "Waorani: From Warfare to Peacefulness." *The World & I,* January 1989.

Smith, Randall. "Report on Cononaco Huaorani Village." October 1991.

Yost, James A. "Assessment of the Impact of Road Construction and Oil Extraction upon the Waorani Living on the Yasuní." Report for Conoco Ecuador Ltd., April 1989.

———. "Twenty Years of Contact: The Mechanisms of Change in Wao ('Auca') Culture." In *Cultural Transformations and Ethnicity in Modern Ecuador,* edited by Norman E. Whitten, Jr. Urbana, Ill.: University of Illinois Press, 1981.

Yost, James A., and Douglas McMeekin. "Reaction of the Waorani to Potential Road Construction and Oil Extraction." Report for Conoco Ecuador, Ltd., November 1989.

CHAPTER FOUR
Books, Articles, Reports, Documents

Comisión de Evaluación del Impacto Ecológico de la Explotación Sísmica en el Bloque 10. "Análisis Impacto Ambiental Producido por los Trabajos de Exploración Sísmica en el Bloque 10 Ejecutado por la Cía. Arco International Oil and Gas Company." Sarayacu, May 29, 1989.

CONFENIAE. "Declaración de Sarayacu." Sarayacu, May 9, 1989.

———. "Plantamientos de la Confederación de las Nacionalidades Indígenas del Ecuador al Señor Presidente Constitutional del Ecuador Doctor Rodrigo Borja Cevallos." Sarayacu, May 9, 1989.

"Ecuadorian Indigenous People Challenge ARCO." *World Rainforest Report,* January-March 1994.

"Indígenas 'retienen' al director de IERAC." *El Comercio,* May 5, 1989.

Kimerling, Judith. *Amazon Crude.* New York: Natural Resources Defense Council, 1991.

McCreary, Scott, et al. "Independent Review of Environmental Documentation for Petroleum Exploration in Block 10, Oriente, Ecuador." Berkeley: Center for Environmental Design Research, University of California, March 13, 1992.

OPIP. "Planteamientos de le Organización de Pueblos Indígenas de Pastaza 'OPIP', ante el Gobierno Nacional Frente al Conflicto de Tierras y Empresas Petroleras Suscitado en la Comunidad de Sarayacu y Otras Comunidades de la Provincia." Sarayacu, May 9, 1989.

"Retenido en Sarayacu director del IERAC." *Hoy,* May 5, 1989.

Robarchek, Clay, and Carole Robarchek. "Warorani: From Warfare to Peacefulness." *The World & I,* January 1989.

CHAPTER FIVE
Books, Articles, Letters, Reports

Chapman, Alex B., Director, Organization Services, Exploration and Production, International, Conoco, Inc. Letter to Randall Hayes, Executive Director, Rainforest Action Network. November 17, 1989.

Coello, Flavio, and James Nations. "Plan Preliminar de Manejo del Parque Nacional Yasuní 'Reserva de Biosfera'." Quito: DINAF, 1989.

Morales, Oscar Valenzuela. "Ecuador: Purchase of Debt to Finance Environment Conservation." Inter Press Service, November 28, 1988.

González, Gustavo A. "Conflicting Conservation and Development Policies: A Critique of the Management Plan for Yasuní National Park in Ecuador." Unpublished thesis.

Labaca, Alejandro. *Crónica Huaorani*. Quito: Ediciones CICAME, 1988.

Nations, James D. "Road Construction and Oil Production in Ecuador's Yasuní National Park." May 1988.

Ortiz de Villalba, Juan Santos. *Los Últimos Huaorani*, 3rd ed. Quito: Ediciones CICAME, 1991.

USAID. "Uso Sostenible de los Recursos Biológicos (SUBIR)." Quito, September 12, 1991.

CHAPTER SIX

Important interviews for this chapter, in addition to those referred to in the text, include Juan Aulestia, Alex Chapman, Marcela Enríquez, Gustavo González, Valerio Grefa, Theodore MacDonald, Hernan Martínez, Michael McCloskey, Evaristo Nugkuag, Byron Real, S. Jacob Scherr, Marijke Torfs, Leonardo Viteri, and Angel Zamarenda.

Articles, Books, Letters, Documents

Adams, John. Letter to Mrs. Philip Kind, Jr. December 17, 1990.

La Campaña por la Vida. "Environmental Imperialism in Ecuador?" Quito, 1991.

——. "History of La Campaña por la Vida." Quito, n.d.

——. Letter to Adrian DeWind, Chairman of the Board of Trustees, NRDC. January 25, 1991.

Christensen, Jon. "Plan to Tap Oil in Ecuador Enrages Environmentalists." *San Francisco Chronicle*, October 9, 1990.

Collier, Peter, and David Horowitz. *The Kennedys: An American Dream*. New York: Summit Books, 1984.

"Condiciones exigidas por las organizaciones no gubernamentales del Ecuador el Estado ecuatoriano y al Banco Mundial." The "Thirteen Points" demands made by the coalition of Ecuadorian indigenous, environmental, and human rights groups. Quito, January 27, 1990.

Cooper, Marc. "Oil Slick." *Mother Jones*, November/December 1991.

Corporación de Defensa de la Vida. Open letter to international indigenous and environmental groups. April 19, 1991.

Corry, Stephen, Director General, Survival International. Letter to Adrian W. Dewind, Chairman NRDC. March 14, 1991.

"Diamond Shamrock to Get New Name: Maxus Energy." *Wall Street Journal*, April 29, 1987.

"Ecuador Steps Up Pace of Oil Development Activity." *Oil & Gas Journal*, March 23, 1992.

"Ecuador's Indians: Counsels of War." *The Economist*, August 25, 1990.

Freeman, Stanley A. Letter to Adrian W. DeWind and John F. Adams, Natural Resources Defense Council. May 31, 1991.

González, Gustavo. Letter to Randall Hayes. March 8, 1991.

Grefa, Valerio. Letter to Robert F. Kennedy, Jr. March 8, 1991.

Gregg, D. E., General Manager, Exploration and Production, International, Conoco, Inc. Letter to Natural Resources Defense Council. November 14, 1990.

——. Letter to Jacob Scherr, February 14, 1991.

Hall, Susan E. A. "Block 16: Interview with Randy Hayes, RAN." Boston: Harvard Business School, 1993.

——. "Conoco's 'Green' Oil Strategy." Boston: Harvard Business School, 1992.

Hamilton, Martha. "Forest's Fate Splits Environmentalists." *Washington Post*, May 15, 1991.

Hayes, Randall. Letter to Jacob Scherr. May 1, 1991.

Karten, Joe. "Trip Report: COICA/Environmentalist Alliance Committee Meeting." November 1991.

Kennedy, Robert F., Jr. "Amazon Crude." *Amicus Journal*, Spring 1991.

——. "Amazon Sabotage." *Washington Post*, August 24, 1992.

——. "Petrofied Forest." *Village Voice*, February 12, 1991.

——. "Presentation to CONFENIAE." Text of speech delivered in Puyo, Ecuador, March 8, 1991.

Kimerling, Judith. *Amazon Crude*. New York: Natural Resources Defense Council, 1991.

——. Letter to S. Jacob Scherr. January 25, 1991.

"Maxus Energy to Become Operator of Block 16 in Ecuador." Press release. October 21, 1991.

Ministerio de Energía and Minas. "Reglamento Ambiental para la Actividad Hidrocarburifera en el Territorio Nacional." Draft. Quito, 1990.

Natural Resources Defense Council. "Lawsuit to Prevent Oil Development in the Arctic National Wildlife Refuge." Direct-mail solicitation, n.d.

——. "NRDC Confirms Opposition to Conoco Oil Drilling in Ecuador's Amazonian Rainforests." Press release. June 1991.

——. "NRDC in Ecuador: Fighting Pollution in the Rainforest." Press release. October 3, 1990.

——. "NRDC Study Exposes American Oil Company Devastation of Amazonian Rainforest in Ecuador." Press release. October 3, 1990.

——. "NRDC's Actions on Conoco's Proposed Oil Development in Ecuador." Press release. July 1991.

——. "Settlement Agreement and General Release." January 1991.

"Oil Wars in the Amazon: An Interview with Leonardo Viteri." *SAIIC Newsletter* 6, nos. 1, 2 (1991).

"Open Letter to the Ecuadorean State and to the World Bank." Open letter from Ecuadorian nongovernmental organizations. January 27, 1990.

Parker, Vawter. Letter to Valerio Grefa. February 28, 1991.

Parlow, Anita. "Worlds in Collision." *Amicus Journal*, Spring 1991.

Petroecuador. "Disposiciones de Manejo Ambiental para las Actividades Hidrocar-
buriferas." Quito, August 1990.

Potts, Mark. "Diamond Shamrock to Split into Two Firms." *Washington Post*, February 3, 1987.

"Producer of Agent Orange Warned, Documents Show," Associated Press, December
28, 1988.

"A Quiet Victory for Robert F. Kennedy, Jr." *New York Times*, June 4, 1985.

Rainforest Action Network. *Action Alert*, December 1990.

"Resolution from the Third National Ecological Meeting." Press release. Puyo, May 12,
1991.

Ridgeway, James. "Jungle Fever: Robert Kennedy Jr., the Oil Companies, the *Voice*,
and Ecuador's Indians: What a Mess." *Village Voice*, July 23, 1991.

Ortiz de Villalba, Juan Santos. *Los Últimos Huaorani*, 3rd ed. Quito: Ediciones
CICAME, 1991.

Scherr, S. Jacob. Letter to D. E. Gregg, Conoco, Inc. December 11, 1990.

———. Unaddressed letter. January 30, 1991.

Scherr, S. Jacob, et al. Letter to E. S. Woolard. October 2, 1990.

———. Letter to James W. Kinnear, President of Texaco. October 2, 1990.

Smith, Joan. "Camelot Kid an Earth Crusader." *San Francisco Examiner*, October 25,
1992.

Springer, Larry D., Director, Public Relations, Environmental Protection Center,
Conoco Ecuador. Letter to Robert F. Kennedy, Jr. October 12, 1990.

Springer, L. D., and A. B. Chapman. Minutes of Feb. 5, 1991, NRDC Meeting in New
York. February 8, 1991.

Tassi, Giovanna. "Todas Las Sangres." In *Naufragos del Mar Verde*. Quito: Abya-Yala,
1992.

Viteri, Leonardo. "La Nacionalidad Huaorani y la Defensa de su Territorio: Pedido de
Solidaridad." Quito: CONFENIAE, 1988.

Woolard, Edgar S., Chairman, DuPont. Letter to NRDC, October 18, 1990.

CHAPTER SEVEN
Articles, Books, Letters

"Amazon Oil Exploration Suspended." *Facts on File World News Digest*, November 13,
1987.

Bledsoe, Jerry. "Saint." *Esquire*, July 1972.

CONFENIAE. "La Confeniae al Gobierno del Doctor Rodrigo Borja." Sarayacu,
May 9, 1989.

Elliot, Elisabeth. *Through Gates of Splendor*. Wheaton, Ill.: Living Books, 1988.

Kozloff, Nicholas. "Los Males de los Huaorani." *15 Dias*, March 1993.

Robarchek, Clay, and Carole Robarchek. "Waorani: From Warfare to Peacefulness."
The World & I, January 1989.

Saint, Rachel. Letter to supporters. May 30, 1959.

Turner, Kernan. "American Missionaries Ordered to Leave Ecuador." Associated Press,
May 6, 1982.

"U.S. Bible Group Leaving Ecuadorean Indians." Associated Press, May 15, 1982.

Yost, James A. *El Desarrollo Comunitario y la Supervivencia Étnica*. Quito: Summer Institute of Linguistics, 1979.

——. "Twenty Years of Contact: The Mechanisms of Change in Wao ('Auca') Culture." In *Cultural Transformations and Ethnicity in Modern Ecuador*, edited by Norman E. Whitten, Jr. Urbana, Ill.: University of Illinois Press, 1981.

CHAPTER EIGHT
Articles, Books, Documents

"Ecuador: Armed Forces Demand Expulsion of Foreigners." Inter Press Service, July 11, 1991.

Ferguson, Douglas. "Sociological Study of the Colonization within Huaorani Territory and Delimitation of the Huaorani Territory." Project proposal. June 1990.

IERAC. Act creating Huaorani territory. Quito, April 3, 1990.

ONHAE. Open letter. Quito, May 23, 1992.

——. "Resoluciones del Congreso de la ONHAE." Shiripuno Center, December 1991.

Rainforest Information Centre. Reports from Work Sessions 1–10. Quito, 1993.

Sierra Club. "Sierra Club Joins Ecuadorian Environmentalists in Denouncing Proposed Oil Development in Ecuadorian National Park." Press release. August 24, 1990.

Vanenzuela, Oscar. "Indians Organize to Defend Their Amazon Homelands." Inter Press Service, October 15, 1988.

Vásquez, Marcela Enríquez, and Byron Real. *Vida por Petróleo*. Quito, Fundación Ecuatoriana de Estudios Sociales, 1992.

CHAPTER NINE
Books, Articles, Documents

Bledsoe, Jerry. "Saint." *Esquire*, July 1972.

Brooke, James. "Oil and Tourism Don't Mix, Inciting Amazon Battle." *New York Times*, September 26, 1993.

"Drillers Are Adapting to the Rain Forest." *Wall Street Journal*, January 5, 1993.

"Ecuador Grants Indians Title to 3 Million Acres." *San Francisco Chronicle*, May 20, 1992.

Europa World Yearbook 1994. London: Europa Publications, 1994.

González, Gustavo. Personal communication. March 18, 1991.

Martz, John D. *Politics and Petroleum in Ecuador*. New Brunswick, N.J.: Transaction Press, 1987.

Nash, Nathaniel C. "Latin American Indians: Old Ills, New Politics." *New York Times*, August 24, 1992.

ONHAE. Open letter. Quito, May 23, 1992.

Smith, Randy. *Crisis Under the Canopy*. Quito: Abya-Yala, 1993.

Stott, Michael. "U.S. Oil Firm Seen Threatening Amazon Tribal Ways." Reuter, September 6, 1993.

World Factbook 1994. Washington, D.C.: Central Intelligence Agency, 1994.

CHAPTER ELEVEN

For the history of Quehueire Ono and background on Mengatohue I relied mainly on the dissertation of Dr. Laura Rival, who was an eyewitness to the creation of the village, and I have used her translations of "ahuene" and "Quehueire Ono" (the latter has been translated elsewhere as "the land that gives much"). As indicated in the text, Rival's paper is the basis for the discussion of Huaorani education. However, I also found useful, and more current, information in a report by Randy Smith, "Education in Huaorani Territory."

Articles, Reports, Documents

Alvardo, Carlos Bay, President of Quehueire Ono. Letter to M. McIntyre, General Manager of PetroCanada. March 8, 1990.

Enomenga, Raúl, President of Quehueire Ono. Invitation to *asamblea*. June 26, 1992.

Ferguson, Douglas. "Report on the Huaorani Project." Quito: Rainforest Information Centre, 1993.

Huaorani representatives. Letter to Dr. Rodrigo Borja Cevallos, President of Ecuador. March 11, 1990.

Parlow, Anita. "Worlds in Collision." *Amicus Journal*, Spring 1991.

Rival, Laura. "Social Transformations and the Impact of Formal Schooling on the Huaorani of Amazonian Ecuador." Doctoral dissertation, London School of Economics, University of London. January 1992.

Sierra Club Legal Defense Fund. *Petición presentada a la Comisión Inter-Americana de Derechos Humanos, Organización de Estados Americanos, por la Confederación de Nacionalidades Indígenas de la Amazonia Ecuatoriana (CONFENIAE) a favor de la población Huaorani contra Ecuador.* San Francisco, 1990.

Smith, Randy. "Education in Huaorani Territory." Quito: Rainforest Information Centre, 1993.

CHAPTER TWELVE
Articles, Letters, Reports

Acción Ecológica. "Irregularidades Cometidas en Relación al Bloque 16." 1993.

Anchundia, Armando. "Error humano, técnico o sabotaje?" *El Universo*, August 12, 1992.

CONAIE. "Informe de la Comisión Técnica de la CONAIE: Derrame de Petróleo del Campo Sacha Norte-1." Quito, August 1992.

CONFENIAE. Declarations from Limoncocha assembly. August 6–8, 1992.

Conoco Ecuador, Inc. "Block 16 Environmental Management Plan." Quito, September 1989.

Holmstrom, David. "Encounter With a Rain-Forest Indian Culture." *Christian Science Monitor*, June 23, 1993.

Kozloff, Nicholas. "Ojo con la Maxus!" *15 Days*, August 1993.

Maxus Ecuador, Inc. "Environmental Management Plan, Block 16." Quito, June 1992.

——. *Nucanchic Naupacuna Rimashcata.* Quito: FEPP, 1992.

Neill, David A. "Botanical Inventory and Revegetation of the Maxus Pipeline Road, Petroleum Block 16, Amazonian Ecuador." Project proposal. May 11, 1992.

"Oil Boom Exploding in the Western Amazon." *World Rainforest Report*, January-March 1993.

"U.S. Oil Firm Builds Road through Amazon Nature Reserve Despite Opposition." Latin America Institute, University of New Mexico, January 19, 1993.

Yost, James A. "Assessment of the Impact of Road Construction and Oil Extraction upon the Waorani Living on the Yasuní." Report for Conoco Ecuador Ltd. April 1989.

CHAPTER FOURTEEN
Articles, Books, Documents, Letters

Borman, M. B., ed. *"The Old People Told Us ..."* Quito: Summer Institute of Linguistics, 1991.

Brooke, James. "New Effort Would Test Possible Coexistence of Oil and Rain Forest." *New York Times*, February 26, 1991.

———. "Pollution of Rain Forest Is Tied to Oil in Ecuador." *New York Times*, March 22, 1994.

Center for Economic and Social Rights. *Rights Violations in the Ecuadorian Amazon: The Human Consequences of Oil Development.* New York, 1994.

Colitt, Raymond. "Green cloud hangs over Ecuadorean oil sector." *Financial Times*, November 30, 1993.

———. "Indians Bring Drilling to Halt at Amazon Well." *Financial Times*, November 2, 1993.

CORDAVI. "Oil in the Ecuadorian Amazon: Water Contamination by Oil Activities." Document presented to the International Water Tribunal. Quito, September 1991.

Criollo, Delfin, and Roberta Borman. *Elberta Queta: Autobiografías Cofanes No. 1.* Quito Publicaciones Cofanes, 1992.

———. *Gregoria Quenama: Autobiografías Cofanes No. 2.* Quito: Publicaciones Cofanes, 1992.

E&P Forum. "Oil Industry Operating Guidelines for Tropical Rainforest." London, April 1991.

Fundación Natura. Minutes from meeting with Ministry of Agriculture and Cofan representatives. August 28, 1991.

International Water Tribunal. Ruling in the case of *CORDAVI vs. Petroecuador, Texaco Petroleum, and City Investing.* Amsterdam, February 20, 1992.

Kimerling, Judith. *Amazon Crude.* New York: Natural Resources Defense Council, 1991.

———. "Disregarding Environmental Law: Petroleum Development in Protected Natural Areas and Indigenous Homelands in the Ecuadorian Amazon." *The Hastings International and Comparative Law Review* 14, no. 4 (1991).

———. "The Environmental Audit of Texaco's Amazon Oil Fields: Environmental Justice or Business as Usual?" *Harvard Human Rights Journal*, Spring 1994.

LeCorgne, D. York, President, Texaco Petroleum Company (Ecuador). Letter to Arthur van Norden, Executive Director, International Water Tribunal. February 7, 1992.

Louisiana Department of Environmental Quality. "Naturally Occurring Radioactive Materials Associated with the Oil and Gas Industry." September 1, 1989.

"Statement of International Delegates: Texaco Week." Quito, July 1993.

Texaco Petroleum Company. "Response to Cordavi's Casedocument." Document presented to the International Water Tribunal. Quito, 1992.

CHAPTER FIFTEEN
Documents, Letters

Faieta, Rossana. "Acta de Reunión." September 9, 1992.

ONHAE. Open letter. Quito, May 23, 1992.

——. "Resoluciones del Congreso de la ONHAE." Shiripuno Center, December 1991.

Martínez, Esperanza. "Encuentro: Estrategia y Alianza popular frente a los impactos petroleros en la Amazonia Ecuatoriana." Invitation to the Coca meeting. September 1992.

"Resumen del trabajo de los grupos." Summary of the Coca meeting. September 1992.

CHAPTER EIGHTEEN
Articles, Books, Documents, Letters

Abad, Boris P. Letter to Rodrigo Davila, Chief of the Environmental Unit, Petroecuador. April 29, 1993.

——. Letter to María Perez, Acción Ecológica. May 13, 1993.

——. Letter to Bill Vourvoulias. December 14, 1993.

Acción Ecológica. "Irregularidades Cometidas en Relación al Bloque 16." Quito, 1994.

——. Letter to Glen Switkes. August 5, 1993.

Avirgan, Tony, and Chris Walker. "Trinkets and Beads." Transcript from film documentary. Sunnyside Productions, 1993.

Brooke, James. "Oil and Tourism Don't Mix, Inciting Amazon Battle." *New York Times*, September 26, 1993.

Colitt, Raymond. "Business and the Environment: Exploiting the Rainforest. Local Indians, oilmen and conservationists have formed an uneasy alliance in Ecuador." *Financial Times*, March 3, 1993.

CONFENIAE. "Genocido Contra Pueblo Huaorani." Press release. October 26, 1992.

"Ecuador: New Blocks, New Mess, New Hope." *World Rainforest Report*, July–September 1994.

"Ecuador Indians Block Offices of Foreign Oil Firms." Reuters, October 27, 1992.

Enomenga, Moi. Open letter. August 27, 1993.

Ferguson, Douglas. Letter to Randy Hayes. April 4, 1993.

——. "Report on the Huaorani Project." Quito: Rainforest Information Centre, 1993.

——. "1990s Bright for Post-OPEC Ecuador." *Oil & Gas Journal*, March 1, 1993.

Hutton, Willliam. Letter to Bill Vourvoulias. September 21, 1993.

Ibrahim, Youssef M. "Departure of Ecuador: The Symbol for OPEC of a Decade in Decline." *International Herald Tribune*, September 19–20, 1992.

"Indígenas presionan salida de compañia petrolera de amazonia." *El Universo*, October 28, 1992.

Kozloff, Nicholas. "Maxus, the Huaorani, and the Politics of Oil Development in Ecuador." Quito: Rainforest Information Centre, 1993.

Maxus Ecuador, Inc. "Acuerdo de Amistad, Respeto y Apoyo Mutuo entre Las Comunidades Huaorani y Maxus Ecuador, Inc." Quihuaro, August 13, 1993.

——. "Plan Integral de Relaciones Comunitarias, Communidades Waorani." Quito, March 1993.

——. Press release describing oil spill. September 8, 1993.

——. "Research Center of the Amazon Basin 'Yasuni.' " Funding proposal. September 1993.

Neill, David, and Edgar Gudino. "Inventario Botánico y Reforestación de la Vía del Oleoducto de Maxus." Fundación Jatun Sacha, December 1992.

ONHAE. "Carta Abierta." October 18, 1992.

——. "Carta Abierta: Pedido del Pueblo Huaorani a la Compañia Maxus y al Gobierno Ecuatoriano." October 1992.

——. Letter to Maxus Ecuador. October 1992.

"Petroleras piden garantias." *El Universo*, October 30, 1992.

Rainforest Action Network. "Oil Assault on Ecuadorian Amazon." *Action Alert*, May 1993.

Salpukas, Agis. "Oil Companies Shifting Exploration Overseas." *New York Times*, November 8, 1993.

"Sixto a indígenas: Póngase en mis zapatos." *El Universo*, October 30, 1992.

Smith, Randy. Letter to Randall Hayes. January 25, 1993.

——. Personal communication. November 6, 1992.

——. Personal communication. December 20, 1992.

——. Personal communication. March 7, 1993.

Stott, Michael. "U.S. Oil Firm Seen Threatening Amazon Tribal Ways." Reuter, September 6, 1993.

Taylor, Eric. "A Brief Dissertation on Love in the Amazon: The Poet Ortega, Maxus Corp. and the Huaorani People." Draft article. Quito, 1994.

"U.S. Oil Firm Builds Road in Amazon Despite Opposition." Inter Press, December 16, 1992.

CHAPTER NINETEEN

Articles, Books, Documents, Memoranda

Acción Ecológica. "Boletín Alerta Verde No. 8." January 1994.

"Ayuda Memoria: Reunión Alicia Durán Ballén—30.09.93: Ayuda Comunitaria Quewere-ono/Kakatado." September 30, 1993.

"Contrato Quehueridiono y Contrato Kakatado." Contract among ONHAE, Maxus, Christian Mission. 1993.

Cherrez, Cecilia, President of Acción Ecológica. Letter to George W. Pasley, Senior Vice-President, Maxus Energy. March 3, 1994.

Enqueri, Ehuenguime. Letter to Paulina Garzón, Acción Ecológica.

Enomenga, Moi. Letter to Alicia Durán Ballén. August 6, 1993.

——. "Manifesto de Moi Enomenga del Pueblo Huaorani de Quehueire Ono al Gobierno Nacional y a la Comisión de Protección de las Minorías Étnicas de las Naciones Unidas." May 28, 1993.

——. Open letter. August 27, 1993.

Petroecuador. "Mapa Catastral Petrolero Ecuatoriano." September 21, 1993.

——. "Séptima ronda de Licitaciones: Empresas Inscritas Región Amazónica." June 1994.

World Factbook 1994. Washington, D.C.: Central Intelligence Agency, 1994.

A Note on the Type

This book was set in Electra, a typeface designed by William Addison Dwiggins (1880–1956) for the Mergenthaler Linotype Company and first made available in 1935. Electra cannot be classified as either "modern" or "old style." It is not based on any historical model, and hence does not echo any particular period or style of type design. It avoids the extreme contrast between thick and then elements that marks most modern faces, and it is without eccentricities that catch the eye and interfere with reading. In general, Electra is a simple, readable typeface that attempts to give a feeling of fluidity, power, and speed.

W. A. Dwiggins was born in Martinsville, Ohio, and studied art in Chicago. In the late 1920s he moved to Hingham, Massachusetts, where he built a solid reputation as a designer of advertisements and as a calligrapher. He began an association with the Mergenthaler Linotype Company in 1929 and over the next twenty-seven years designed a number of book types of which Metro, Electra, and Caledonia have been used widely. In 1930 Dwiggins became interested in marionettes, and through the years he made many important contributions to the art of puppetry and the design of marionettes.

Composed by American-Stratford Graphic Service,
Brattleboro, Vermont

Printed and bound by Quebecor Printing Martinsburg,
Martinsburg, West Virginia

Designed by Cassandra J. Pappas